D0011380

James Kynge first went to China as an undergraduate in 1982, when he studied Chinese in a university located between the Yellow River and the birthplace of Confucius. In those days, the country was still in the early stages of its long recovery from the excesses of Chairman Mao's Cultural Revolution, and un-authorised contact between Chinese and foreigners was banned. Nevertheless, it was a formative experience. He returned to China soon after graduating from Edinburgh University in oriental languages in 1985 and has lived and worked either in the mainland or in countries near it ever since.

During nineteen years as a journalist in Asia, he has spent over a decade reporting from China, latterly as China bureau chief for the *Financial Times* from 1998 to 2005. His experiences during that period, during which the country shifted from the periphery to a central position in world affairs, inform the material in this book. He speaks Mandarin fluently and has travelled all over the country, visiting every province and region.

Kynge is the recipient of several awards for journalism, including a Business Journalist of the Year award (London) in 2004 and a European Online Journalism award in 2003; *China Shakes the World* is the winner of the 2006 *Financial Times* & Goldman Sachs Business Book of the Year Award. He is a regular speaker, lecturer and broadcaster on China, featuring on the BBC, CNN, National Public Radio, Deutsche Welle and other broadcast media. He lives in Beijing with his wife and three children. This is his first book.

CHINA SHAKES THE WORLD

The Rise of a Hungry Nation

JAMES KYNGE

PHOENIX

A PHOENIX PAPERBACK

First published in Great Britain in 2006
by Weidenfeld & Nicolson
This paperback edition published in 2007
by Phoenix,
an imprint of Orion Books Ltd,
Orion House, 5 Upper St Martin's Lane,
London, WC2H 9EA
A Hachette Livre UK Company

9 10 8

© James Kynge 2006

A CIP catalogue record for this book
is available from the British Library.

ISBN 978-0-7538-2155-8

Typeset at The Spartan Press Ltd,
Lymington, Hants

Printed and bound in Great Britain at
Mackays of Chatham plc, Chatham, Kent

The Orion Publishing Group's policy is to use papers that
are natural, renewable and recyclable products and
made from wood grown in sustainable forests. The logging
and manufacturing processes are expected to conform to
the environmental regulations of the country of origin.

www.orionbooks.co.uk

To Lucy, Tom, Ella and Ollie.

CONTENTS

ACKNOWLEDGEMENTS

This book was researched and written over a year and a half from mid 2004, but it is the product of many influences and impressions formed during an association with China that goes back to 1982, when I arrived in Jinan, Shandong province as a wide-eyed student. I am indebted, therefore, not only to the many people who helped in several ways with the book project itself, but also to those who have shown me kindness, hospitality, wisdom and many corrective prods in the years since China became my fascination. I wish to thank the teachers and administrators of Shandong University's foreign students' department in the early 1980s for their generosity and humour during difficult times. I am also indebted to the Edinburgh University Chinese department's inspiring lecturers, in particular William Dolby and John Scott.

My career as a journalist would never have got off the ground had it not been for Graham Earnshaw and Mark O'Neill who took me under their wings in Beijing 1985. Since then, countless others have helped shape my evolving understanding of China, at times by teaching me things I did not know and at others by challenging my point of view. Among these, I feel particularly grateful to Robert Thomson, Jasper Becker, Li Jiehua, William Kazer, Gui Minhai, Andrew Higgins, Jane Macartney, Jean-Pierre Cabestan, Andrew Browne, Wang Xiaohong, Fang Xinghai, Graham Hutchings, Song Fengming, Yu Yongding, Li Yang, Hu Angang, James Harding, John Pomfret, James Miles, Karin Finkelston, Cao Siyuan, Xu Zhongbo, Andy Rothman, Xu Xiaonian, Zhang Weiying, Wang Rujun, Hong Huang, Zhang Xin, Hu Shuli, Anthony Galsworthy, Richard McGregor, Mure Dickie, Andrew Yeh, Adam Williams, Clinton Dines, Peter Batey, David Mahon, Jeorg Wuttke, Nicholas Lardy, Denis Simon, David Shambaugh, Liu Chaowei, Wang Wei, Wang Min, Ge Xiaomei, Xing Houyuan, Patrick Horgan, Shi Junbao, as well as Joe Studwell and Arthur Kroeber at the excellent *China Economic Quarterly*. Needless to say, the opinions within are my own and I take responsibility for them.

My greatest debt in researching the book is to Yang Li who, first as a colleague at the *Financial Times* and later as a full-time researcher on this project, showed enormous resourcefulness, intelligence and good humour in tracking down elusive facts, securing meetings with many hard-to-get-to characters and helping me understand what we experienced. She alone knows the many places in which it would have been more accurate for me to have written 'we' instead of 'I'. Alia Malik also did sterling and much appreciated work researching several issues of context and economic history.

Many friends supplied generous advice, support and insights during the ups and downs of the writing process. Among these, I am particularly thankful to Tim Clissold, David Murphy, Jim McGregor, Rob Gifford, Nancy Fraser, Zhang Lijia, Calum Macleod, Catherine Sampson, Charles Hutzler, Gerry Bourke and Rupert Wingfield-Hayes. An old friend, Keith Abel, did a fastidious job reading drafts and in telling the truth with sensitivity. I also wish to thank Ion Trewin and Anna Hervé at Weidenfeld & Nicolson, and Linden Lawson, Ilsa Yardley and David Atkinson, as well as my agent, Felicity Bryan, for the judgement, support and the patience they showed an often frustrating first-time author.

My many excellent former colleagues at the *Financial Times* have been an unfailing source of inspiration and intellectual stimulation. I thank Richard Lambert for posting me to China in the first place, Peter Montagnon, John Thornhill and Dan Bogler for the endless care they took to keep the phone lines open and the story ideas flowing, and Graham Watts, Victor Mallet, Guy de Jonquieres for their help at crucial times. I am also very grateful to John Ridding who, having engineered the time for me to write, spared plenty of his own to debate many of the issues and arguments.

My parents, to add to their countless indulgences over the years, put up a 'cuckoo' who was writing about one appetite while developing another during several glorious weeks in Potto. My love and gratitude go to them, as well as to Marian and Howard Rogers and Lucy and Iain Nicholson, for their hospitality and endless good cheer.

This book is dedicated to Lucy, who, throughout the writing of it, as in all things, made the difficult parts easier and the distant closer by. It is also to our wonderful children, Tom, Ella and Ollie, for whom China is quite simply home.

ONE

By the time I got there, there was only the scar. A scar of ochre earth twenty-five times the size of a football field. A dozen excavators pawed ponderously at the soil as if absently searching for something lost. The place where one of Germany's largest steel mills had stood since before World War Two was now reduced to a few mounds of twisted metal scrap. I approached a man in worker's overalls by the side of the road. He was hoisting a huge metal segment of a pipeline onto the back of a truck. After he had settled it in place, I called over to him. He said he had dislodged, lifted and loaded fourteen segments like this already and now there were only three left, enough for another week's work. Then it would all be over. I asked him where the pipeline was going. He straightened his back and made as if to throw something in a gentle arc far into the distance. 'China,' he said.

The rest of the equipment had gone earlier: the oxygen converters that were housed in a shed 60 metres high, the hot rolling-mill for heavy steel plates that stretched out over one kilometre, a sinter plant, a blast furnace and a host of other parts. They had all been packed into wooden crates, inserted into containers, loaded onto ships and then unpacked again near the mouth of the Yangtze River. There, on the flat alluvium beds of that mighty river, they had been reconstructed exactly – to the last screw – as they had been in Germany. Altogether 250,000 tonnes of equipment had been shipped, along with 40 tonnes of documents that explained the intricacies of the reassembly process.[1] The man in overalls shook his head at the convoluted nature of it all. 'I just hope it works when they get it there,' he said.

The ThyssenKrupp steel mill in Dortmund once employed around 10,000 people. The communities of Hörde and West-falenhütte, where workshops clustered around chimneys that could be seen from all over the city, had depended on it for generations. People had made iron here for nearly 200 years and when the drums of German conquest rolled in 1870, 1914 and 1939, it was this corner of the Ruhr Valley that supplied first Prussia and then the German empire with field guns, tanks, shells and battleship armour. A pride in practical things was evident everywhere. A stumpy-looking, nineteenth-century iron blast furnace, with a notice explaining that it had been brought over from England, stood as a monument by one of the gateways to the former plant. Nearby, a plaque memorialised a local engineer.

But on a warm, bright afternoon in June 2004, Hörde was clearly no longer the pounding heart of the Ruhr. The place looked laid-back, becalmed. A few people sat in the sun outside an ice cream shop on Alfred Trappen Street, digging to the bottom of their sundaes with long spoons. Up the road, women fished into a wire basket outside Zeeman Textiel, a discount store, inspecting T-shirts for 99 (euro) cents. There were three solariums in the vicinity and a tattoo parlour advertising its ability to emblazon the characters 'Ai' 'Fu' 'Kang', the Chinese characters for 'Love', 'Wealth' and 'Health', onto the bodies of its customers. But both the solariums and the tattooist were shut.

I had come to try to understand how life was changing now that the steel plant was gone. But my inability to speak German was a handicap. I tried calling on local officials but they were unwilling to talk. People on the street, when approached, seemed to find my questions unwarranted. So I went to the Lutheran Church and phoned each of the five pastors listed in a leaflet to invite them for a coffee. Pfarrer Martin Pense was busy, Pfarrer Klaus Wortmann was out of town, Pfarrer Bern Weissbach-Lamay did not answer and Pfarrerin Angela Dicke would have been happy to help but it was a holiday, so . . . sorry. Pfarrer Sven Fröhlich, a softly spoken man, was ready to give me a few minutes on the phone.

The death of the steel mill, he said, had been the slow but inevitable result of a loss in competitiveness. In the early 1990s, when efficient South Korean steel plants were undercutting the world, Hörde steelworkers were agitating to work a thirty-five-hour week. Then the reunification of West and East Germany took its toll by forcing the government to raise taxes and by acting as a drag on general economic activity. By the mid 1990s, the ultimate fate of the Hörde plant had become an issue of debate. To start with, the management reacted as managements generally do: it discussed merging with a competitor to derive operational synergies, cost reductions and improved competitiveness. But by 2000, when global steel prices were in a slump, all talk of rescue faded away. There seemed to be little that could be done.

Pfarrer Fröhlich said that the Lutheran church's congregation had moved away as thousands of steelworkers lost their jobs and the community, though not poor, had sunk into a kind of numbness. Young people did not seem to feel the pull of religion in spite of the strenuous efforts, evident in the church newsletter, to lure them into all sorts of community activities. 'Our identity is lost,' said Fröhlich. 'And that is the most important thing that can be taken away from somebody. It could take more than a decade to recover it.'

According to ThyssenKrupp, the Hörde plant would have been closed regardless of whether a buyer for it had been found. But others have had their doubts. The Chinese pounced so quickly on the purchase, signing to buy it just one month after the plant was idled, that some in Hörde suspected a behind-the-scenes deal. Whatever the truth, it was not the Chinese acquisition so much as the events that were to follow that stunned the local population. As if out of nowhere, nearly a thousand Chinese workers arrived. They dossed down in a makeshift dormitory in a disused building in the plant and worked twelve hours a day throughout the summer, seven days a week. Only later, after some of the German workers and managers complained, were they obliged to take a day off out of respect for local laws.

Their industriousness alone was enough to give the hardened workers of the Ruhr pause for thought. But there was something else. Locals started to notice the Chinese deconstruction teams high up – 40, 50, 60 metres above ground – on exposed walkways, swinging up ladders and clinging from scaffolding poles – all without the use of safety harnesses. The spectacle became a local media sensation. Some referred to it as the 'ultimate Chinese takeaway' and on the day that a reporter from Deutsche Welle, the German broadcaster, was there, a Chinese worker was spotted dangling by a thin wire from the top of the 98-metre-high Hörde

Fackel chimney. 'Have the Chinese acrobats come to town?' he asked in his dispatch.

By the end of 2002, in less than one year, the Chinese had finished the dismantling job – a year ahead of the schedule that they had agreed with ThyssenKrupp and a full two years faster than the German company had initially estimated the job would take. Shortly before it was time to leave, a diplomat from the Chinese embassy in Berlin arrived to address the labourers. 'The Chinese are known in Germany for washing dishes and running restaurants,' he said. 'When our companies want to do business here we sometimes have to beg just for an appointment. But through your work you have earned the Chinese people some face.'

A few weeks after that, they pulled out, having invited local German officials and site managers to a banquet cooked in four different styles reflecting the four home towns of the deconstruction team chefs. The dormitories and kitchens they had been using for a year were left scrupulously clean and tidy, save for a single pair of black safety boots. These boots, it turned out, bore the brand name of 'Phoenix' and were made in China.[2] That was curious, said Germans who had worked at the steel mill, because the plant the Chinese had just taken away was also called 'Phoenix', in commemoration of the way that Dortmund had risen from the ashes of bombing raids in 1944. Nobody could tell, however, whether the single pair of forgotten boots was an oversight or an intentional pun.

Eighteen months after the Phoenix's migration, I stood in the lounge bar in 'Zum Brauhaus', a hostel on Alfred Trappen Street. It was a simple place with pinewood tables, upright chairs, photographs of local football teams on the wall and a fruit machine in the corner that had attracted the attention of a stolid woman with a fleck of mayonnaise on her upper lip. At a table behind her, a teenage girl wearing a blank expression sipped a pint of lager. I stood by the bar, where the landlady introduced me to a man called John. He had been born and brought up in the UK, in the northern industrial town of Bolton, and had been posted to Germany with the British Army a few years after the war. He married a German girl and they moved to Dortmund, her home town, after he left the army. He had worked in the steel mill for more than twenty years but, now that it had gone, he took a philosophical view of its departure. The Chinese economy was booming, whereas Germany's had reached a plateau. If they could put the Hörde plant to profitable use, then maybe it was a good thing that they had bought it, he said.

But there was no denying that the Phoenix's loss was keenly felt. You could see the psychological displacement in a small park at the lower end of Alfred Trappen Street. There, around a monument to a synagogue that was destroyed during the war, groups of unemployed steelworkers sat under spreading beech trees with their cans of lager in plastic bags. John held a thumb to his lip and made a sucking sound. A future without heavy industry was going to take some getting used to, he said. Nobody had a clear idea of what would take its place. The only thing that the local authority had come up with so far was a plan to redevelop the area that the steelworks had occupied into a lake larger than the Binnenalster in Hamburg. It would feature four small islands and a tombolo. Around the sides there would be the moorings for a marina, rows of upscale restaurants and nearly 200 hectares of parkland. But so far the marina scheme had not received a positive reception.

As John was talking, another former steelworker, a large, powerfully built man in his forties, joined the conversation. 'Let me ask you,' he boomed. 'Do we look like yachtsmen to you?'

The flight of the Phoenix made Hörde one of the first communities on earth to feel the convulsive force of a rising China. Before that, it was true, there had been plenty of soundings emanating from Asia's rising giant, but few of them had amounted to more than tremors on the seismic scale. In 2001, when the buyer of the Phoenix was negotiating the deal, China had not yet joined the World Trade Organisation and, although its economy was certainly a driving locomotive for Asia, it had yet to develop a world-class punch. Indeed, my assignment as a journalist for the *Financial Times* in Beijing had been taken up mainly with domestic issues. I had spent a lot more time researching and reporting on how the world was affecting China than on how China was affecting the world. The story then seemed to revolve around the large inflows of foreign investment, the latest intrigues among the modern-day mandarinate that ruled from within a forbidden compound in the centre of Beijing, and whether or not you could or should trust the official statistics.

Then, quite suddenly, or so it seemed, China became an issue of daily international importance. It is difficult to pinpoint when, exactly, that transition took place; perhaps it was late in 2003, or maybe it was early the next year. I could not be sure. In any case, it was unlikely that there would have been any single moment when everything changed. An object as large as China cannot turn on a sixpence. Nevertheless, in my imagination at least, there may have been a tipping point. It occurred during the several weeks from mid February 2004 when, slowly at first but with mounting velocity, manhole covers started to disappear from roads and pavements all over the world. As Chinese demand drove up the price of scrap metal to record levels, thieves almost everywhere had the same idea. As darkness fell, they levered up the iron covers and sold them to local merchants who cut them up and loaded them onto ships to China. The first displacements were felt in Taiwan, the island just off China's southeast coast. The next were in other neighbours, such as Mongolia and Kyrgyzstan. But soon the gravitational pull of a resurgent 'Middle Kingdom' was reaching the furthest sides of the world. Wherever the sun set, pilferers worked to satisfy China's hunger. More than 150 covers disappeared during one month in Chicago. Scotland's 'great drain robbery' saw more than a hundred vanish in a few days. In Montreal, Gloucester and Kuala Lumpur, unsuspecting pedestrians stumbled into holes.

It was not the first time that a great power had telegraphed its arrival in an unusual way. The first inkling the British had of the thirteenth-century Mongol invasion of Europe, for example, was when the price of fish at Harwich, a harbour on the North Sea, rose sharply. The explanation for this, people learned later, was that the Baltic shipping fleets, abruptly deprived of sailors required to fight the enemy approaching by horse from the east, had remained at its moorings. That had reduced the supply of cod and herring to Harwich, and prices had risen accordingly.

Sitting in my office overlooking the Avenue of Eternal Peace, Beijing's main thoroughfare, I fancied I could actually *see* some of the economic forces that China was conjuring before it sent them hurtling around the world. People were buying cars at such a rate that, week by week, the traffic on the avenue became noticeably more clogged. The buildings on the far side of the road that were Soviet-era apartment blocks when I started my assignment had become high-rise towers with marble foyers and glass and chrome exteriors by the time that I finished it. Bicycles, once ubiquitous, were disappearing. On the pavement outside my ground-floor window, the sibilant touts who peddled pirated DVDs out of the corner of their mouths had proliferated. Even the 'Friendship Store', a state-owned relic from the first blush of China's opening to the world, had changed. Its staff, who in the early 1980s presented an aspect of studied indifference to their customers, had mellowed in the intervening years into an attitude of rumpled nonchalance. The sleepy patisserie that occupied one corner of the store and used to sell some of the only croissants in the capital when I was a student in 1982 had, by the early twenty-first century, made way for a Starbucks that offered blueberry muffins and tiramisu.

The changes that I could see from my window were multiplied a million times across the country. Together they were the trappings of a transformation that had lifted more than 400 million people above the poverty line of one US dollar a day since reforms began in 1978. Over the same period, the economy had recorded an average annual growth rate of 9.4 per cent, the highest of any large economy in the world. Whereas in 1978, private telephones were virtually unheard of, by 2005 some 350 million people had mobile phones and more than 100 million were accessing the Internet. And the magnitude of that change is not unusual. It has been repeated in many fields of human endeavour.

What *is* new, however, as the manhole cover episode suggests, is that in many different ways, the events reshaping China are no longer merely resonating on foreign shores but actually changing the way the world works. It is said that around two hundred years ago Napoleon warned that people should: 'Let China sleep, for when she wakes, she will shake the world.' There is no record of the context of this admonition, and the quotation itself may be inaccurate or even apocryphal. But, if the French leader did indeed say those words, he was far ahead of his time. It is not that China has been asleep for the last two centuries – far from it. Though, it is certainly true that the renaissance currently transforming the world's most populous nation marks the end of a long era of decline and weakness for the Chinese nation. The energies now released – and on display outside my office window and in countless other places all over a vast country – have started to shake the world. This book aims to explore the ways in which trends and events within China are being projected as influences onto the outside world. It seeks to link cause and effect, tracing external convulsions back to their internal combustions. So, from Dortmund, I travelled back to China to discover the source of the energy that had removed the Hörde steel plant.

The sea voyage of the ThyssenKrupp steel mill ended 5,600 miles away from Hörde at a small, windswept port on the alluvium beds of the lower Yangtze River. The water was wide and sluggish here, and deep enough for all but the largest sea vessels to dock. A few hundred metres inland from the riverbank, the plant had been reassembled. I recognised it immediately. It looked somehow cleaner than in the photographs I had seen of it in Germany, although that may merely have been an illusion created by the white sands and metallic grey skies surrounding it.

The company that had bought the plant was called Shagang, 'sand steel' after the distinctive physical environment in which it had blossomed from its humble beginnings as a village workshop in 1975. China's entire national steel output had then been scarcely more than that of Dortmund alone. In the intervening years, though, business had taken off. The workshop's expansion had first consumed the village that built it and then usurped the neighbouring town. Now everyone in the area seemed in thrall both to steel and to the former peasant farmer with a rudimentary education who had turned a backyard furnace into one of the world's most efficient producers. His name was Shen Wenrong.

I stayed at the Steel Town Guest House, just down the street from the Sand Steel Hostel. The receptionist told me that everyone was thankful to Shen. Without him, she said, this place would be nothing. Now it was full of the incongruities of industrialising China. A five-star hotel with an external mural of mythical goddesses in floating gowns was under construction in the reed beds by the river. Its name, locals said, was to be 'Heavy Industry Hotel'. Not far away, a restaurant called 'Sweet Water' stood beside mounds of stinking rubbish rotting in a canal. Wide new boulevards had been built in another part of town, but a dearth of manhole covers had turned driving into a slalom with consequences. And in front of a sports hall, there was a scale replica of the iron bull that stands in front of the New York Stock Exchange on Wall Street. On its plinth, a poem written by Shen Wenrong had been carved into granite:

> The bull will rush forward without whipping,
> Once in flight it covers a thousand miles.
> We ask the golden bull; Why are you like this?
> But the bull can fly over oceans too –
> Only then should you call it a miracle.

The town's name was Jinfeng and it had the air of a temporary encampment. Most of its inhabitants were migrant workers, the peasant farmers who flooded in from their villages to find work for around 40 cents an hour. There were about 30,000 of them in Jinfeng and shortly after dawn they tramped in long silent lines to the steel, cotton and glass factories that held the promise of a future free from the thousand-year tyranny of their fields. At dusk the factories would disgorge them back to their dormitories; a sullen, twilight army. The local economy bore the imprint of their presence; shops selling hard hats, metal toecap boots and lengths of rope lined their route to work. There was also a discount garment shop for those who wanted to smarten up before triumphant trips home. A pair of leather shoes with a fashionable square toe was on sale for $4 and patterned T-shirts were going for 10 cents.

A bit further on, I dropped into a liquor store and was attracted to the poetic names on several bottles of white spirit. 'One Drop Fragrant' (90 cents), 'Cool River Destiny' (75 cents), 'Eastern Crossing' (95 cents), 'Boiling Ditch' (60 cents), 'Drink Happy 100 Years' ($1.10 cents). The last one I looked at was called 'Ordinary' and it cost 20 cents, but just as I picked it up the shopkeeper called over to me. 'Don't drink that. You couldn't stand it. It's for migrant workers,' he said.

Later that afternoon, near the Steel Town Guest House, a white truck moving at the speed of a milk float came down the road playing a jingle and a recorded message from a speaker on its roof. 'Jinfeng Cinema. Outstanding Song and Dance. Travelling Performance. Five O'Clock Start. Don't Miss It,' the message said. In the passenger seat, a young woman with rouged cheeks and her hands interlaced in front of almost naked breasts was 'casting the beautiful eye' to passers by. On the other side of the road, a truck carrying iron ore juddered to a halt, its driver and passengers craning to get a better view.

Before coming to Jinfeng, I had spent weeks trying to secure an invitation to Shagang to see Shen. But at every step I had been thwarted by a man called Wu. When I phoned him to request a visit, he suggested that I send a fax. I did. But he told me it needed alterations. I made them. Oh, and there should be a list of questions that I wanted to ask, he added. I wrote them. When my documentation was finally to his specifications, the stalling took a different tack. Things were busy now, he said. Next year might be a better time to visit. Besides, Jinfeng had no good hotels . . . and transport was inconvenient.

In the end, I just went. At the forbidding iron gate to the plant, three stern guards with uniforms and peaked hats stood in a pillbox. I told them I needed to find Shen's office. They smiled, pointed it out from the mass of long, low factory buildings and allowed me to walk straight in. It was an open-plan, communal space and as soon as I came through the building's main door, I found myself standing in the middle of it. I had not seen pictures of Shen but I had been told that he was a big man, with the ham hands of a farm labourer. Getting my bearings, I turned around a couple of times taking in the rows of staff sitting in cubicles and staring at computer screens. Then, suddenly, I noticed that a couple of feet behind me, through a glass divider, was a big man poring over documents at a desk. A small line of staff, all clutching papers, had formed into a queue next to him. As each person reached the front, the large man would grab their papers, study them intently for a minute and then issue orders in a low, growling voice. It had to be Shen. I walked over to join the queue, but just as I was nearing the front, a man came over to ask what I was doing. It was Wu. He smiled in a resigned way and said he was delighted to see me. However, he said, it was not clear if Shen would be working today. In any case, I had better go with him to a separate office and fill out forms, make a formal request. But by now I was standing three feet away from the man I had been hoping for months to meet. I was not going to be budged.

When Shen looked up and saw an unannounced foreigner at the front of his morning business queue he seemed neither surprised nor pleased. He just stared at me over the top of his reading spectacles for some time and then, with an impatient wave of his hand, told me to sit on a low wooden stool by his side. His desk was no bigger than a schoolchild's; very different from the wide, polished, hardwood 'boss platforms' that Chinese corporate chieftains normally awarded themselves. Its glass surface was piled with two stacks of paper and in between them was a Perspex holder containing a few cheap biros. There was no photograph of his wife or children, no mementoes of business success and no computer. Shen seemed to prefer doing business in physical form, in the here-and-now. Many of the line managers and other executives who had stood in front of me in the queue had been clutching reports that were handwritten or typed on sheets of A4.

As I told him why I had come, he cut me off in mid sentence and told me to wait in a back room. Half an hour later, he reappeared. We sat around a meeting table and he told me to dispense with formalities and just get on with asking whatever it was that I wanted to know. I asked him why he had bought the Thyssen-Krupp steel plant. 'I needed a horse that would run fast and not eat much hay,' he said. 'When the next crash in world steel prices comes, and it will certainly come in the next few years, a lot of our competitors who have bought expensive new equipment from abroad will go bust or be so weighed down by debt that they will not be able to move. At that time you will see that this purchase was good.'

Shagang bought the steel mill by paying its price in scrap: $24 million. Its transportation by land and sea from Dortmund had cost $12 million and its reconstruction (plus the purchase of 1½ square kilometres of land) cost another $1.2 billion.[3] All told, it came in at about 60 per cent of the cost of buying a new plant and, by reconfiguring it, Shen was confident he would be able to squeeze 3 million more tonnes of annual output from it than the Germans had managed in Dortmund. When it started producing at full tilt, it would more than double Shagang's current capacity, catapulting the company into the ranks of the world's top twenty producers.

If Shagang had decided to buy a new plant, not only would the cost have been far greater but also it would have taken about three years to make and one or two years to assemble. By comparison, Phoenix was indeed a fast, low-maintenance horse. Shen said he had the advantage during negotiations with ThyssenKrupp because, although steel prices worldwide were in a trough in 2001, he knew that demand in China was set to balloon over the following two to three years. The Germans, he said, were just happy to find a buyer. They could not have been expected to foresee that an extraordinary upsurge in Chinese demand in 2003 and 2004 would propel global steel prices to levels at which Phoenix in its original Dortmund setting would have made a handsome profit.

All in all, the Germans had been very co-operative, Shen said. Both he and Qi Guangnan, the chief engineer who had packed up the plant in Hörde, had an admiration for their technical knowledge and their trustworthiness. And clearly, they had loved their factory, said Qi. He recounted how a big, middle-aged German who showed him around had started sobbing at the door of the sinter plant. 'He had worked there for twenty years,' Qi said. But the great thing about the Phoenix plant, as far as the Chinese were concerned, was that back in Germany it had supplied steel to Volkswagen, the car maker. In China, few firms as yet had the technology to make automobile-grade steel. There was a market to be had in substituting for the expensive imports of auto-grade steel, especially now that car sales nationwide were in an unprecedented boom. Volkswagen itself had a large plant in Shanghai, which was not too far away from Jinfeng. Shen's vision, then, was simple. Cars designed in Wolfsburg would still be built with steel made from Dortmund's fine technology – only the whole process would unfold within the span of delta where the Yangtze meets the sea.

As I left, I was accompanied to the gate by Wu, whose resigned expression was accentuated by the weight of his bushy eyebrows. He had been with Shen since they grew up and, as we walked through the plant, he spoke of the memories he was seeing in his mind's eye. The place where we stood on the factory forecourt had been a bed of reeds when he and Shen had first started out. And somewhere lost in the mass of buildings was the site of the farmer's shack where Shen had lived out a childhood as poor as it was possible to be in one of the world's most impoverished countries.

I thanked Wu for taking me around. He said it had been no problem. 'Only next time,' he said, 'send a fax.'

One aspect of the steel mill saga that intrigued me was how Shen had managed to leave behind his humble beginnings and, without any training in business, rise to run one of the world's most competitive steel companies. People to whom I spoke in Dortmund had assumed that their steel mill must have been bought by a Chinese state-owned enterprise, or perhaps some sinister arm of a totalitarian state. This type of perception was widespread in Europe and the United States. The conventional wisdom seemed to be that the Chinese companies acquiring equipment or technology in the industrialised world were somehow agents of the Communist government, or at least financed by state banks with loans they would never have to repay. Indeed, some of the corporations that sought to buy equipment, companies and assets overseas did fall into this category. But in the case of Shagang and Shen, such a characterisation did not match with reality. The story of Shen's rise belonged to a different tradition, and one that was much more instructive about the forces transforming China.

To understand these forces better, it is necessary to delve into a crucial, yet often misunderstood, passage of history. In the popular imagination, the launch of China's economic reforms in 1978 was a planned, top-down affair managed by a man who is often called the 'architect' of the country's emergence, Deng Xiaoping. According to this version of events, Beijing has all along been cleverly manipulating a master plan that has delivered structured, gradual free-market reforms. But the reality has not been so neat. Many of the key events and occurrences that propelled progress towards capitalism were, in fact, either unplanned, unintended or completely accidental. It is undeniable that the 1980s, the decade of Deng, brought genuine and deep-seated change that improved the lives of hundreds of millions of Chinese. But on closer inspection, it turns out that much of the crucial impetus behind the creation of wealth during this period sprang not so much from the implementation as from the miscarriage of central government policies.

At the outset, the reforms were precipitated by a payments crisis.[4] The first thing that Deng tried to do after winning his power struggle with Chairman Mao Zedong's successor, Hua Guofeng, was to try to carry out the priorities listed in the so-called 'Ten-Year Plan for Economic Development'. He had drawn up this document in 1975 but political infighting and the rise of the 'Gang of Four' led by Mao's demonic wife, Jiang Qing, had stalled its passage through the bureaucracy. The plan boiled down to a huge shopping list: approval for the importation of twenty-two complete industrial production units at an average cost of over $500 million each, amounting to a total outlay of $12 billion – equivalent to the annual incomes of roughly 24 million Chinese in those days. Deng gambled that these purchases could be funded by the discovery of big new oil deposits. Chinese companies, assisted by foreign engineers, were already feverishly at work sinking wells in promising locations all over the country. But, unfortunately, little oil was found. Many of the purchases had to be postponed, but those that had already been paid for left a gaping hole in the state's finances.

Deng was forced to improvise to coax growth out of an economy that had only just started to recover from the Cultural Revolution, the decade of Maoist madness that had officially ended in 1976. He brought in Chen Yun, an expert at defusing economic crises, to conceive of new strategies. Chen's view was that the activism of farmers, who comprised some 700 million of China's then population of 1.1 billion, had been suppressed for too long under the system of agricultural communes instituted by Mao. From 1979 onward, farmers could form smaller 'work groups' to cultivate fixed parcels of land, reaping the benefit – or sorrow – of their harvest. A key tenet of the new policy, however, was that such work groups would not be single families and the land they tilled would remain state-owned. But, in one of the first of several important acts of creative disobedience,[5] farmers took the new policy as a licence to start cultivating family plots. Local officials knew exactly what was going on, but they could also see that the activism of the peasant farmers had been unleashed and that it was consigning the lassitude of the communes to history. The impact was immediate. By 1984, the national grain harvest rose to 407 million tonnes from 305 million in 1978, and meat became more widely available.[6]

Similar types of subterfuge attended China's prototype private businesses. In areas around the Pearl River Delta bordering Hong Kong and in Zhejiang and Jiangsu provinces to the north and south of Shanghai, people began to form companies that were socialist and state-owned on paper but capitalist and privately owned in reality. The main ruse employed to conceal this disobedience was semantic acrobatics with the word 'collective'. When Mao had used it, the word meant that a company was entirely owned by the state but by more than one branch of it. In its new incarnation, however, 'collective' could also mean a collection of private, or partly private owners. It was a fig leaf that came to be known as 'donning the red hat' and it would not have fooled anyone had it not been for the complicity of local government officials. They were willing to allow such sophistry to flourish because they soon saw that 'red hat' collectives could be the most dynamic job creators and tax payers in their districts. Often, of course, they had the additional incentive to co-operate that came from direct shareholdings. Within a few years, an unsanctioned amalgam of 'red hats', collectives and 'township and village enterprises' had become by far the fastest-growing sector in the national economy.

The willingness of local government officials to disobey Beijing was therefore a crucial ingredient in the free-market reforms of the 1980s. And the artifice did not end with that decade. It was to continue well into the 1990s, notably with the establishment of thousands of unlicensed 'development parks'[7] to which local governments attracted corporate investors by offering a package of frequently illegal incentives. Taken together, then, these realities suggest that Deng was not so much the omniscient architect of free-market reform that he is often hailed to have been. A significant part of his success can be attributed to the disobedience of local government officials, farmers and entrepreneurs towards central government policies. Deng's contribution was not that he conceived of all the strategies that would lay the foundations for China's economic take-off, but that he was willing to ride with whatever homespun formulae seemed to yield the growth the country so desperately needed. This was no mean achievement; a phalanx of conservative ideologues in Beijing kept constant vigil from the wings, ready to convert the slightest mishap into an argument for revisionism.

Understanding the haphazard nature of much that happened in the 1980s assists in appreciating where men like Shen came from. Chaotic times throw forth heroes. Several of the entrepreneurs who by the late 1990s were driving Mercedes, flying first-class to the World Economic Forum in Davos, Switzerland and sending their children to the best British public schools started at the bottom of the social pyramid in the early 1980s. In fact at that time, misfortune – particularly if it came in the form of unemployment – could be the ultimate blessing. The payments crisis brought on partly by Deng's spending binge in the late 1970s was matched by an urban employment crunch. Some 7 million educated young people who had been sent to the countryside to 'learn from the peasants' during the Cultural Revolution were by the late 1970s and early 1980s flooding back to the cities. As they were assigned to their work units, many of those with lesser educational achievements could not find a job. Beijing felt it had no choice but to allow them to indulge in minor private business.

Thus did the unemployed – and in some cases the unemployable – of the early 1980s get their feet onto an escalator that would within two decades deliver some of them to the highest echelon of wealth. Li Xiaohua, now a portly man in his mid fifties, started out selling watches from a bag on the streets beneath the office block that he now owns. There had been no job for him when he returned from a Cultural Revolution assignment to 'repair the earth' in a frigid northeastern province near the Russian border. The watches business was never going to take off, so he caught the train to the coastal resort of Beidaihe, sank all of his savings into a US-made iced drinks dispenser and prowled the beach for customers.[8] Another salesman's job and some canny property investments later, he found himself in 1994 as the number two tycoon on a list of the richest people in the country. Since then he has slipped back down the rankings, but he does not lack for consolations. One of them was parked in a garage beneath his office: a red Ferrari with the licence plate 'A 0001'. 'It was the first to be imported,' he said.

Even richer than Li in the mid 1990s was Mou Qizhong,[9] who had emerged from jail in 1979 without a job, a 'work unit' or any apparent prospects. He took a loan to start a suitcase company selling ornate brass alarm clocks to shops in Shanghai and made a reasonable profit. Then came his pièce de résistance; he had heard that a regional airline, Sichuan Airlines, needed planes but had no cash to buy them with. The Soviet Union, he knew, had planes but lacked manufactured products. So he brokered a deal – 500 rail carriages crammed full of instant noodles, shoes, garments and other stuff in exchange for four Soviet passenger aircraft. The audacity of the 'socks-for-jets' transaction delighted Beijing, which hailed Mou as one of the country's 'Ten Best Private Entrepreneurs' and a 'Reform Hero'. But his star was burning too brightly. Bearing an uncanny physical resemblance to Mao, he cultivated the likeness by brushing his hair in the same manner as the late Great Helmsman and by letting it be known that he did not much mind being called 'Chairman Mou'. His ideas grew delusional; he talked seriously about blasting a hole through the Himalayas and using giant turbines to blow moist, rain-filled Indian air to parched parts of China. A scheme to launch satellites on Russian rockets haemorrhaged cash, driving his firm towards insolvency. Finally, the fraud inspectors closed in and in 2000 Mou was sentenced to life imprisonment for a foreign exchange scam.

Mou and Li were the luminary agents of a broader trend. Deng had said that 'some people should be allowed to get rich first', but he left the question of who these people were largely to chance.

For much of the 1980s those selected by the rounds of social roulette were mostly the 'getihu' (single body unit), or self-employed. I got to know several in Beijing in 1985 and became friends with one, Meng Ke. He lived in an old courtyard house behind the Fine Arts Museum in central Beijing and was from a good family. His grandfather, an octogenarian who kept a copy of Confucius's 'Analects' by his austere wooden armchair, had been a ranking official in the central bank before the 1949 Communist revolution. But Meng was cut from a different cloth. He was not interested in economics, politics or literature; his conversation revolved around whether 'Hilton' cigarettes were superior to 'Camel', and why 'Beijing Beer' should only be drunk if it had a white label. Why? I asked once. 'Because the other stuff is horse piss!' he replied.

Meng was officially classified as 'waiting for employment', which meant he was allowed to become a 'getihu'. He opened a hole-in-the-wall noodle restaurant just across the street from his courtyard home and, with almost no competition, made quick money. For several months he made the noodles, waited on the tables and ensured a steady supply of white-label Beijing Beer. After a while, though, he tired of the work and hired someone to do it for him while he assumed the role of landlord. He had a name card printed:

> MENG FAMILY
> COLD NOODLES
>
> *Meng Ke*
>
> Chairman, President and CEO

Meng lacked the application but, if he had stuck at it, he could have made it big. Many of China's corporate luminaries were in 1985 a lot worse-off than he. Liu Chuanzhi,[10] who as chairman of Lenovo, the Chinese computer company that bought the personal computer division of IBM in 2004, was at that time just starting out as a sales agent for 'Big Blue' in China. He would later recall how in those days he lived in a tiny communal space at the back of a bicycle shed and had to dry his socks over a coal-burning stove in the middle of a single room used by the whole family. When he attended his first IBM sales agent meeting, he was wearing a suit borrowed from his father. Liu Yonghao,[11] who by 2005 was the largest individual shareholder in the China Minsheng Bank, the country's first private bank, was, back in the mid 1980s, using a bit of cash borrowed from relatives to start raising chickens on his balcony. Chickens had eggs which hatched more chickens and, through various permutations, Liu soon became head of New Hope, the largest animal feed group in China. He used money earned from that business to buy his stake in Minsheng, which is now listed on the stock market.

Lu Guanqiu,[12] whose Wanxiang company had become so successful by 2005 that it was making auto parts for General Motors, was in the mid 1980s just starting to make gimbals in his oil-slicked smithy. Li Shufu,[13] the founder of Geely, a private car maker which by 2005 was outselling some of the world's best-known brands, was, at the time that Meng sold cold noodles, just starting to piece together a refrigerator using parts bought with a 2,000 renminbi (rmb) loan from his father. Li Dongsheng,[14] who in 2003 acquired Thomson, the French electronics company, for TCL, a private electronics and white goods manufacturer, spent much of the 1980s producing magnetic tapes with a Hong Kong businessman in the back of an agricultural machinery storehouse. Zong Qinghou,[15] whose Wahaha group had by 2005 turned into a formidable competitor to Coca-Cola in China, was in the 1980s selling ice creams (only ice, no milk) priced at less than a US cent each on the street.

The list goes on. Every rags-to-riches story was different, but chance and hardship were common denominators. In his village on the lower Yangtze, the particular hardship that Shen had to endure was the death of his father when Shen was in his late teens. His mother was left with four boys and two girls to support in the aftermath of the twentieth century's worst famine; some 30 million people had starved to death in the late 1950s and early 1960s. Shen's family were peasants on a 'people's commune' where grain was rationed to its members according to a points system which rewarded labour with food. Shen, the second son, was tall and broad and physically strong and was therefore of more use in the fields than in a classroom at school. People who knew him said that when he was first pulled out of school and assigned to a production brigade, he worked as if driven by the anguish of misfortune.[16] But with so many unproductive mouths, his family was always short of work points and often could eat only one meal a day.

He soon learned, though, that the work points were a red herring. The people on the commune who ate well were not those who laboured the hardest but those who had the cosiest connections with the managers of the grain store. Acting on this insight, he cultivated Zhang Wenzhong, the head of a production brigade, and benefited in two crucial ways from this contact. The first was through the handouts of food that Zhang would sometimes give him. The second was a recommendation when an opportunity presented itself for Shen to apply for a factory job. Around that time, word had got out that a local cotton factory was considering hiring 'mud legs', as peasant farmers were called. That leap from the field to the factory was the biggest and most important of Shen's career. People in factories earned cash, not points, and they could save money and had prospects for promotion.

Initially, what marked Shen apart in the textile mill were the fruits of his agricultural labour. He could lift and carry 100-kilogram bales of cotton with ease. But as time passed it became clear to his superiors that he was much more than a workhorse. He had a quiet, determined temperament and a shrewd intelligence. By the mid 1970s, when his next big chance presented itself, he had risen to a senior rank in a factory that had thousands of employees and was committed to further expansion. But it could not expand without the steel needed to build new workshops, machinery and housing. Steel was strictly rationed in the aftermath of the Cultural Revolution and in chronically short supply all over the country. So Shen, with others, decided to take matters into his own hands and build a secret backyard furnace.

Jinfeng was then a very small town, no more than a speck on the map north of Shanghai which even Chinese would have been hard pressed to find. It was inconceivable that so lowly a place would be able to win over the bureaucrats in distant Beijing to provide approvals for a new steel plant. So the cotton factory bosses turned obscurity to their advantage. While Beijing was preoccupied with power struggles and the impending death of Chairman Mao, they conferred with local officials and made the calculation that if they just went ahead and built their small steel workshop, nobody in Beijing would notice. They turned out to be correct. The workshop they made was the crudest type imaginable. Technologically, it was on a par with the nineteenth-century British blast furnace that stood as a monument outside the Phoenix plant in Dortmund. It consumed scrap metal scavenged from the surrounding countryside and smelted it into iron bars which workers pulled by hand out of the furnace.

Shen spent much of his time there, fascinated by the process and trying to think of ways to make money out of the changes stirring all over the country. The communes had by then been disbanded and tens of millions of small entrepreneurs were taking their first steps. Demand for steel in the early 1980s was rising all along the eastern and southern coastal strips. Shen could see which way the wind was blowing, but he had to find a product which was simple to make and had an assured market. He noticed that when peasant farmers made money, the first thing they spent it on was a bigger house. He also knew that China's cramped cities, enduring the highest population densities in the world, would have to expand outward. His conclusion was that the future lay in window frames made not from wood but from iron. He sent engineers to Shanghai to tour around the window frame industry leader, a state company called Xing Hu, with instructions to copy down as much of the technology and processes as they could get away with. Wu, who accompanied the engineers on that trip, explained how they did it. 'They prepared everything in advance so well that as soon as they saw part of the manufacturing process, they would understand quickly how it was done. Then they boiled down the things they did not know to one or two questions because they knew that if they asked too much, the other side would get suspicious.'

Within a few years, Shagang was the second-largest window frame maker in the country and its sales were starting to challenge those of Xing Hu itself. Shen, however, did not rest on his laurels. He heard from a Hong Kong businessman in 1987 that a 75-tonne electric arc furnace capable of producing 250,000 tonnes of reinforced steel bars a year was up for sale in a town called Bidston, near Liverpool. The UK industry, squeezed by foreign competition and restrained by a mature home market, was already in decline. But a British industrial cast-off was in those days a state-of-the-art facility in China.

Shen borrowed heavily to finance the purchase, and had to sell equity to a Hong Kong investor. But opposition to the whole plan was building among government officials and even within the ranks of his own workers. During one meeting in Jinfeng, a worker shouted out that the idea of buying the Bidston plant was 'like putting the hens to flight and breaking all the eggs'. The Vice-Minister of Metallurgy made a special trip all the way from Beijing to persuade Shen to change his mind. Even large state companies had not been daring enough to acquire untested foreign equipment and have it shipped back and reassembled in China. Operations like this, said the Vice-Minister, were akin to 'trying to eat the sky'. But Shen would not listen. If the equipment did not work, he told a massed meeting of workers in Jinfeng, they could put it in a museum. 'You can hire me to stand outside and sell the tickets,' he said at that time.[17]

His gamble came to within an inch of failure. The plant was bought and reassembled in China. But the whole operation took three years, during which time inflation had spiralled almost out of control, millions of anti-government protesters had taken to the streets in large cities all over the country and Deng had responded by ordering the People's Liberation Army to massacre the people in the streets around Tiananmen Square in central Beijing. The economic consequence of the 1989 crackdown was a state of nervous stagnation and Shen, lumbered with heavy interest payments on his loans, was faced with the prospect of selling steel at below cost into a glutted market. Then, out of the blue in early 1992, Deng embarked on what became known as his famous 'southern tour'. Like the emperors of old, he travelled with a retinue of mandarins to inspect the situation beyond his sequestered leadership compound in Beijing. Everywhere he went in the Pearl River Delta bordering Hong Kong, he was fêted. At first, conservatives in Beijing tried to suppress his message, but soon the news leaked out that he was exhorting people to 'be a little bolder, go a little faster'. It was if a touch-paper had been lit. In a few brief weeks, the whole country had shifted gear and Shagang was perfectly positioned to ride the boom that followed.

This boom would carry Shagang along the path that eventually reached Dortmund. Chinese and foreign investors alike took Deng's message of the 'southern tour' as a rallying cry for faster economic liberalisation. Foreign direct investment began to flood in to coastal areas, the Hong Kong stock and property markets rallied, China's own stock markets – one in Shanghai and the other in Shenzhen – were founded, southeast Asian nations began to sell more resources to the emerging giant in their midst and in 1995 China's economy grew at over 14 per cent in a single year. But all this was relatively insipid compared to the cyclonic forces that were unleashed in the first few years of the twenty-first century.

The appetite that was to start feasting on the world in 2003, 2004 and 2005 was in its extent and nature utterly different to that which followed the 'southern tour'. It was nothing less than the total transformation of a large continental economy, a transition through time, space, technology, culture and ideology all at the same time. China had for centuries been the world's biggest economy and it was now emerging once more, but along lines unprecedented in its history. This cauldron of change, along with the combustions and eruptions attending it, were set fundamentally to alter the world in which we live in a myriad different ways. I set out in 2004 to look for a place that would encapsulate many of the changes taking place in China, somewhere which could serve as a symbolic epicentre of the energies remaking the country and, by extension, the world. Far up the Yangtze's turbulent course from the alluvium beds of Shagang, I felt I found it: a place largely unknown to the world it was already helping to reshape. Chongqing.

TWO

Chungking, China's wartime capital, is marked on no-man's map. The place labeled Chungking is a sleepy town perched on a cliff that rises through the mists above the Yangtze River to the sky; so long as the waters of the Yangtze flow down to the Pacific, that river town will remain. The Chungking of history was a point in time, a temporal bivouac with an extra-geographical meaning, like Munich or Versailles. It was an episode shared by hundreds of thousands of people who had gathered in the shadow of its walls out of a faith in China's greatness and an overwhelming passion to hold the land against the Japanese. Men great and small, noble and corrupt, brave and cowardly, convened there for a brief moment; they are all gone home now.[1]

That excerpt is taken from *Thunder Out of China*, the 1946 classic by Theodore H. White and Annalee Jacoby, two reporters for *Time* magazine who spent a few years in Chungking, or Chongqing as it is now called, during World War Two. The city they recall was, for a while, an American household name. It featured in Hollywood movies and romantic novels. Its fate was the focus of stormy Congressional debates and it was not unusual for the clocks above hotel receptions in New York and Washington to show the time in London, Paris and Chungking.

White and Jacoby traced the tribulations of General Joseph Stilwell, or 'Vinegar Joe', who had been dispatched by Washington to aid the ailing forces of Chiang Kai-shek. Chiang, the leader of the Kuomintang, or KMT, was later to lose a civil war against Mao Zedong and flee in 1949 to set up a 'free China' on the island of Taiwan, just off the mainland's southeast coast. But at the time that Stilwell and America came to his assistance, his energies were still fully absorbed fighting the Japanese, to whom he had surrendered his capital, Nanking. From Nanking, he retreated up the Yangtze

24

River with a flotilla of junks carrying dismantled factories and power plants, and did not call a halt until he was over a thousand miles into the embrace of China's interior. The place where he unloaded his junks, where he set up his 'temporal bivouac', as White and Jacoby called it, was a walled town of brick and bamboo dwellings that straggled down to a river wharf.

Stilwell's house can still be seen in Chongqing today. A Spartan, solidly built place with wartime wooden floorboards, it stands high on a cliff overlooking the misty river and is now a museum. The photographs on the museum's walls depict the tenor of that time. 'Flying Tiger' American airmen who flew dangerous supply missions over the Himalayas stand square to the camera, cigarettes lolling from the corner of their mouths. The Chinese and American infantry soldiers who built the 'Stilwell Road' into Burma are shown bathed in sweat as they cut a trail through the thick, malarial jungle. Stilwell himself looks thin, stooped and almost kindly in his thick-rimmed spectacles, while Chiang is stern and immaculate in his generalissimo's uniform. But the pictures that intrigued me most were of Chongqing itself. They show a town reduced to rubble and charred remains by the repeated raids of Japanese bombers. I peered into the grainy, black-and-white prints, but it was difficult to spot more than a few buildings that had been left standing on the narrow littoral next to the river. Even more difficult, though, was to reconcile these scenes with the vista of the modern city visible from a museum window.

Chongqing's role as a footnote in world history is over. It is no longer merely 'a point in time', a focus for outside ambitions or a forward position in an international theatre of events animated from Tokyo, Washington and Nanking. It is now the centre, at least symbolically, of a trend that is reshaping the world. The city is engaged in a revival more far-reaching than its wartime destruction. A tumult of construction is under way, an outpouring of energy that eclipses everything before it. The area where the swath of rubble is shown on the old museum photograph is now a zone of high-rise, glass and concrete office buildings, neon-lit shopping malls and restaurants selling hot pot, the spicy dish for which the city is famous.

The easiest way to describe the transformation under way in

Chongqing is by comparing it to Chicago in the nineteenth century. The 'city of the century' then was to the birth of American nationhood what Chongqing, in many ways, is to the renaissance of China in the twenty-first century. Chicago was a gateway to vast and largely undeveloped lands to its west, a hub where the traffic of roads, rail lines and waterways converged, and a centre for business where ambition eviscerated risk. Chongqing, also, is all of these things. The location of both cities was preordained by natural features, in Chicago's case by its proximity to Lake Michigan and the rivers that feed it and in Chongqing's by its position on the confluence of the Yangtze and Jialing Rivers. But the drive behind both places is the vitality of a population that migrated to live and work there.

Caught up in their booms, neither city could be described as aesthetically pleasing. H.G. Wells, the author, was appalled by the abattoirs in Chicago's northern suburbs which slaughtered live-stock from all over the Midwest. He wrote of an 'unwholesome reek' as his train passed by the slaughterhouses and stationary carriages packed with 'doomed cattle'. Although some observers saw in Chicago 'a concentrated essence of Americanism', Wells found it 'one hoarse cry for discipline' and, as he travelled through the final fathoms of smoke and grime into the 'large emptiness of America', he described the city retreating into the distance as a 'dark smear in the sky'.

Chongqing presents a similar aspect today. As I approached it from the air, it was lost in its own pollution. The river mist that White and Jacoby remember creeping over their 'sleepy town' has become a blanket of industrial smog, acrid to the taste, enveloping everything. I thought I could even discern it curling into the corridors of my hotel. Beyond the hotel windows was a ceaseless clamour; the pounding of jackhammers, the churning of cement mixers, the impatient clarion of car horns, the cries of the hawkers in the back alleys and the gurgle of pipes that spew a billion tonnes of untreated sewage into the Yangtze each year. Amid the hubbub, people were infused with purpose. Middle-class women in leotards pounded the running machines in a fitness centre visible from a main street through ceiling-to-floor windows. Around the corner, a group of businessmen, all dressed in black, disappeared into the faux baroque doorway of an establishment called 'The Rich Club' to have their drinks poured, vanities massaged and passions quenched by country girls offering the 'three accompaniments'.

Nearby, in a hot pot restaurant, an extended family celebrating a birthday party had grown red-faced on rice spirit. As the drink flowed, the singing began. The songs were high-pitched and nasal, and the tunes jaunty. I imagined they were imports from villages in the mountains around the city. Outside on the roadside, as I stood making notes, a high school student with halting English approached me with her mother a couple of steps behind. She wanted me to get her out of this place. The pollution was lethal, she said, and everyone was being poisoned. Quiet tears started to roll down her cheeks. Her mother tugged at her arm, embarrassed at the display of emotion, but the girl persisted as the tears flowed more freely. I could see that the air was bad but I was puzzled as to why this should cause grief. Then she told me; her father had died recently of throat cancer. She stood on the pavement next to a giant plastic-and-velvet Santa Claus imitating the hoarse, barking way he used to talk.

The raw human effort that girded nineteenth-century Chicago and propels Chongqing today underpins the two cities' most revealing similarity; the speed of their expansion. When Chicago was transforming the Midwest and helping to turn America from a coastal to a continental economy, the rapid pace of its physical and population growth became a much mentioned phenomenon. Charles Dudley Warner, a famous travel writer of that time, wrote: 'there is in history no parallel to this [meteoric growth]. Not St Petersburg rising out of the marshes at an imperial edict, nor Berlin, the magic creation of a consolidated empire and a Caesar's power.'[2] His friend Mark Twain, also a frequent visitor, also recalled the city's changing visage in his book, *Life on the Mississippi*. 'We struck the home trail now, and in a few hours were in that astonishing Chicago – a city where they are always rubbing a lamp, and fetching up the genii, and contriving and achieving new impossibilities. It is hopeless for the occasional visitor to try to keep up with Chicago – she outgrows her prophesies faster than she can make them. She is always a novelty; for she is never the Chicago you saw when you passed through the last time.'[3]

Impressive though Chicago's transformation must have seemed then, its dimensions pale next to those of Chongqing today. Herein lies the key to understanding why China's emergence is different and unprecedented. Although it is following a path of the industrialisation and urbanisation blazed by the United States during the nineteenth century, Japan since the 1950s and several other nations in more recent times, the sheer scale and speed of its renaissance puts it in a class of its own. The appetites that are correspondingly released are of a power that is only just starting to be felt around the world, and yet they are already forceful enough to pluck a steel plant whole from the middle of the German city it used to nurture.

Chicago, then known as the fastest-growing city on earth, took the fifty years until 1900 to increase its population to 1.7 million people. Chongqing is growing at *eight* times that speed. In the six years from 1998, it grew by 1.7 million people, or an average of nearly 300,000 new inhabitants a year. Most of these people were migrants from the countryside who came to seek employment in factories, or as maids, labourers or a thousand other jobs that hold the promise of an urban future and a new life for themselves and their children. To accommodate this human tide, the city proper has had to expand in size by at least 20 square kilometres in each year since 1998. In 2004, as the migration from rural areas accelerated, some 25 square kilometres of new houses, factories, roads, railways, ports and other urban infrastructure had to be built. The same again was happening in 2005. The result of this has been that, since 1998, the city has grown, in population terms, by the equivalent of three Dortmunds, two Birminghams and a couple of Detroits. If the future bears out the conservative predictions of its urban planners, the city will leap from a current 4 million inhabitants to 6.6 million by 2010 – or more than the combined population of the eleven cities that make up Germany's industrial Ruhr.

Chongqing city is the focal point of a larger area designated as a 'municipality', and it may be that at some time in the future much of that municipality, which is now comprised mainly of towns, villages and farmland that hold a total population of around 32 million, will agglomerate into a single conurbation. If it does so, it may lay claim to being the largest city on earth. But at the moment, the most extraordinary thing about Chongqing is that it is not necessarily exceptional. Urbanisation on a massive scale is happening in towns and cities all over China and the process is not expected to abate at any time in the foreseeable future. This trend, taken in its entirety, is awe-inspiring. In 1949, the year of the revolution, the number of Chinese cities with a population of more than one million was only five, and those with between 500,000 and one million inhabitants numbered just eight. In 2000, the last year for which figures were available, those numbers had risen to forty and fifty-three respectively.[4] Japan, by contrast, has only six cities with more than one million inhabitants.

Yet China's urbanisation is only in its infancy. There are roughly 400 million people living in towns and cities at the moment, but in 2050 that number is expected to have risen by between 600 and 700 million to reach a total of one billion or 1.1 billion.[5] Even at that level, China may be only slightly more than 70 per cent urbanised, compared to prevailing rates of around 90 per cent for the UK and the US, just over 80 per cent for France and Germany, and 77 per cent for Japan. The investment required to settle so many people in an urban environment is impossible to calculate with any accuracy, but it is clear that worldwide demand for steel, aluminium, copper, nickel, iron ore, oil, gas, coal and many other basic metals and resources may remain strong for as long as urbanisation in China unfolds at a rapid clip.

The momentum behind the process shows no sign of exhaustion, at least in the foreseeable future. The reason for this lies within another of China's most salient characteristics, something I call the compression of developmental time. What this means, on a human level, is demonstrated by someone I met in Chongqing, a young woman called Huang. She had a dimpled smile, a face that betrayed her feelings and a job selling low-end real estate to out-of-towners who wanted to move, as she had done, to the big metropolis. A miniature pink mobile phone hung on a ribbon around her neck. But 110 kilometres away in the village of her birth, she was the daughter of a peasant farmer who fed plump white ducks on a small pond and tilled a half-acre plot of land. The family house was an old stone structure, and it was so typical of peasant dwellings that it was faithful to the very origin of the Chinese character for 'home', which shows the symbol for 'pig' beneath the symbol for 'roof'. In a back room beyond the kitchen, a pig sat in a sty beneath an open latrine. There was nothing unusual in this. Many of the farmhouses around Chongqing had a similar arrangement.

Huang's home and village had barely changed in hundreds of years. But the rise of modern urban centres like Chongqing had meant that in the two hours it took for Huang to travel between her old home and her new life, she traversed centuries of developmental time. This time warp effect is a crucial propellant of China's economic rise. Back in the village, where land to population ratios are among the lowest in the world, families often have little more than a subsistence income. Over 700 million people are thought to get by on less than $2 a day. That provides a huge pool of labour that is willing to work at pre-industrial wages in factories capable of producing goods at a speed that is thousands of times faster than was possible during the UK's Industrial Revolution some 230 years ago. The productivity that results from this compression of developmental time is spectacular, and it guarantees that as long as there are factories being built in places such as Chongqing, there will be robust demand for the labour of farmers' children.

The wages of migrant workers have risen considerably since reforms began in 1978, especially for those who work in factories along the east and south coasts. But, in historical terms, they remain paltry. During the early stages of the Industrial Revolution in the UK, the British parliament triggered riots by rejecting the Weaver's Minimum Wage Bill, a piece of legislation that would have lifted the wages of handloom operators above the prevailing 8 shillings for an eighty-four-hour week.[6] But in Chongqing today, offering such a wage might trigger a disturbance for the opposite reason. Adjusted for time and converted into renminbi, those 8 shillings would now be worth 1,300 a month, or about double what a semi-skilled migrant worker could expect for a similar number of hours. Even in the booming factory towns in Guangdong province near Hong Kong and in the Yangtze basin, 1,300 renminbi a month is still an attractive salary. In nineteenth-century Chicago, too, workers were far better compensated than they are in China today. For instance, a worker in a lumber yard in Chicago in the late 1850s could expect to get between $10 to $15 a month in the dollars of the day.[7] Converted to current values, that is the equivalent of between $196 and $294 a month – or between one and a half and three times the current Chinese wage for a similar manual job.

The marriage of cheap labour with modern factories does much to make China competitive and that competitiveness justifies the huge investments required to carry forward the process of urbanisation. But those are not the only forces behind the burgeoning appetite. Another is that when it comes to infrastructure, China is remaking itself in the image of its superpower mentor, the United States – only more quickly and on a larger scale. Sometimes the resemblances are uncanny. It is no accident that Chongqing seems to mirror Chicago in days gone by. Its city planners and transport experts have spent months travelling the United States absorbing the detail of how efficiencies are created by modern cities and infrastructure. 'The dream of becoming like Chicago is too delicious a dream,' said Chen Zhigang, one of the city's senior urban planners.

Chinese planners have learned their lessons well. They know that the US interstate highway system is reckoned to have reduced the costs to American companies of producing goods and services by over $1 trillion in the first forty years of its operation since 1956. So in the late 1990s, they started to build their own. The roads are numbered in ways similar to those in America, so the big artery that traverses China from east to west is not Route 66, but Route 312. The signposts along the highways have the same white letters on a green background. And just as in the US, new roads are spawning their own auto-centric micro-economies. There are repair shops, car washes, petrol stations, fast-food restaurants and 'leisure centres' providing prostitutes for long-distance truck drivers.

In some places, the new expressways have opened up vast new markets. The city of Wuhu, a river port on the Yangtze's middle course, was a backwater as recently as 1998. When I first went there at that time, it took me six hours along a bone-jangling, pot-holed road to reach it from Hefei, the provincial capital. When I did the journey again in 2002, it took an hour and a half and Wuhu had been transformed. In just four years, four expressways, a road and rail bridge over the Yangtze and a river port had been built. It was now possible, the vice-mayor told me, to reach 250 million people within eight hours of the city centre. 'That is the population of America,' he said with a smile.

The only real difference between China's expressway system and the US Interstate is that, when it is done, China's will be longer. Although only around 30,000 kilometres have thus far been completed, Beijing plans by 2030 to have laid 86,000 kilometres, a few thousand kilometres more than the existing US system. At the same time as it builds its highways, it is also recreating an upscale version of America's great nineteenth-century railroad boom. It has plans for a high-speed track to link Beijing to Shanghai and is near to completing the Qinghai-Tibet railway, an engineering challenge that recalls the building of the US transcontinental railroad through the Sierra Nevadas. Nearly 800 miles of the Tibet railway run at more than 14,500 feet above sea level and over 500 kilometres of track are laid on permanently frozen soil. Its longest tunnel, built through more than 3 kilometres of rock, is longer than any carved through the Sierra Nevadas by the thousands of Chinese coolies who had arrived in California after fleeing war and famine in China in the 1860s.

Of course, not all the feats of Chinese infrastructure have been inspired by American example. The dream of building a dam to span the Yangtze stretches back about eighty years to Sun Yat-sen, the founder of the KMT and the first of several Chinese leaders to see the country's biggest river not as a silken, elegiac thread but as a sinew, a muscle, that if flexed could lift the nation from poverty.

If the water power of the Yangtze and Yellow Rivers could be utilised by the newest methods to generate electrical power, about one hundred million horsepower might be obtained. Since one horsepower is equivalent to the power of eight strong men, one hundred million horsepower would be equivalent to the power of eight hundred million man power . . . Manpower can be used only eight hours a day, but mechanical horsepower can be used all twenty-four hours . . . If we could utilize the water power in the Yangtze and Yellow rivers to generate one hundred million horsepower of electrical energy, we would be putting twenty four hundred million men to work! When that time comes, we shall have enough power to supply railways, motor cars, fertilizer factories and all kinds of manufacturing establishments.[8]

(Sun Yat-sen, speech, 1924)

In 2003, the Three Gorges Dam was built and Sun's dream, if not his optimistic mathematical calculations, was realised. The Chinese project drew comparisons with the Hoover Dam which, built in the 1930s across the Colorado River, had helped create a whole new regional economy from nothing and raised a city, Boulder, out of a stretch of desert. The Hoover Dam was 221 metres high, 379 metres long and able to generate 2,080 megawatts of electricity – an engineering wonder of the world. But the Three Gorges, which spans the Yangtze River a few hundred kilometres east of Chongqing, is six times as long and eight times as powerful as the Hoover. And it is by no means a one-off. Scores of dams larger or around the same size as the Hoover are planned for construction across the upper reaches of the Yangtze, the Mekong and the Salween as they tumble down from the tablelands of Tibet. In each year since 2004, China has built enough power plants to supply all the electricity needs of a large European economy such as Italy's or Spain's.

The Three Gorges has spin-off benefits too. The reservoir it has created will by 2009 stretch all the way upriver to Chongqing, eliminating the rapids and currents that made the KMT's retreat from Nanking so perilous. In 2004, the lake was filling up and by 2009 ocean-going vessels will be able to travel all the way from the sea to Chongqing, a distance of 1,250 miles. The city is building two large container ports in anticipation of an upsurge in traffic.

When this happens, the changes it brings could be similar to those wrought by the construction of the Erie Canal in the US in 1825. The Erie was an essential foundation in American nationhood, opening up the Midwest to commerce by reducing the cost of shipping grain between Buffalo, Detroit, Cleveland and New York by 90 per cent from the day that it started operating.[9] It is interesting to note, however, that the cost of shipping a tonne of wheat one kilometre along the Erie in 1825 was around 120 times higher than the cost of transporting a tonne of merchandise one kilometre down the Yangtze in 2005, calculated by adjusting dollar values over time. The reasons for this include improvements in boat technology, logistics and fuel efficiency.

Taken together, these advantages describe one aspect of China's supercharged emergence. Centuries of developmental time have coalesced into a concentrated vigour. People paid less than they would have been during Britain's Industrial Revolution are being put to work in factories equipped with up-to-the-minute machinery. The manufacturing competitiveness thus created is the main lure behind a massive factory-building boom that is itself driving the migration of young workers from the countryside to hundreds of cities, such as Chongqing. Their arrival, coupled with that of tens of millions of others seeking non-factory jobs, is forcing cities to expand at speeds that are unprecedented in human history. The whole process is facilitated by the construction of a transport infrastructure that is set to be the equal of America's. Such are the sources of some of China's world-shaping energies and appetites.

China is absorbed in laying the infrastructural underpinnings of a future superpower. It is already commonplace for observers to extrapolate from current growth rates that China will surpass the US as the world's largest economy sometime around 2040. This prediction assumes, of course, that the graphs tracing the country's current trajectory continue their unrelenting ascent. Those who make this assumption do so partly because of the long-range prospects for development that are evident in places such as Chongqing. Another common justification for predictions of greatness is historical determinism – the belief that because China was the world's economic superpower for most of the last two millennia, it is destined to be so again.

It may transpire, however, that events do not conform to neat extrapolations. In the second half of this book, I try to show why linear predictions of a manifest Chinese destiny may be flawed. As for historical determinism, the facts are by no means as straightforward as they may seem. Leaving aside for the moment the broader philosophical question of whether history is hard-wired to repeat itself, the issue of whether China was ever truly an 'economic superpower' is itself open to debate.

Certainly, its technological prowess has been awesome. Long before the dawn of recorded history, the Chinese mastered techniques not developed in Europe until thousands of years later. Silk fragments discovered recently date from 4,000 years ago – 2,000 years before sericulture spread to the Roman empire. Another discovery suggests that as early as the sixteenth century BC in a bronze foundry in the northern province of Henan that covered an area of 10,000 square metres, the Chinese may have had a prototype of the industrial process, complete with the subdivision of labour that would not become widespread in Europe until the Industrial Revolution. In addition, it is well known that although bronzes were made in the Near East earlier than in China, the single-casting techniques developed in settlements on the central plains and the sophistication of the finished items remained unrivalled for hundreds of years.

As in any country, China's development went in fits and starts. There were hundreds of years during which little of worth appears to have been invented, followed by an apparently sudden flowering of creative talent. Perhaps the greatest outpouring of such talent came from the tenth to the thirteenth centuries. The inventions from this time include several technologies that either remain in use today or have lapsed from modern life only relatively recently. The windmill, the lock gates that control the flow of water in canals, mechanical clockwork, power transmission by a driving belt, water-powered metallurgical blowing engines, hempspinning machines, gear wheels, sternpost rudders for ships and water-powered trip hammers for forges are all technologies that originated in China and spread around the world. Other inventions such as gunpowder, printing and various astrological devices were also in evidence in China before they gained currency in the West.

In more modern times, the examples of ships and porcelain provide further evidence of China's technological superiority. Fifteenth-century shipyards in China made ocean-going wooden traders three times larger than anything the British put in the water before the 1800s. The largest of these vessels, one of the 'treasure ships' used by the Ming dynasty admiral Zheng He on his trading missions to Asia and Africa, weighed a staggering 7,800 tonnes. Nothing approaching that size was built anywhere else in the world until more than 400 years later, when the British engineer Isambard Kingdom Brunel defied legions of sceptics by constructing his 'Great Ship' out of iron in the middle of the nineteenth century.

The example of porcelain shows a similar, enviable precocity. The exact date of porcelain's invention in China is a subject of controversy, but it is clear that by the thirteenth century, techniques were well advanced. By the sixteenth century, most of Europe's ruling classes were in thrall to this mysterious material which combined a translucent luminosity with a hardness that allowed Chinese artisans to make ceramics that were almost eggshell thin. So enraptured were some of Europe's princes, monarchs and barons by porcelain that the flow of funds from aristocratic coffers to the pottery town of Jingdezhen in central China swelled over time into a flood. One noble, Augustus the Strong of Saxony, spent 100,000 thalers – or enough to pay the annual salary of a thousand skilled craftsmen – to buy porcelain in the first year of his reign alone.[10]

The economic impact of porcelain imports was such that many of the most powerful families in Europe threw themselves into a desperate quest to discover how the wonderful material was made. They had only vague, second-hand accounts which had trickled back from China to go on: a special clay was required and it had to be fired at very high temperatures. More than that was guesswork. By 1705, a replica had been achieved in France, a so-called 'soft paste'. But it was instantly recognisable as inferior to the real thing.

Augustus the Strong, however, was both resourceful and determined. He set up what would now be called a research and development programme – though one with medieval characteristics – in his castle at Meissen. His researchers worked as captives and his chief technician, Johann Böttger, may have been in fear of his life having made the earlier blunder of promising his impatient patron that he could turn base metals into gold. Alchemy he never managed, but he did, through luck, stumble upon the right ingredients for porcelain. He mixed a certain type of fine clay found near a place called Colditz with alabaster in 1708. It happened that Colditz clay was identical to Chinese kaolin, the hitherto secret ingredient that made porcelain so hard and glassy. Although it would be some years before Meissen porcelain could compete with the exquisite artefacts of Jingdezhen, the discovery nevertheless helped alleviate Europe's first, but not its last, balance of payments crisis with China.

Later, however, the creativity that led to Chinese innovations such as porcelain seemed to dissipate. In the late eighteenth and early nineteenth centuries China lost the technological lead it arguably had held for millennia. This decline was partly relative; the Industrial Revolution had thrown up a tumult of ingenuity that spread across much of Europe. But it was also partly that China itself was growing stale. Theories as to why this happened abound. One suggests that the rigidity of an imperial examination process that channelled intellectual energy into literature and neglected the sciences had an impact on technological inventiveness. Another maintains that a sharp growth in population made it cheap to hire workers, thereby inhibiting the development of labour-saving machinery. A third points out that deforestation deprived China of adequate supplies of wood, its primary energy source. A fourth theory had it that the regular military campaigns along China's northern and northwestern frontiers diverted funding and focus away from peacetime pursuits. The Chinese government, for its part, blames its slide from technological pre-eminence on the rapaciousness of Western powers that attacked Chinese ports, peddled opium to its people and occupied parts of its territory. All of these theories would seem to contain a measure of validity. However, the work of Angus Maddison, a leading economic historian, shows that the decline, in terms of individual prosperity, started long before the eighteenth century.

The zenith of Chinese prosperity was in the Tang dynasty (AD 618–906), an era that is also regarded as a golden cultural age. Some of the most moving poetry dates from that era and the ceramic likenesses of courtesans, horses and camels fashioned then remain unsurpassed in their beauty. In those days, the country had several cities with a population of over half a million, whereas Europe's proudest urban centres could boast of only tens of thousands of residents. The Tang was also an age of inter-nationalism. The Silk Road ran from the central city of Chang'an, or modern-day Xi'an, to the central Asian cities of Samarkand, Bukhara and beyond. The ports of Quanzhou and Guangzhou on the south coast were heavily engaged in trade, mostly with south-east Asia. Foreigners were present in numbers that were not to be equalled until the first half of the twentieth century. Not only did some 25,000 Turks, Afghans, Tajiks, Jews, Zoroastrians and Christians reside in Chang'an, but non-Chinese even occupied senior administrative, military and commercial positions. In south-ern trading cities, foreigners may have been even more numerous than in Chang'an. Perhaps as many as 100,000 non-Chinese may have lived in them during the first half of the Tang, before xenophobic massacres in 760 and 879 drove numbers down.[11]

But a couple of hundred years later, according to Maddison's figures, things started to slowly deteriorate. By 1400, Chinese were still richer on average than Europeans and the size of their economy was also larger than that of Western Europe. At that time, Chinese earned an average of $500 each (calculated at 1985 values) spread across a population of 74 million people, meaning that gross domestic product amounted to the equivalent of 37 billion 1985 dollars. Western Europeans, by contrast, were earning $430 per head and had a population of 43 million, so their overall economic output was worth $18.4 billion. In 1820, however, China's per capita income remained at around $500, but Eur-opeans were by then earning on average some $1,034 each. By 1950, the difference was even more dramatic. The Chinese were by then earning around $454 per capita, less than they had done in the fifteenth century. Europeans, by contrast, were pulling in an average of $4,902 each.[12] Even though Europe's population was still smaller than China's, the value of its economic output was larger by several multiples.

These figures show why it might not be appropriate to regard China in history as an economic superpower, at least by con-temporary standards. For hundreds of years the country was locked in a cycle of growth without development. Its people, on average, were living the same lives in 1950 as they had done a millennium earlier, in spite of obvious changes in technology, customs and politics. The only impetus behind the expansion of the Chinese economy during those centuries seems to have been the increase in the size of its population. But this did not bestow prosperity and vitality to the people; rather it intensified competition for limited resources, inflated the death tolls from periodic famines and natural disasters and forced the government to expend more and more energy on social control. In short, though China was certainly a large economy and often the largest economy on earth, the lives of the majority of its people rarely rose above the level of subsistence.

There were other ways, too, in which China's realities were not consistent with the image or idea of an economic superpower. In common usage, the word superpower implies a projection of influence. But China, since the Tang dynasty, has dwelt largely within itself. Although it traded with the outside world, the volume of this trade as a percentage of the size of its economy has been small – no more in the nineteenth century, for instance, than around one per cent of its gross domestic product. Therefore, the effect it had on the world around it was mostly that of a large, brooding presence that fought protracted wars along its borders. This was noticed at various times by various Western commentators but Adam Smith may have summed it up best in his 1776 masterwork, *The Wealth of Nations*.

China seems to have been long stationary, and had probably long ago acquired that full complement of riches which is consistent with the nature of its laws and institutions. But this complement may be much inferior to what, with other laws and institutions, the nature of its soil, climate and situation might admit of. A country which neglects or despises foreign commerce, and which admits the vessels of foreign nations into one or two of its ports only, cannot transact the same quantity of business which it might do with different laws and institutions.[13]

It is neither a coincidence nor a surprise, therefore, that China's economic ascent since Deng started reforms in 1978 has been accompanied by a level of openness to foreign commerce that is reminiscent of the golden age of the Tang. The fruits of this policy are also visible in figures: in 1975 – the nadir in well over a thousand years of economic history – Chinese earned on average just 7.5 per cent of the income of Western Europeans. But by 2000, there had been a startling turnaround, and incomes were back up to about 20 per cent of European levels.[14] Which, to put it another way, means that Beijing has succeeded in turning the clock back to about 1850 – the last time that the wealth gap was so narrow.

The process by which China is turning back the clock and joining the world is not pretty or forgiving. It is full of human suffering, alienation and longing. And it starts with men like Wang Qiling, the head of a family of migrant workers. Wang, a slight, wiry man with eyebrows set in a frown, works as a caretaker at a weekend cottage rented by Westerners in a beautiful village on the outskirts of Beijing. The village grew up in the Ming dynasty (1386–1644), when its inhabitants were charged with guarding and tending the tombs of the emperors' favourite concubines. But after the Ming succumbed to an invasion of Manchu nomads from the northern steppes, the tombs fell into disrepair. Bricks from their perimeter walls were pillaged to build houses and the land inside them was used to plant fruit trees or crops. In recent years, one large, intricately carved marble slab that used to be an offertory platform to a concubine's spirit has become a makeshift ping-pong table for village boys.

Wang's home is far from Beijing, in a part of China that is so different it could be another world. He comes from the village of White Horse in a rural county several hours' drive from Chongqing, a place famous for 'hua jiao', the peppers that make 'palace treasure chicken' and other dishes taste numbing on the tongue. His birthplace is hot and humid, full of the shade from broadleaf trees and the sounds of insects. On the outskirts of Beijing, though, the air is dry, the winters long, the food strange and the locals mostly unfriendly. In particular, the couple who own the cottage next door to the one he tends are unpleasant, simply because they can be. They tell him to his face that his thick southern accent, which mixes up the tones that are essential to understanding Chinese, hurts their ears. They tell him he speaks worse than the

40

foreigners he works for and that he should go back home, leaving the concubine tomb village to the people for whom it was intended.

When a macaque monkey which they kept tethered to a tree by their house broke free one day and bit Wang seven times, the couple saw no reason to apologise. They, after all, were successful people with a 100 cc motorbike who had given up working in the fields, borrowed some money and bought a sauna business in the nearby town of Changping. To them, Wang embodied the life they had left behind. He was a person of no consequence, a peasant. In his own way, however, Wang was engaged in the same project as his neighbours. He had walked out of his home village for the same reason as all of the 120 million people who make up the 'blind tide' of migrant workers. To escape. He had left his home, his wife and his teenage son for seven straight years because his job as a caretaker offered some hope of finding a path out of the myriad humiliations of poverty. Whatever the drawbacks of his current work – the loneliness, the way he missed seeing his son grow up and the strangeness of watching weekend guests spend the equivalent of several months' of his salary on an afternoon barbecue – they were not as bad as the memories of a childhood without enough food.

The escape that Wang was plotting was not his own but his son's. Without education or skills beyond farming, his own life was already set in its trammels. But his son had a chance at a future. Ever since he was born he had been costing his father extra; his name, Sifa, was a pun on the words for 'four fine' because, being the third child, his birth had marked the violation of an official quota that limited farming families to two children. The fine for breaking the quota in those days was 400 renminbi, the equivalent of about a year's income and an amount that Wang had been proud to fork out. Sifa had repaid the investment, excelling at school and becoming the first person from White Horse village ever to make it to university. He did not go to a prestigious campus like Peking or Tsinghua universities in the capital but his enrolment at college represented a first step on the single-plank bridge over the chasm that separates those who work with their brains and those who use their hands. All in all, though, it cost around 10,000 renminbi a year to keep Sifa at college – more than Wang's annual salary.[15]

That meant that at times Wang's daughters also had to help pay the bills. They were migrants too. One had joined the army of more than 20 million other migrant workers who had found employment in several new cities clustering along the waterways and highways of the Pearl River Delta near Hong Kong. The other, Qiping, had been a nanny to an English family, first in Beijing and then after that for a few years in London. She had come to the capital in the mid 1990s, several years before the 'blind tide's' high water mark. It was a daring move, one which her mother at the time had resisted on the grounds that it was not safe for a young country girl barely out of her teens to try to make a living in an unfamiliar metropolis. But Qiping had insisted, and things had gone her way. The family she worked for were kind to her, and she loved the children whom she looked after. In London they all lived in a nice house next to a park. Looking out over the park's well-tended lawns and arboretums, she did sometimes wonder why so much good agricultural land was being allowed to go to waste.

The most difficult thing about the UK was the cost. Although she was lonely she avoided making friends because of the outlay it entailed. Even a cup of coffee could set you back the equivalent of a week or more of spending money in White Horse. She saved everything she earned and in the four years that she lived in the UK, she did not buy one article of clothing. Even though she had a husband in China, she never phoned him. When he called her long-distance, she would berate him: 'Why do I have to endure loneliness here, away from my family and everything? To make money! But you are wasting our precious money on phone calls,' she remembers telling him on the phone. He would counter that he was using IP cards to call her because they were cheaper than the usual rates. He had to hear her voice, he would say. 'I am keeping these IP cards as a token of our love,' he told her once.

Aside from helping with Sifa's education, Qiling also kept some of her money for herself. Her savings – like those of all young female migrant workers – had a value beyond their nominal worth. Young women in rural China have to contend not only with the privations of poverty but also with an entrenched patriarchal system. When a rural woman marries, she leaves her own parents behind and becomes the property of her husband's family. 'A woman marries outward, in the same way that [waste] water is thrown from the house,' as an old saying puts it. She is expected to work for and obey everyone in the male line – her husband, his father and his brothers. Her only hope of changing this disenfranchised state is to give birth to her own power base, a son. But even if she manages this, she has to maintain vigilance towards her mother-in-law, who is often wary over her daughter-in-law's growing influence. The mother-in-law/daughter-in-law relationship has been a mainstay of literary tragedy, and for good reason. Although family hierarchies have loosened up in the cities, the countryside remains a cruel place for young women joining society.

Suicides among young rural women rank as one of China's greatest social ills. The number of women who commit suicide – about 500 a day on average – is much higher in both absolute and relative terms than in any other country. Some 56 per cent of the world's female suicides are in China, according to a study by the World Bank, Harvard University and the World Health Organisation.[16] This figure, of course, does not include the very large numbers who try to kill themselves but fail. Swallowing pesticide, which is readily available, is the most common means employed. It yields a quick and intensely painful death, which can be averted if the woman's stomach is pumped in time. Although the general cause of suicide is a feeling of hopelessness and rejection, the trigger is often physical abuse. Newspapers are full of stories of gruesome matrimonial violence.

What women lack most in rural China is power and status, as the prevalence of suicide shows. The money that they earn, therefore, in factories on the coast or as housemaids and nannies in the large cities, or as prostitutes in bars, 'leisure centres' and motels all over the country is often spent on their return home in compensating for this deficiency. They buy things that confer an aura of importance. When Qiping got back from Richmond Park with the fruits of her youthful labour, about $10,000, she spent it on a house. Not just any house, but a four-storey, white-tiled building with 120 square metres of space on each floor. She could have fitted her London bedroom into one of its toilets. There was a large, flat-screen TV in one room, complete with a branded sound system. Elsewhere there was a DVD player and mod cons which she never used. The house had used all of her savings and some $5,000 in borrowings besides. But it was definitely worth it. Everyone now knew that she was a woman of substance, not a person to be trifled with. It was surely no accident that the home of her brother-in-law, just across the road from her own, was a full storey shorter than hers.

The story of Qiping is not quite typical. Most migrant workers are not nannies and they do not generally go abroad. They toil in factories in the Pearl and Yangtze River Deltas, or in steel towns such as Jinfeng, making heavy industrial goods or the things that fill the shelves in Wal-Mart, Metro, Target, Carrefour and other hypermarkets around the world. Few of them get welfare benefits, many work shifts of 12, 15 or even 18 hours a day and most of them earn Industrial Revolution wages. But still there are millions upon millions of rural people who are willing to do such work, not because they are attracted to it but because they are driven to it by the material and social privations bequeathed by Chinese history. Centuries of poverty and oppression have made village life in China anything but a rural idyll. Thus, people such as Qiping, her sister and her father in the concubine tomb village near Beijing are, in some sense, not so much economic migrants as émigrés from a cruel past.

THREE

The train sat for a long time at the station and when it finally did depart, it seemed to creep, so that the moment of movement was all but imperceptible. My first inkling that the journey from Chongqing had started came when the play of platform shadows on the net curtains of my 'soft-sleeper' compartment slipped slightly in their frame. The indistinct outlines of people hawking chicken legs and tea eggs from trolleys then slid slowly out of view. Other, more fleeting images took their place; underwear flapping on a suburban washing line, a man shovelling coal and, a few minutes further down the track, a donkey standing by stones in a quarry. As the train quickened, the snapshots blurred and the rhythm of the rolling stock grew louder. And then, after a certain time, that rhythm no longer registered in the consciousness and the compartment seemed to fall still. Only the tremor of water in teacups on the table by the window supplied a sensation of flux. As on all long journeys in China, an air of suspended time seeped through the carriage, lending candour to conversations between travellers whose destinations would mark the end of their acquaintance. I sat, as so often before, looking out of the window and thinking about the size and complexity of the country parading past outside.

Out of Chongqing, the track quickly runs into mountains and through an impressive series of tunnels. Later, it travels into country that opens out onto the flood plains of the Yangtze. The natural scenery changes but in every direction throughout the journey, one thing is constant. People. Their presence and weight is everywhere. Even in the spaces between the factories, towns and villages, people could be seen moving to and fro on bicycles, tractors, carts, buses, cars and trains. The vista from the train window was rarely uncluttered by development. The pressure of population was such that the smallest parcels of cultivatable land high on mountain ledges and on the verges of roads had been put to agricultural use. On this journey, as on many others over the years, I wondered how the pervasive presence of people has shaped China's experience and moulded the national consciousness. I remembered a young woman I knew some eighteen years earlier in Tokyo. The daughter of a high-ranking cadre in Beijing, she had been sent to Japan for language study. We met at a night school crammer. One evening after classes, our conversation turned to the Great Leap Forward, the three years of Mao-inspired chaos that resulted in a famine in which at least 30 million people are thought to have died. 'It was a good thing that they died,' she said. 'There are just too many people in China.'

It is difficult to separate people from the influence of the population that surrounds them. And yet the urge is insistent. How does a national populace of 1.3 billion, the largest in the world, affect politics, economics and society? What of the psychological impact, accumulated over centuries, of living as a single unit within a number so forbiddingly huge? Most of the Chinese to whom I have addressed these questions have shrugged, as if they were futile or the answers blatantly obvious. Nevertheless, intimations of a profound legacy are everywhere, embedded in human behaviour, in the attitude of the state towards order, on every page of a turbulent history and in the governing relationships of commerce. Numbers possess a power that transcends the mechanics of mathematics. In the distant past, 'wu ren chu' (no people places) denoted the boundaries of the Chinese world; the grasslands, steppe, mountains and desert to the north and west beyond which everything was alien and hostile. By contrast, the world within the central plains was ordered by numbers and remains so today. Almost every phenomenon, principle, policy and directive is broken down into constituent parts. Babies are said to 'roll over at three [months], sit up at six and crawl at eight'. The link between nature and human activity is also numerically expressed. The following rhyme, conjured in the mists of history but still recited in Beijing today, calibrates the interaction of humans and climate in nine-day periods that follow a big freeze around the time of the lunar new year:

First ninth, Second ninth, don't let your hands show,
Third ninth, Fourth ninth, people are walking on ice;
Fifth ninth, Sixth ninth, stand on river banks and watch the
    willow (buds);
Seventh ninth, the river ice splits;
Eighth ninth, geese arrive;
Ninth ninth and add one ninth, ploughing oxen are
    everywhere on the land.

Human affairs are also arithmetically ordered. The 'one China principle', 'two whatevers', 'three character classic', 'four modernisations', 'five elements', 'six desires', 'seven emotions', 'eight immortals' and 'the stinking ninth category' are all terms in common usage. And as issues evolve, it is often the content rather than the matrix that alters. When the Communist Party decided that the 'dictatorship of the proletariat' should no longer be one of the 'four cardinal principles' of its ideology, it replaced it with something else rather than upset symmetry by reducing four principles to three. Officials are mesmerised by numbers because their career achievements are assessed by statistics, a reality reflected in the adage that 'statistics make officials and officials make [up] statistics'. The ability to memorise and regurgitate numbers and numerical sequences is another staple of successful officialdom. I remember one quarterly briefing of economic figures held by Li Deshui, a senior official in the National Bureau of Statistics. Staring straight ahead and without any apparent notes, he threw out hundreds of figures, all quoted to at least one decimal place, in response to an avalanche of unscripted questions. Later, when official printouts of the statistics came through, I checked them against the notes I had taken during Li's performance. He had been 100 per cent accurate.

The awe reserved for numbers is quickened when it comes to mathematical relationships and, of these, none is more alluring than multiplication. Always somewhere in the love affairs of foreigners with China down the ages there is the promise of the quantum leap. It was there when the Jesuits in the sixteenth century planned to convert 150 million souls – an opportunity bigger by multiples than any that existed in Europe. It was also evident in the fever of British merchants in the mid nineteenth century when one English merchant observed: 'If we could only persuade every person in China to lengthen his shirttail by a foot, we could keep the mills of Lancashire working around the clock.' In a similar vein, William Taft, US Secretary of State and later President, said in 1905 that 'one of the greatest commercial prizes of the world is the trade with the 400,000,000 Chinese'.[1] In the modern era since the process of 'reform and opening' began in 1978, some $550 billion of foreign direct investment has flowed in, a lot of it accompanied by dreams of exponential growth. 'I can envision the day when over half the automobiles sold in the world are sold in Asia and perhaps even in China,' said Joe Gorman, chairman of TRW Inc., the US's biggest manufacturer of auto parts, in one typical comment. 'If China were by the year 2010 or 2020 to have as many autos as the current per capita auto population of Germany today, there would be 500 million autos.'[2]

Chinese officials, cognisant of the enchantment of numbers, like to boggle the mind on overseas trips. Bo Xilai, the Minister of Commerce, told European officials in 2005: 'China is a big family. We have 200 million middle school students. Every day 22,000 girls get married; 44,000 babies are born. We eat better since we opened China's door. Every day we eat 1.6 million pigs and 24 million chickens. Our Premier not only wants young people to have a chance to study and grown-ups to have jobs, he also has to take care of 20 million kids in kindergarten and 12 million people aged 80.'

But if foreign businessmen arrive in China transfixed by size and scale, many of them depart haunted by the concept of share. They envisage being able to sell their product to a multitude of Chinese and then watch as the hoped-for multitude is sliced and diced into morsels. Only certain sections of society are willing buyers of most products and reaching them is made difficult by layers of local protectionism. When a market is finally found, aggressive domestic competitors have usually got there first. The fabled billion-person market is frequently reduced to a fraction in the figment of a dream. It has been ever thus. Chinese history is very much less the story of multiplication than of long division. The experience of having to share scarce resources among so many people has at times been inconvenient and at times traumatic. It has left an imprint not only on people like the young woman I met in Tokyo, but also on the language. The counting word for people, for instance, is 'mouth'. Rather than ask someone 'How many people are there in your family?', you should say, 'How many mouth-people do you have?' The low ratio of land to people has made the adequate provision of food a pressure felt by every dynastic ruler.

For emperors, famines were not only disasters that could, and frequently did, cause rebellion. They were also the ultimate insult; emperors were 'tian zi', the sons of heaven, and as such they were the link between the earth and the celestial authorities that controlled the rain, wind and temperature. Thus droughts, floods, famine and other natural disasters were often seen among the people as evidence that heaven had withdrawn its favour from its son – that the emperor had lost 'tian li', heaven's mandate. For example, according to one legend, the emperor Shangtang of the Shang dynasty (1766–1122 BC) decided to sacrifice himself after the country had suffered seven years of drought. He chose self-immolation on a pyre of firewood as the preferred manner of his death, but at the very instant that the wood was lit, the celestial powers took pity and made it rain, thereby putting out the fire and ending the drought with one stroke. Although the story of Shang-tang is a myth, there is nothing fanciful about the crucial relationship between land, population and power during the last three or four thousand years. The perceived loss of 'heaven's mandate' was seen as legitimising revolt and many a rebel leader, including Mao Zedong, has been swept to power at the head of a peasant army galvanised by hunger and the promise of handouts of land.

The key decisions made by such rebels after they took power always involved how much land to redistribute from the landlords to the peasant farmers, and what level of agricultural tax to levy. These simple choices did much to determine the economic future and social structure of the empire, as well as the nature of the ruler's power base. If land was parcelled out too liberally, the emperor risked losing the allegiance of the elite. But if it was not doled out enough, the peasants would remain impoverished and liable to rise up again. If taxes were too light, the imperial coffers would be strained and the emperor's authority weakened. But if they were too heavy, the masses could grow disgruntled and threaten the survival of the dynasty. Faced with the need to strike such a delicate balance between available food and demanding mouths, most new rulers made only cosmetic changes. But Mao, the founder of the modern era, was different. His approach was not only revolutionary, but unprecedented. He identified his power base as the rural peasantry and urban masses and ordered the persecution of landowners, capitalists and anyone else with a bad 'class background'. No quarter was given, no balance struck; within three years of assuming power, he had decapitated the rural elite and presided over the murder of an estimated 2 million land-owners. Mao did not recognise any authority greater than his own, so the tempering tradition of 'heaven's mandate' had no truck with him. But most decisively of all for the future of China's economy, he scorned the notion that the scarcity of land was a restraint on population growth. Every mouth, he said, was attached to two arms. People could always produce more than they consumed.

The population explosion that Mao encouraged has had far-reaching consequences. The number of people living in the main-land shot up from an estimated 582.6 million at the time of the 1953 census to an official estimate of 1.295 billion now. (The real number is almost certainly higher, but nobody knows by how much.) Anyone who had the temerity to warn the 'Great Helms-man' of his folly, such as the Chancellor of Peking University, Ma Yinchu, was summarily dealt with. Ma's 'New Population Theory', which warned of catastrophe, was denounced and the professor himself was purged. Only after Mao had died and the Party had changed its mind on population, did the politburo see fit to rehabilitate Ma, who by this time was nearly 100 years old. In the twenty-two years that his advice had gone unheeded, China's population had grown by 325 million.[3] It was not Mao who had to pay for his excesses but the masses he claimed to have liberated. In the 1980s, the state intruded into the most private realm of human behaviour, decreeing that urban families could have no more than one child while those in the countryside were restricted to two or, in some cases, more. Female infanticide, long a gruesome outcome of the fierce competition for resources, became more widespread. More common, however, was the abortion of female foetuses following ultrasound scans. One result of this has been a startling imbalance in some demographic segments of society between boys and girls, and a thriving illegal trade in brides.

Economically, population forms China's most basic paradox. It is at once its greatest strength and its gravest frailty. An unparalleled stock of human capital allows it to assume the characteristics of several countries at once. Its huge pool of low-cost, diligent factory workers arouses envy across the developing world and yet China is not merely a giant sweatshop. Mainland universities produce more graduates each year than the US. Though only a fraction of the population could currently be called consumers, the promise of a vast domestic market grows more real as the middle class (estimated at between 100 million and 150 million people in 2004) expands. In any case, recent history has proven that it is the prospect of a large market, rather than its existence, that is the key to luring foreign investors. Nevertheless, these strengths are offset to some considerable degree by the old oppression of numbers. Although China is currently poised to overtake the UK to become the world's fourth-largest economy, on a per capita basis it ranks just above the world's poorest nations, with an average income of just over $1,000 a year. Even if the country's gross domestic product one day becomes as large as that of the US, simple mathematics ordains that its people at that time will on average be only one-sixth as wealthy as Americans. At current relative rates of growth, the size of the Chinese economy will match that of the US a few years before 2040. But at that time too, the children of Mao's population explosion in the 1960s, 1970s and early 1980s will be into their retirement years. In fact, by 2040 around one-third of the then population – or some 400 million people – will be over the age of sixty. It may be that China grows old before it is rich.

However, the most important impediment of population is a variant of the challenge that emperors since time immemorial have had to deal with (and Mao so singularly failed). In the past, the balance each dynasty strove for was that between food and mouths, but the last twenty-five years of development may have banished this concern forever. The crucial equilibrium now is that between people and jobs, and so far it has proven elusive. Even when the economy grows at 9 or 10 per cent, it fails by a margin of several million to create the 24 million new jobs required each year. Thus, while China appears to the rest of the world to be enjoying an amazing growth bonanza, the officials working behind the high walls of their leadership compound in Beijing feel trapped in an endless employment crisis.

This creates an unyielding pressure for growth that influences every economic plan and strategy, and can leave Beijing with little room for compromise in its deliberations with trade partners. Barely a week goes by without some incident of labour or social unrest somewhere in the country, and some of these flare-ups are serious. If the growth rate were to drop dramatically, these convulsions would be almost certain to intensify. As economists in Beijing are fond of saying, China is like an elephant riding a bicycle. If it slows down, it could fall off and then the earth might quake.

The pressure of population combines with other features of life in China to create the salient characteristics of corporate China. Chief among these is a tendency among companies to carry on producing, or even expand production, long after any discernable profit margin has vanished. This behaviour is partly down to the mesmerising attraction of trying ever harder to win a bigger share of the 'billion consumer' market, but it is by no means as simple as that. The issue is of critical importance, though, because it helps demonstrate why it is that most manufactured products in China are in chronic oversupply – and, by extension, why so many of them are extraordinarily cheap. Virtually any manufacturer selected at random might illuminate the causes behind these various phenomena, but, before I left Chongqing I reconnected with Lifan Motorcycle, a company I had been following for some years. The more I learned about it, and the exploits of its remarkable founder, Yin Mingshan, the more I came to see it as a case study of how Chinese manufacturers often manage to undercut the prices of overseas competitors by a third or 40 per cent or even more.

Yin's career, like that of many self-made entrepreneurs, has been far from orthodox. It started when he emerged from prison feeling, as he put it, like Sun Wu Kong, the Monkey King. In the classic novel *Journey to the West* by Wu Cheng-en, the Monkey King is flung into a furnace by his enemies but instead of dying an agonising death he emerges burnished like metal, his eyes blazing and his muscles as strong as hawsers. 'It was as if the thing that I feared most was behind me. My patience had been trained and my judgement was clear; just like Sun Wu Kong,' Yin said the first time I met him.[4] We sat on wooden, hard-backed chairs around a circular table at Lifan's corporate headquarters. There was one chair between us. Yin leaned back and stretched his legs out as if he found the hours immediately after lunch a little wearying. Visible through the windows were motivational slogans painted in red on the white walls of his factory. 'He who does not feel hardship and fatigue is not a Lifan person' said one. 'If you do not work hard today, you will search hard for a job tomorrow' warned another.

Yin does not look like an ex-convict or, for that matter, the Monkey King. He is tall, a little stooped and possessed of an avuncular bearing. A pair of large black-rimmed spectacles dominates his face, giving him a professorial air. He was locked up in 1961 for so-called 'counter-revolutionary' activities, one of the most vaguely defined and yet most serious forms of crime. His parents had come from landowning capitalist families and Yin was thus a member of the 'black five categories': people from whom no good could be expected. Therefore, when a twenty-one-year-old girlfriend of his who had an uncle in America applied to leave China, the vengeful Communist officials of the day were incensed. 'America was the enemy. I was twenty-three and the girl and I were good friends. That meant that she was a traitor and I was part of an escaping-to-the-enemy-traitorous-clique,' he remembered.

Yet in prison Yin did not harbour a grudge. His recurrent thought was that he had wronged Chairman Mao and he wanted the Party to forgive him. When the prisoners were ordered to feed swine, he would grab the biggest bucket of swill. When they had to empty the public toilets he would strive to fill up his nightsoil cart quicker than his peers. 'I only dreamed of being a person again,' he said. But class enemies and traitors were not shown leniency, no matter how they behaved, and Yin stayed behind bars for nearly twenty years. When he was released in 1979, it had nothing to do with his good behaviour. One day, a letter arrived. It explained that there had been a mistake. The Party was rehabilitating him. And that was it; no apology, no compensation. But to Yin, it was a miracle. Deng Xiaoping had seized the reins of power in Beijing and started to put right some of the worst excesses of Mao's rule. Some twenty years later Yin had become one of China's most successful private entrepreneurs, but he still shook his head at the memory of how audacious Deng had been in overhauling Mao's legacy. 'There were still plenty of officials in those days who believed that everything Mao did was correct,' he said.

It had not been easy, however, for an ex-con in his forties with no work experience to find a job, even if he did feel like Sun Wu Kong. But, as with so many entrepreneurs of the 1980s, Yin's poor employment prospects turned out to be a blessing. He was allowed to start up a private business selling books and made a tidy profit. By the end of the decade, his personal wealth was far greater than that of those who had remained on the state payroll. What was more, he could see which way the wind was blowing. He had noticed that people doted on their bicycles, delighting in the smallest differences; a saddle that had a tartan cover, a new type of bell or a bob of rabbit fur for the end of a keyring. He perceived that the whole of society was straining at the moorings of enforced egalitarianism. Motorbikes would be the next big thing, just as they had been in the early days of Japan's industrial take-off. In 1992 he sold off his warehouse of books and raised $15,000 to set up the Chongqing Hongda Motorcycle Fitting Research Institute, a company of eight people including his wife and son.

The word 'Hongda' in his company name was not a mistake. It was a statement of intent. Yin wanted to build a world-beating company. He wanted to imitate the success of the great Japanese corporations Honda and Yamaha by driving them out of the Chinese market. When he had done that, he would take them on in the wider world. But somehow he had to get from his oil-slicked workshop in a suburb of a run-down secondary city to a point where he could challenge motorbikes bearing brands recognised around the globe. There was little time to spare. Both Honda and Yamaha were selling well in China, building their reputations and status. Yin took what he saw as the only feasible route: he copied designs and stole technology. Yamaha engines had recently become available locally following a licensing deal the Japanese company had forged with Jianshe Industrial, an old armaments firm which only forty years earlier had made the machine guns and cannon used to resist Japan's wartime encroachment. As part of the licensing deal, local repair shops were set up which had access to a full range of Yamaha spare parts and the know-how to fix faults. Yin went to these shops, bought their parts and picked up tips from the mechanics who worked there. Within a few months of reverse engineering he had built a replica Yamaha engine. 'To start with, we completely copied other people's stuff,' he said. 'In 1994 we made our own engine for the first time. It was not a copy. In 1995 we did three of our own engines. The Japanese never imagined that the traditional Chinese manufacturers would develop so quickly. They were quite aloof and condescending, like the Americans before Pearl Harbor.'

But in reality, there was little the Japanese could do. Government restrictions meant that Yamaha, Mitsubishi and Honda were not free to set up their own factories where they wanted; they had to form joint ventures with state-owned partners who were chosen for them by the government. They were also told they had to transfer technology to their partners as an entrance fee into a vast potential market. In addition, they were allowed to exercise only loose control over their marketing and a network of suppliers. But the lure of a billion Chinese swapping their bicycles for motorbikes seemed to override their misgivings. Yamaha got fully into bed, creating a fifty-fifty joint venture with Jianshe, a typical offspring of socialist planning that had 18,000 workers on the payroll and another 35,000 either on pensions or in some other way dependent on the factory. All of the dependants had to be paid for out of current revenues because the concept of pension funds did not exist in China in the early 1990s. Decision-making at the plant was diffuse and sluggish and every initiative was costly. However, these problems, thorny though they were, paled next to the issue of intellectual property.

The factory leaked its technological secrets like a sieve. Components suppliers who were supposed to be discreet and loyal were actually engaged in a roaring trade selling parts out of the back door to counterfeiters. Yamaha found it hard to get a grip on how serious the problem was until it brought out its flagship model, the 100ml four-stroke Jinbao, in 1995 after years of preparation. Then the full horror was revealed. Within months of its launch, exact replicas were being made in thirty-six factories throughout the country. The worst of it was that even though the copies were nearly identical, they were sold for around 6,000 renminbi each, compared with the 18,000 rmb that Jianshe-Yamaha was charging for the Jinbao.

By the mid 1990s, piracy was becoming an all-too-common phenomenon. Once it had infected an industry, it spread like a virus up the value chain and leapt from company to company. By the early years of this century it was endemic, no longer a peripheral handicap to doing business but a fact of life that almost every company in virtually every sector was forced to consider or confront. Various estimates had it that American, Japanese and European companies may have been losing more than $60 billion a year through Chinese piracy of one sort or another.[5] By necessity such estimates were rough, but if they were anywhere near accurate it meant that the loss to Western companies through intellectual property theft was far in excess of the total flow of foreign direct investment into China. In 2004, for example, foreign investment amounted to $56 billion.

Some rip-offs were systematic. Almost every time a Hollywood blockbuster was cut, it would appear on DVD in China before it had been released in the same format in America. To accomplish this, pirate networks had to have operatives under cover in the film companies that they were ripping off. DVD copies seen in Beijing often bore intermittent warnings saying 'Studio screening only. Copying strictly forbidden.' Another victim of chutzpah has been the book publishing industry. A sixth volume in the series of Harry Potter novels appeared in China months before J.K. Rowling had written it. When the real *Harry Potter and the Half-Blood Prince* did appear in English, several pirates competed to translate it and sell it online. A number of translators, unhappy with the way the book ended, wrote their own denouements.

Similarly, a series of 'how-to' business books written by Paul Thomas, a Harvard Business School professor, became a mini publishing sensation in Beijing in 2004. As his fame grew, he lent his reputation to other books by writing prefaces, and everyone seemed to be winning. But then it emerged that there was no professor at Harvard that fitted his description, and the books bearing his illustrious name had been written by students paid the equivalent of one-third of a US cent per word to make it all up. Fake books, it turns out, are big business. Several publishers, including state-owned houses, had over 100 bogus titles on the market in early 2005.

Other counterfeits are either tragic or comic, or both. Golf clubs have been widely pirated but with varying degrees of success. A bag full of impressive-looking clubs can cost less than one-tenth of their price in the US or Europe, but some snap mid shot, releasing the head of the club to chase the ball down the fairway. Other fakes are even more dangerous. Kettles blow up, electrical transformers short-circuit, medicines have no effect, brake pads fail, alcohol poisons those who drink it and fake milk powder has had the effect of starving several babies to death.

For many foreign companies, however, the problem is not sub-standard knock-offs so much as fakes that faithfully replicate the quality of the original. Motorbikes aside, the car industry has provided a prominent case study for this kind of abuse. Chery Automobile did not exist when Volkswagen, the market leader, launched its popular Jetta car in the late 1990s. But thirty-three months after starting at zero with a new company in the city of Wuhu on the banks of the Yangtze River, Chery had made its first car, a four-door saloon called the Chery that bore more than a passing resemblance to the Jetta, which at that time was China's best-selling car. Suspicions were immediately raised, partly because Chery's main investor, SAIC, was a joint venture partner of Volkswagen and partly because one of Chery's top executives used to make the Jetta in China for Volkswagen's subsidiary Audi. Volkswagen launched an investigation and found their own original parts inside the Chery. They wrote and spoke to executives at Chery, which is owned by the Wuhu city government, and eventually the Chinese company agreed not to use any more original parts.

But Chery's intellectual property tangles were not over. GM, which is also partnered with SAIC, is suing Chery for $80 million for piracy following its launch of a compact car, the QQ, which GM claims is a dead ringer for the Spark, a popular car produced by GM's subsidiary Daewoo. Chery denies all wrongdoing and says officially that it welcomes the case, which is to be held in a Beijing court. But while both sides wait for their day in court, the QQ – which has a price tag of $3,600 – is selling like hot cakes and the Spark, costing twice as much, has yet to win much of a following.

Whatever the interplay of right and wrong, the commercial result of piracy is always the same: rapid value destruction across a wide range of manufactured products. This is true not only for established goods, but also for new technologies; and evidence of an unremitting downward pull can be found both in individual examples and in aggregate prices of manufactured items since 1998. Regardless of the breakneck growth in the wider economy or the prevailing inflation as measured by broad indices such as the Consumer Price Index, the average prices of manufactured products have fallen each year. In some cases, the declines have been significant. A 29-inch flat-panel television that cost 6,000 renminbi in 1998 was going for just under rmb 2,000 in late 2004. Colour-screen cellphones were a new, trendy product in 2001 and were priced accordingly at around rmb 6,500; by late 2004 they too were trading at under rmb 2,000. Domestic brands of DVD players, all configured to play counterfeit DVDs, hit the market in 1998 at rmb 3,000 but cost around rmb 500 by late 2004. Set top boxes, which allow viewers to access satellite television, started selling for around around rmb 2,300 in 2000 but were going for around rmb 700 in late 2004.[6] Each of these products represented a new foreign technology which, once introduced to China, suffered a swift destruction of value that was due in part to piracy.

The problem, though, as Yin in the late 1990s was starting to discover, was that piracy had a way of returning to haunt those who had once thrived on it. With the technological barriers to entry non-existent and capital freely available, more and more motorbike manufacturers were springing up, each of them following the trail that Yin had blazed to prominence. By 1998 there were over a thousand motorbike factories in China producing some 15 million units a year – 5 million more than were sold. As unsold bikes filled warehouses, vicious price wars erupted until profit margins were completely obliterated. But the big players, still transfixed by a vast potential market, refused to alter their strategy. Liang Xueben, the general manager at Jianshe-Yamaha, told me in that year that he was committed to maintaining market share.[7] Only 3 per cent of Chinese owned motorbikes, he said. One day the market would take off and amazing profits would be had. Yamaha could not afford to cede ground to upstart domestic competitors now.

Eight years later, the hoped-for boom in sales had not materialised and the problem of oversupply was more acute than ever. Yin was disillusioned. Almost all of the value had been stripped out of the industry and he had begun telling people – only half in jest – that he would soon start selling his motorbikes by the kilogram, like pigs. 'The ex-factory price of our cheapest model is rmb 25 per kilo. That is a bit more than a kilo of live pig,' said one of his deputies, Yang Zhou, during another of my visits to the plant. A more pertinent comparison, however, might be with the cost of the metal and other components that go into building a motorcycle. At a sales price of around rmb 2,500, a motorbike costs only a shade more than its scrap value; the other inputs such as engineering, labour, development costs, brand, distribution and the experience and vision of the company's executives are rated as valueless. 'Clearly this is not healthy. It is malignant competition,' Yang says.

In a normal market economy companies cannot go on selling at below cost for years. Banks start to worry about their ability to repay the debts and eventually call in their loans. But China is not a normal market economy. It does not have a functioning bankruptcy law, so the liquidation of insolvent companies is difficult. In addition, banks are awash with liquidity; Chinese people save an average of around 40 per cent of their income and the supply of money in the economy is well over double the annual gross domestic product. This means that banks often have more deposits than they can find borrowers to lend to, and are therefore less than vigilant about calling in suspect loans. Aside from this there are other concerns. A senior provincial banker with the Industrial and Commercial Bank of China, the country's largest bank, told me that precipitating a bankruptcy by recalling loans from an insolvent company was inimical to the interests of the bank. The knock-on effect would be palpable as that company's suppliers were also pushed under, he said. Unemployment would rise, potentially causing a slump in consumer spending and endangering social stability. 'It is much better to wait for the next upturn in the market rather than cause a slump across the board,' the banker said. The ubiquity of this attitude is revealed by an extremely low level of Chinese corporate bankruptcies by international standards.

This peculiarity leads to another, one that is shaped partly by the ever-present lure of selling to the mythical 'billion'. Under market economy conditions, when a company encounters oversupply of the product it makes, it generally pulls in its horns. But in China this happens only rarely. A more common response is to continue producing at the same rate while looking around for another industry sector to diversify into. On one trip to the Pearl River Delta, I went to visit the world's largest maker of microwave ovens, a company called Galanz. From there, I went a few miles up the road to Midea, one of the world's biggest manufacturers of air-conditioners. Both companies were classic examples of their type. Each had started off as a humble workshop in the early 1980s making products that looked like prototypes from the Industrial Revolution. In Midea's case this was a small electric fan with blades that had been beaten into shape with a hammer on a wooden bench by the company chairman (it now sits as an artefact in a glass cabinet in the company museum). But when I visited in 2001, the glory days of patriarchal leadership were over and both companies had run into a quagmire of oversupply. Their margins were sinking fast, and executives from each reckoned the other was operating at a loss. But their response to this predicament surprised me. Galanz, the microwave maker, decided to expand into air-conditioners and Midea, the air-conditioner maker, was moving into microwaves. Never mind that nationwide demand for air-conditioners lagged supply by 10 million units that year and microwaves were similarly oversupplied.

I asked Yu Yaochang, Vice-President of Galanz, how come the banks were willing to support such a diversification. 'The banks only care if your company is getting bigger and stronger. If you expand production you are increasing scale and reducing unit cost. That is bigger and stronger. And anyway we are the biggest local company. If they don't lend to us, who are they going to lend to?' Such reasoning helps to create the salient characteristic of the Chinese economy: that almost all (around 90 per cent in late 2005) manufactured products are in chronic oversupply. Midea, for example, was in addition to its core product of air-conditioners also making bread makers, coffee pots, refrigerators, dishwashers, smoke extractors and microwave ovens. Haier, one of the country's most famous consumer electronics companies, counts insurance, pharmaceuticals, personal computers, mobile phones and a chain of noodle restaurants among the eighty-six products with which it is involved. D'Long, a scandal-tainted company listed on the Shanghai stock exchange, makes everything from tomato ketchup to car parts.

So when the profit margins on Lifan's motorbike business were squeezed, Yin's response was not to retreat but to attack. He branched out into buses, mineral water, paint thinner, imported wine, newspapers, duck-down jackets and a successful Chinese football team that bore his company's name. He had been reading management books by Jack Welch, the then CEO of General Electric, whose photograph could be seen on the cover of pirated translations of his books selling all over China. Diversification, he said, helps a company weather downturns in the business cycle. Nevertheless, it was clear that if his core business of motorbikes was to survive, he would need to find a new source of revenue and sales growth. The answer was obvious: exports. Any company that could survive in the cauldron of Chinese competition, surely had a chance overseas. His selected battleground was Vietnam, where Lifan came face to face with Honda. The Japanese company's market share was around 70 per cent in Vietnam when Lifan made its first forays, but Yin had the obvious advantage of price. His opening salvo was to offer bikes that looked virtually identical to those of Honda but cost one-third as much. It proved a powerful lure and within three years, Lifan had outstripped its old rival.

Yin's early childhood was spent listening to the percussion of Japanese bombing raids on Chongqing and watching the smoke rise from fires that raged through the back alleys. Yet his rivalry with Honda and Yamaha appears devoid of nationalistic sentiment or any trace of revenge. In fact, he expresses admiration for Honda, in particular. 'As Isaac Newton said, "I stand on the shoulders of giants,"' he comments without irony. In fact, I developed a sense during our meetings over the years that Yin sees himself and Soichiro Honda, the late founder of the Japanese company, as kindred spirits. Both started their careers tinkering with engines in oil-slicked garages. Neither had much of a formal education and both knew well the sting of ostracism from the Establishment. (Honda's career was all the more remarkable because he operated outside, and sometimes in opposition to, the tight nexus between the Japanese government and large corporations.)

The irony was, though, that while Lifan started by copying Honda, the Japanese company ended by imitating its Chinese rival. The loss of market share in Vietnam had rattled Honda, which hastily established a production base on Hainan Island, Chinese territory just across the sea from Vietnam. There it used an almost exclusively Chinese business model; it benefited from cheap Chinese labour and sourced almost exclusively from mainland parts suppliers – many of which were churning out the third- or fourth-generation descendants of copies of original Japanese parts. But it did the trick. Honda was able to slash prices in Vietnam by about half and claw back some market share because of the superior cachet of its brand. The company also won success on another front. A long-standing lawsuit against Lifan for using the name 'Hongda' bore fruit and Lifan had to pay out rmb 98,000.

But the battles are far from over. Japanese companies are known for financing their forays into export markets by charging more for their products at home than they do abroad. Chinese corporations are the exact opposite. Many of them, Lifan included, export as a means of staying afloat at home. Yang Zhou, Yin's deputy, says the profit margins on bikes sold in Africa, Iran and Latin America can be as high as 10 per cent in some cases, whereas margins in China are wafer-thin or negative. In Nigeria, for instance, the company can sell for rmb 6,000 a bike that goes for half that in China.

Although his sales in the UK are minuscule, Yin was wondering how to build his brand among the British public. Unexpectedly, he started talking about football, tossing out the names of almost the entire England squad followed by each player's transfer fee. Then he asked me whether I thought he should buy a UK club as a means to build his brand. I asked him which one he was thinking of. 'Lan-che-si-te,' he said, but the name was unfamiliar to me. It was not Manchester United because that is 'Man-lian' in Chinese and anyway he had heard that Rupert Murdoch was once prevented from buying Man U, so he was sure that he would also be barred from snapping up a British 'national treasure'. Unwilling to reveal my ignorance of a club he may have taken a shine to, I asked whether he reckoned they were good enough at football to carry the Lifan name. 'Well, they might not be very good but they are quite cheap,' he said. 'Ten million maybe. Twenty, max.'

My journey from Chongqing ended at a terminus of China's industrial revolution, a place where the hundreds of thousands of products made in factories like Yin's ended up. It was called Yiwu. Only fifteen years ago, this small town in the middle of Zhejiang province on China's eastern seaboard had been distinguished by little but its unusual name. Yiwu means 'loyal crow', but when you ask local people why, you get a range of different answers. Nobody seemed to care much anyway. There is too much going on. In less than two decades, it has transformed itself from a sleepy backwater into one of the busiest places in the country. Even though it remains little known outside China, Yiwu has become the largest wholesale market in the world.

The scale of the place is dizzying. Some 34,000 stallholders sit in one vast exhibition hall after another selling around 320,000 different types of product. Almost every category of manufactured item made in the factories of the Pearl and Yangtze River Deltas is on sale in hangars covering an area of 1,500 hectares. I had been urged by Chinese friends to visit Yiwu in order to marvel at the prices. They had told me that if you took the price of the best bargains in the cheapest market in Beijing and then halved it, you would be getting close to the cost of buying the same things in Yiwu.

On my way to the exhibition hangars in the morning, I passed the Hiyat Hotel. It had a dusty glass frontage in bluebottle blue, a golden laughing Buddha by the front door and a polystyrene Santa Claus in the lobby that looked as if it was about to topple over. I started to wonder why the hotel company that owns China's tallest and grandest hotel, the eighty-eight-storey Jingmao Tower in Shanghai, had bothered to invest in a tacky, two-star establishment in Yiwu. Then I noticed the spelling. The Hiyat, of course, had nothing to do with the Hyatt.

I walked on for a few hundred metres until I came to a shopping mall selling fashion accessories. The first shop was advertising leather bags made in Italy by the famous brand, Gussi. They cost $11 each but, the shopkeeper said, you could always bargain a bit. Nearby, there were three stores in a row. One was called VSL, another LYS and the third SYL. They all had on their walls a large photograph of a youthful Yves Saint Laurent with his trademark thick-rimmed spectacles.

In another corner there were Lacoste rip-offs, again all close to each other. One was called New Crocodile, another Crocodile of the Yangtze, a third Crocokids and, the last, Croc Croc. I walked into one of the shops and asked the assistant whether the real Lacoste branded products were being sold in her shop or in France. 'The French crocodile and the Chinese crocodile are the same brand. They have merged,' she said. Then she waved dismissively at the rival shops nearby. 'They are all fakes, those ones, you can easily tell.'

A bit further on there were three shops with lettering in the same distinctive tall and thin format that Dunhill uses. One was called Denghaoli, another Dunbaolu and another Doctortoh. It was relatively easy to understand that they were all trying to be like Dunhill. But others in a different corner presented a puzzle. I had to think for a while about 'Woershaqi' before I assumed it must have been a derivative of Versace. 'Wearesaatchi', a bit further along, was a bit easier. Another outlet had come up with the idea of using an ice cream brand to sell haute couture. The shop sign read: 'Haagendess', but there was not an ice cream in sight. Only leather bags.

As I left the shopping mall, I bumped into a group of policemen.

I asked them how so many fake brands could be allowed to do business so openly. China had agreed when it joined the World Trade Organisation in 2001 to stamp out piracy. They looked at each other and then looked back at me. One of them took the cigarette out of his mouth and used it to point at the wall just feet away from the 'Crocodile of the Yangtze'. 'See that plaque. There is a number on there. You can try calling that if you have a complaint,' he said.

The plaque read: 'Smashing Fakes Hotline. Call: 32157.' I called and a woman answered. She told me that I had come through to the wrong city. This was Jinghua and I needed Yiwu, she said. 'Try 5558853,' she added. A man answered but he told me that the hotline I had reached was not for reporting fakes but for consumer issues. I needed to speak to the fakes inspection brigade, he said. 'Try 5324716.' He said the number quickly and then hung up. I had my mobile phone wedged between one hunched shoulder and my ear and my notebook resting on a raised knee. I just got the numbers down before I overbalanced. When I called, a man answered. He acknowledged that I had got through to the fakes hotline but added that he was too busy to talk. 'I am writing a report,' he said. I told him I wanted to inform him of brand copyright violations but he repeated that he was busy. 'Try 32157,' he said, referring me back to the number I had started with.

I had no desire to go round in a circle again so I left the shopping mall and walked the remainder of the distance to the main wholesale market exhibition hall. In the foyer, I was immediately confronted by a large sign standing near the escalators. 'Value Quality. Honour Credibility,' it said in giant gold characters on a red velvet background. It was signed by the Yiwu municipal government, the same people who were supposed to be running the anti-fakes hotline.

Inside the exhibition hall, it was just as my friends had foretold. The prices were unbelievable. A certain type of tea mug we used at home, which is normally bought in shops such as Ikea for at least $1, was on sale in Yiwu for 5 cents. A graphite titanium tennis racquet that appeared to be of medium to good quality was going for roughly what a tube of tennis balls would cost in the UK – $7.80. The famously cheap toasters Wal-Mart sells across the United States for $11 each would have seemed outrageously over-priced in Yiwu, where they can be bought for half that sum. A Chinese-made DVD player that had caused a minor sensation in America when it was put on sale at $29 was effortlessly undercut in Yiwu. An unbranded motorised drill, the spitting image of a Black & Decker product, cost $12, with a full set of drill bits thrown in. A sledgehammer was going for $1.40, an axe for chopping wood for $1.20. And so it was across the board. Almost every product was on sale for about one-half, one-third, one-tenth or even less of the lowest price available in the cheapest discount stores of Europe and America. What's more, the quality of these items seemed in no way inferior to the products on sale at stores around the world. In many cases, in fact, they were the same goods.

Yiwu offered a glimpse at the source of the discount store phenomenon sweeping the developed world. Half an hour walking around its cavernous exhibition halls was enough to destroy any mystery as to how Wal-Mart, Target, Home Depot, Tesco, Metro, Carrefour, Lowe's, Best Buy, Royal Ahold and several other dis-count retailers are able to offer goods so cheaply. In fact, I began to be impressed not at their capacity to discount but at their ability to get away with charging hefty mark-ups without incurring a consumer backlash. All of the large discount stores sourced mer-chandise in China, and they all owed their rankings in the upper echelons of the world's 500 largest corporations in part to the fat margins they earned from procurement in China. Total procure-ment of wholesale goods by foreign retailers was expected to reach $60 billion in 2005, according to official Chinese estimates. If you make the highly conservative assumption that these goods are sold in the developed world for double the cost of their procure-ment, then it appears that at least a staggering $120 billion worth of merchandise sold in European and American discount stores comes from China.

But the big discount houses are not the only ones getting in on the act. Yiwu was full of freelancers. Individual traders from all corners of the globe were strolling from one booth to another making bulk orders of buttons, jewellery, ornaments, white goods, electronics, cutlery, crockery, sports equipment, car parts, agricultural machinery, industrial plants and hundreds of thousands of other products. A few years ago the number of foreign traders resident in Yiwu was in the low hundreds, but now there were over 5,000 of them. The business had boomed after the quality of the stuff on offer had improved. I met Barry Beaumont from New Zealand at a stall selling oil paintings. His friend was lifting one canvas after another from a stack of hundreds on the floor, looking at it for a second or two and then tossing it aside – either into a pile to be bought or onto a stack of rejects. Sometimes he would ask Beaumont for his opinion on an artwork before deciding on which pile to put it. Most of the paintings were copies of famous originals by van Gogh, Constable, Dalí, Chagall and Monet. Beaumont and his friend had no illusions that they were buying anything other than 'good crap; the type of thing you might find hanging near the loo in a coffee shop'.

'They are painted by the locals around here for 20 [renminbi] each, so you buy them from the stallholder for 25,' Beaumont said. 'To start with they will ask you for 140 each, so you need to bargain them down. It takes time and they are tough, so generally I leave the bargaining to one of the girls.' He pointed to three heavily made-up, middle-aged Chinese women standing a couple of metres away. 'They are much tougher than us,' he added. 'The Chinese don't mind selling cheap to Chinese but they will never give a foreigner the same price.'

Beaumont had started coming to Yiwu seven years earlier after a business he had in New Zealand failed. To begin with he bought agricultural machinery, metalworking equipment and industrial tools for cutting and working plastics. At first he did not want to risk anything but small orders. But things went well and now he did not bother with consignments of less than $10,000 in value. If you bought a hundred of anything in Yiwu, you could get the price down by a reasonable margin, but if you bought a lot of a thousand, you might be able to get as much as 50 per cent off, he said. The Chinese manufacturers expected to make only a 2 or 3 per cent margin on what they sold and the exporting agents rarely tried to make money off the clients. The main reason they were in business was to reclaim a government VAT rebate of up to 17 per cent of the product value. The real profits, Beaumont said, were earned by those who knew how to distribute and sell goods once they had been shipped to their target markets. Some people were taking profits of 100 per cent but Beaumont was contenting himself with a 30 to 40 per cent mark-up in order to build a reputation with his customers. Still, things were getting more competitive now as people from all over the world began to discover Yiwu and places like it across China. Over time, this would mean that the hefty profits that discount stores derive from China will start to shrink, as will the commissions and mark-ups of middlemen in places such as Hong Kong, where agents add nearly 30 per cent to the cost of every mainland product that passes through the territory.

But while such things may change on the periphery, the world's cheapest market is set to endure. Yiwu is the point at which the collected energies of China's industrial transformation converge. Its low prices are the final expression of a hundred different realities, reforms and trends that underpin the prowess of a rising giant. The presence China projects across the world originates primarily from the strengths that Yiwu symbolises. This is because throughout history, the big shifts in the global power balance and in the hierarchy of nations have all been accompanied – or, often, preceded – by a whole set of new price signals. In many of its conditions, China's ascent now mirrors that of the US in the second half of the nineteenth century. Not only does Chongqing's transformation resemble that of a youthful Chicago and the construction of China's infrastructure replicate America's in both its concept and even in aspects of detail, but also the movement of the sons and daughters of farmers to factories along the coast echoes the mass migration of young people from Europe to the New World some 150 years ago. New communications technologies – in the US a century and a half ago it was railways, in today's China it is the internet and digitalisation – are creating quantum leaps in productivity. International flows of capital and expertise from Great Britain to the US in the nineteenth century and in modern times from the industrialised nations to China are lubricating the process of change.

In those days – as today – price shifts were a harbinger of the economic, political and social changes to come. The period from 1873 to 1900 is known as the era of 'deflationary boom' because prices of agricultural and manufactured items fell almost across the board in the US.[8] The opening of the prairies to agriculture sent the price of grain plummeting across the developed world, causing rural unrest throughout Europe, the depopulation of the country-side and a crisis among the British landowning classes which was to reverberate throughout the increasingly egalitarian twentieth century. Similar changes hit industry. Andrew Carnegie, the Scottish-born US industrial baron, took a new steel technology, called the Bessemer converter, from Britain to the US in much the same way as Shen Wenrong transported the Phoenix plant to China from Germany. From 1872 to 1898, Bessemer steel prices fell 80 per cent in the US, and Carnegie commented prophetically: 'The nation that makes the cheapest steel has other nations at its feet.' Indeed, British industry found it hard to adjust to the relentless cycles of deflation in manufactured products, and many companies went bust. From 1875 to 1896, British prices fell by an average of 0.8 per cent every year. Nevertheless, living standards improved for most British people because of the sharp increase in the number of inexpensive imported goods. By the end of the century, the situation was so pronounced that Theodore Roosevelt, the US President, was able to comment:

Even if the United States were not so blessed with raw materials, the excellence of her manufactured products guaranteed her dominance of world markets. Current advertisements in British magazines gave the impression that the typical Englishman woke to the ring of an Ingersoll alarm, shaved with a Gillette razor, combed his hair with Vaseline tonic, buttoned his Arrow shirt, hurried downstairs for Quaker Oats, California figs and Maxwell House coffee, commuted in a Westinghouse tram, body by Fisher, rose to his office in an Otis elevator, and worked all day with his Walden pen under the efficient glare of Edison light bulbs.[9]

A century later, it is China that is exporting deflation in manu-factured products and it is Americans and Europeans who are increasingly living out their lives assisted by a cornucopia of products made in China. As an early signal of a shift in the distribution of geopolitical power, it seems unmistakable.

FOUR

Yiwu and markets like it are just specks on the map of China. But they represent the sources of a global economic phenomenon. Nobody could look at the prices there, and the range of goods on sale, and fail to wonder what would happen to manufacturers in the rest of the world when the full force of China's industrial revolution hit their factories and shopping malls. Or, maybe, this was merely alarmism. Perhaps Europe and the United States would weather the oncoming Chinese typhoon with no more discomfort than they had betrayed when the Japanese economic miracle went global in the 1970s and 1980s. I decided to take my own soundings on the contours of things to come by visiting to one of the oldest manufacturing towns in Europe, a place called Prato in Italy not far from the historical city of Florence.

Prato had every appearance of a typical Tuscan market town. In the stillness of early evening, shadows swept across the russet roofs of the old town and onto the rough-hewn stones of the central piazza. Flocks of doves swooped and wheeled around marble statues of founding fathers and then flew off to low green hills in the distance. Church bells chimed with a measured, funereal rhythm, drawing a stream of mourners for Pope John Paul II, who had died a day earlier in Rome, towards the Cathedral Santo Stefano. The men were in blazers and the women in long dresses, and when they reached the cathedral's flagstone steps, they stopped to greet friends or relatives with a word or a kiss on each cheek. Children with their hair damped and neatly parted waited for their parents and then accompanied them through the heavy wooden doors. Inside, candles illuminated the main points of piety: the alcoves of saints, the choristers in their lace ruffs and, by the altar, a life-size photograph of the Pope in his latter years gripping a staff with both hands. It was several degrees cooler inside than out, and some of the women in thin blouses shivered and hugged their arms as they made their way up the aisle.

Everything, in fact, was how it should have been in a well-to-do, self-respecting town in northern Italy. Except for one feature. Walking in the opposite direction to the Catholic faithful – towards the western suburbs – were people marked apart by their bearing and appearance. They strode purposefully through the crowds singly or in twos, keeping their gaze downcast in the manner of locals who have no need to navigate through familiar surroundings. It was clear they were not tourists; they had no cameras or bags and they wore simple clothes. They were, it turned out, members of a large immigrant population of Chinese. Since they started to arrive in Prato some fifteen years earlier, they had transformed the destiny of one of Italy's oldest industrial towns and changed the lives of its indigenous population.

I walked along behind one man. As we moved, the surroundings altered. We passed a hairdresser with Chinese characters in the window, a supermarket with trays of fungus and lichee out front, several shops offering cheap overseas phone calls, an apothecary for ginseng and other herbal remedies, a leisure club with flashing neon lights, a bookshop stacked with martial arts comics and a restaurant called 'Golden Sea'. I began to feel as if I had returned to China, perhaps to one of those places such as Qingdao or Weihai which used to be foreign treaty ports in the early twentieth century and still today combined European architecture with Chinese life. Prato had a population of 180,000 and, out of these, around 20,000 were Chinese.[1] They lived according to their native culture in an enclave the locals seemed to have vacated. The only obvious concession to their adopted country I could detect was a shelf full of books in a supermarket promising short cuts to fluency in Italian.

The man I followed stopped outside a supermarket called Xiaolin. He joined a knot of other men who stood peering intently at a wall on which various notices, all in Chinese, flapped in a light evening breeze. The wall held the reason for their presence. Printed or handwritten on the notices were advertisements for jobs. A car mechanic was needed in a nearby town, a restaurant down the street was seeking a waiter, and a shop required a cashier. Most of the advertisements, though, were for 'buyigong', or 'cloth garment workers'. Each notice had telephone numbers written on strips that hung from the bottom of the paper. The men stared at each one in turn, but none of them ripped off a number. 'Buyigong' was not for them, one said. You had to have skills. You had to be able to cut cloth according to patterns you were given and you could be fired for the smallest mistake. The men standing outside Xiaolin were looking for something more menial; general work such as sweeping the floors, doing the garbage, cleaning the machinery and stacking the finished garments into piles.

One man from Shenyang in the northeast of China started to speak. He had grown vegetables in a greenhouse on the outskirts of his home city, but since arriving in Italy he had gone from one general work job to another. His last job had required eighteen hours of work a day, he said. Overhearing him say this, his friend, a heavy man who had been slumped over a railing nearby, jerked upright with indignation. He was wearing dark trousers, a black jacket and a white shirt. His face was crumpled into folds beneath the eyes, as if weathered by interlocking rivulets of fatigue. 'Eighteen hours?' he asked. 'More like twenty. Then four hours' sleep, then twenty hours again, and then again. It is like that month after month. We get 600 euro a month. That is about what you need to survive here. If you can really cut down on food, maybe you can save about 50 to 100 euros a month on that wage. But it is exhausting. Mostly what you dream of all day is being able to sleep.'

There was a pause while the others in the group took in the big man's outburst. Some nodded their heads. Others carried on staring at the wall. Then one, a small man with a southern accent, said something in an almost inaudible voice: 'People from the northeast are lazy.'

The heavy man glared at him. He bunched a fist and took a step forward. But everyone else was laughing, and suddenly he softened. Instead of fighting, he said: 'The northeast used to be the heavy industrial base of all China. We used to lead the whole country making military equipment when you bastards from the south had your backs towards heaven in the paddies.'

'If that is the case,' said the southerner, 'why don't you go back and start making tanks again?'

'If I did,' the heavy man said, 'you'd be the first to be marched in front of them.'

By this time, a woman had joined the group. She was also from the northeast and had held a lowly position in a local government. She had an open, cheerful face and a way of speaking that sounded as if she was making intellectual observations. 'You know, it is generally thought that people from cities such as Shenyang in the northeast are better-educated than those from the south,' she said to nobody in particular. But those words seemed sage enough to end the altercation.

The men and women outside Xiaolin that April morning were illegals. They had come to Prato as part of 'snakebodies' led by 'snakeheads' to Europe. In other words, they had made the perilous journey from China by train, truck, on foot and by sea as part of a small, terrified group that had entrusted its fate to the Chinese gangs who run the world's largest people-smuggling networks. At the places where their journeys had begun, there were children, parents, wives and others who were depending on them to send money home. At their destinations there were walls plastered with tatty job adverts representing hope for a better life.

I asked one of the men by the wall to tell me what his journey had been like. He demurred. Members of the snakebody are sworn to secrecy by the snakeheads who arrange their trips. I had to persuade him by agreeing to use a false name and to camouflage other aspects of his journey. After a series of meetings and interviews, for which I paid him some money, the story of how Huang came to be in Prato slowly emerged.

In the mid 1990s, Japanese demand for soft-shell turtles was surging and farmers in Fuqing county, in the southeastern province of Fujian, were well placed to benefit from the new fashion. Much of the county was too waterlogged for agriculture but turtles could be raised in freshwater pools excavated out of the marshes. Huang's father duly invested, and everything was going fine until late 1997 when the Asian financial crisis struck. Turtles are a luxury, the type of thing businessmen eat when they are trying to impress someone. So the price plummeted as the whole of southeast Asia tightened its belt and Japanese demand eased. Huang's father's business began to unravel. By late 1999, he was bankrupt and his creditors in the underground banks that service a thriving grey economy in southern China were getting restless. These banks, though illegal, were actually run by the local government and so when Huang's father could not pay up, the officials threw him into the basement of a local government building that doubled as a jail.

There he had to stay until someone could pay his debts. There was no chance of legal redress because his loans had been illegal in the first place so Huang began to consider his last option. Going abroad would mean having to leave behind a wife and a ten-year-old son. But there were plenty of precedents in Fuqing that suggested the perilous journey to a foreign shore could pay off handsomely. You could tell at a glance which households had a son or daughter earning good money in Europe or America; their houses were the tallest in the neighbourhood and the construction of extra storeys sped up or slowed down in tandem with the ebb and flow of remittances from overseas. So Huang went again to the moneylender to whom his father was in hock and agreed a further loan on the understanding that if his trip overseas failed to yield the necessary funds, the lender would seize all of the property of Huang's extended family. Then, after some discussions between the moneylender and a local snakehead, it was agreed that Huang would leave a few months later for England.

As he told me these things, we sat in the corner of a café looking out onto the tiled roofs of old Prato. Life in Fuqing with its unofficial prisons and soft-shell turtle farms seemed so far away as to be barely imaginable. But every time Huang mentioned the moneylenders, his face tightened. 'They are not like the state banks. They know everything about you. You can never escape from them,' he said. 'They know how many beers you have in your fridge and how many of those bottles are just half full.'

In June 2000, he had been ready to leave. But news of a tragedy spread through the community. Fifty-eight Chinese had been found suffocated to death in the back of a tomato van as it tried to cross into the UK through Dover. The Dutch driver had closed the air vents to prevent the noise of his human cargo from escaping.

The crackdown that followed in Fuqing made everyone nervous.

Police inspectors from Beijing went from house to house, interviewing people and trying to find the snakeheads who were responsible for arranging the passage of the young men and women to Europe. Strangely, though, the Dover tragedy did not damp the desire among people to try for a new future abroad. Consequently, the price of passage went up. The snakeheads demanded that Huang pay another $3,000 on top of the $12,000 he had already handed over. He had no choice but to borrow more, this time from his father's elder brother, so that by the time he finally set off in September 2000, he was carrying with him the hopes of an imprisoned father, a mortgage on two houses and the goodwill of his uncle.

A snakehead supplied Huang with a passport and a Chinese exit stamp and told him that it was now too risky to attempt travelling to northern Europe; the police had tightened up since the Dover tragedy. He would be heading to the south – maybe to Italy, maybe to Spain – with several travelling companions also driven by a mixture of obligation and misfortune. One woman among them was four months pregnant and none of them was over thirty years old. In Beijing, they were told they would take the Trans-Siberian train, crossing into Russia at Blagoveshchensk, a busy town on the Chinese border. They had no Russian visas so they were packed into crates as freight. The box that Huang was told to slither into was half full of blue anoraks, so it made a fairly comfortable bed. The holes between the wooden panels allowed him ample air to breathe, and when the temperature plunged as the train thundered through the Russian night, Huang burrowed deeper into the anoraks.

Several hours later a snakehead who spoke Russian and had a relationship with the train's guards helped him get out of the crate. His group of fellow stowaways then spent a few more days sitting amid the freight. Sometime before Moscow, the snakehead got a call on his mobile phone. He turned to the group and told them that getting off at Moscow would be too risky. They would have to jump off the train while it was still moving and head across country. Huang looked at the pregnant woman, but there was nothing to be done. The snakehead waited until the train slowed down near some signal points and then slid open the door. They leapt onto a grassy verge next to the tracks and everyone survived the jump, though the pregnant woman was weeping silently by the time they regrouped in a hedge bottom. The snakehead worked his mobile phone and within a few hours, a white van arrived to pick them up. They drove for days, stopping at night in nondescript houses by the side of the road.

Suddenly, without warning, the snakehead told them to get out and walk. Dusk was falling and there was a mountain range ahead of them. Huang thought it might have been the border of the former Yugoslavia. They were about to cross into a war zone on foot. They walked all night; a local man guided them, first through forests and then through mountain passes in silence. Once, one of the snakebody asked where they were and the snakehead snapped: 'We haven't come to see cultural relics. What are you asking for?' On the other side of the mountain, they rested in a white house on a hillside that had mattresses on the floor but no other furniture.

A truck came to pick them up that evening and they drove again all day. The house they were lodged in this time was more comfortable. It had running water, furniture, a kitchen and a room with bunk beds. They stayed there for a week before being packed off for the last leg of their journey – a trip in the hold of a cargo ship from a small port somewhere on the Adriatic to Sicily.

Such sea voyages were among the most dangerous parts of the whole journey. During the week I was in Prato, the local Chinese newspapers gave front-page coverage to one operation that had gone wrong. The Italian coastguard had intercepted a ship sailing from Malta to Sicily and the snakehead, desperate not to be caught, had forced his charges to jump into the sea at gunpoint. According to the testimony of some of the survivors, several members of the snakebody told the snakehead they could not swim. But he made them jump anyway and some are thought to have drowned.

Huang's sea crossing was uneventful and at last his ship docked. In the back of the van that drove them to Milan, he had been too tired for emotion and still too scared to relax. From there he had spent the next four years in Bologna, Rome and, recently, Prato always doing menial jobs such as sweeping, stacking, washing and lifting. When the authorities in Fuqing saw he had begun settling his father's debts in regular instalments, they let his father out of the makeshift prison. His father and he then set about paying off the debt to the father's elder brother. By the time I met Huang in April 2005, he was almost debt-free but he could not go back home. His son was fifteen years old and his school fees were too expensive. He had not seen him since he left China and when he spoke of him, his voice cracked. 'Everything is for my son,' he said.

I was not surprised to find Chinese in Prato. In fact, they were part of the reason I had come. It struck me that their presence offered a potentially telling insight into the competitiveness of European manufacturing in general. Prato had been the centre of the European textiles for more than 700 years and its brand was enriched by a history that no advertising could buy. Centuries of Florentine courtiers, including Machiavelli – the most sharply dressed of them all – had swathed themselves in its cloth. Prato also had designers that were second to none in the industry, and a glamorous list of clients: Armani, Prada, Ferré, Gucci, Max Mara, Patrizia, Pepe, Banana Republic, Valentino and Versace had all done their shopping here. Now, with the presence of the Chinese, it had another enviable advantage – access to probably the cheapest and most determined labour force in the world. Men, such as those outside the Xiaolin supermarket, for example, were willing to work nearly double the hours of their Italian counterparts for about half the compensation. A Chinese cloth and garment cutter, for instance, would expect to take home about 1,000 euros for a month of six-day weeks at fifteen hours a day, without any pension or welfare payments.

So, my thesis was this: if, blessed by this confluence of good fortune and hard-earned expertise, Prato could not compete with textile towns in China, then what hope, ultimately, was there for the rest of a European industry which employed around 2.7 million people in twenty-five countries and had a turnover of 225 billion euro a year.[2] And, by extension, what would the outlook be for the rest of European manufacturing?

Prato's early experiences, I learned, had been positive. The first illegal immigrants began to arrive in the mid to late 1980s and, according to an artist who was among the first to arrive, children on the streets would look at them as if they were extraterrestrials. The numbers then were relatively small and they were absorbed naturally by the town's textile factories. But by the early 1990s, they had become a potent economic force of some 10,000 cheap and often skilled workers. The combination of Italian flair and Chinese labour fostered a mini-boom and the number of textile companies rose to around 6,000 in the mid 1990s from some 4,000 at the start of the decade. But the local Italian bosses had no way of knowing at the outset quite what they had let themselves in for. It would not have seemed worthy of note to them then that most of the people they employed to sweep the floors, cut the cloth and sew on labels came from Wenzhou, probably the most entrepreneurial place in all China.

Wenzhou is a port city in the province of Zhejiang south of Shanghai. A ring of high mountains that stand between it and the rest of China have inculcated into its people something of an enclave mentality. For centuries they have been more likely to look outward than inland for their opportunities, rather in the same manner as people from Goa, Malacca or Djibouti. Free trade has been their lifeline, and the city was one of the last places to submit to Communist rule after the 1949 revolution. Indeed, Communism always seemed an alien contrivance. During the Cultural Revolution – when merely talking about private enterprise could land you in a labour camp – some Wenzhou families owned their own farm animals, traded on the black market or provided services for a fee. With the advent of free-market reforms, the city was among the first to blossom and today it is a national centre for several industries, including shoes, agricultural valves, lighters, spectacles and garments, for which it seems to have no comparative advantage aside from the sheer force of will. Its businessmen are daring, diligent and sometimes ruthless. But what makes them unusual is the degree to which they work together. Thus if a Wenzhou businessman in some far-flung corner of China or somewhere else in the world has an idea that he thinks will fly, he can usually call upon quick, concessionary financing from an informal network of relatives and business associates.

This is what happened in Prato. After a few years working on the factory floor, one after another of the Wenzhou workers decided to set up businesses on their own. The numbers of Chinese-run firms registered at the House of Commerce in Prato rose from 212 in 1992 to 1,753 in 2003. Indeed, the same thing was happening elsewhere too. In Empoli, a Tuscan town that makes leather goods and garments, several hundred Wenzhou businesses also sprang up and in the Emilia-Romagna region embracing Bologna, Modena and Reggio Emilia, the number of Chinese-run factories also proliferated.[3] Stories of how immigrant labourers in threadbare clothes walked off the factory floor one week and set up in competition with their former bosses the next began to fill the business pages of local newspapers. Of course, there were ups and downs and success did not always come easily to Prato's newest type of entrepreneur. Wang Liping, for example, raised money from associates and relatives in Wenzhou to finance the purchase of a $35,000 container of thread. But when it arrived in Prato, he discovered it was too thick for Italian spinning machines. 'I lost every cent I invested,' he said. But six months later he tried again, this time borrowing from different associates. Now he runs a business selling thread and sewing machine accessories with annual revenues of around $1 million.

Another entrepreneur, Wang Yihua, a young woman with a company called Great Fashion, came to Italy in 1989 after a journey organised by snakeheads. On her first attempt, she had been caught hiding in the train's toilets in Erlian, a town on China's border with Mongolia, and police sent her back home with a severe warning. But a few months later, still aged nineteen, she tried the same journey again and was successful. Now she drives a soft-top Volkswagen with furry dice dangling from the mirror, wears designer sunglasses and speaks fluent Italian. As well as the Chinese workers in her factory, she has also employed an Italian designer.

For a while, everyone seemed to benefit from Prato's growing associations with China. The cheap thread and cloth that was coming out of Wenzhou, Nantong, Hangzhou, Suzhou and other textile towns was available not only to start-ups like Great Fashion but also to the long-established companies of the Pratese. As costs went down, business flourished and it seemed as if this mid-sized town in Tuscany had found an elusive formula, a way of harnessing the energy of a rising China to serve its ends. The local government embraced its unexpected good fortune. It set up an immigrant service centre to help those who arrived – illegally or otherwise – with their first few steps in Italy. It recognised the Wenzhou chamber of commerce in Prato as a local organisation and cemented a sister-city pact with Wenzhou in China. As a demonstration of sincerity, Prato even funded the restoration of a Ming dynasty temple in Wenzhou by craftsmen sent over from Italy.[4]

But the bonhomie was not sustainable. The illegal immigrants-turned-entrepreneurs began to put their former Italian bosses out of business. Of the 6,000 or so textile companies that existed in 2000, less than 3,000 remained in mid 2005. Several Italian companies with more than a hundred years of history are hanging on by a thread. The main reason for this is that whereas in the past only one part of the process of making a garment was outsourced to China, now almost every step in the production process is being moved offshore. As spinning, weaving, cutting and sewing moves to Wenzhou, the Chinese factory bosses in Prato are better suited to the transition than their Italian counterparts.

The typical Prato textile business resembles Wang Yihua's Great Fashion. She produces 'ready-to-wear' garments for an Italian brand holder, but the only functions performed in Italy are the design and the sewing of the brand holder's label onto finished garments that return from China. The factories back in Wenzhou are so large and efficient that they need only a week from the time they receive a new design by e-mail from Prato to the time they dispatch the shipment of the finished garments back to Italy. Even allowing for Prato's unusual source of cheap immigrant labour, the cost differentials between China and Italy remain huge. 'The euro is so strong these days,' said Wang. 'Chinese workers in Prato are earning about about ten times what they would back in Wenzhou.'

The municipal authorities in Prato seem unsure of what to do. The boom that Chinese labour had helped to create is turning to bust. Seven hundred years of textile tradition are in danger of extinction, and along with them Prato's links with its past. The meaning of this realisation came to me as I sat in the office of Francesco Delfino, general manager of the province of Prato, in the Palazzo Banci Buonamici. It struck me that everything around us had been founded on cloth. Outside the window was a statue of Francesco di Marco Datini, a fourteenth-century cloth merchant and philanthropist. The building in which we were seated was an old textile palace with trussed ceilings and alabaster statues of Roman emperors looking out from alcoves in the main hall. Delfino was philosophical about his town's visitation from China. He could see the diligence and agility of the people from Wenzhou, but he could also see, first in their arrival and now apparently in their gradual departure, that they threatened an indigenous culture. He did not know what the future held but he was sure that, somehow, the Pratese would find a way through.

Prato's predicament is common throughout the European textile trade and in all of Italy's artisan industries. In Biella, a wool town near Piedmont, Chinese competition is forcing closures of factories that have lined the river there since the thirteenth century. Other companies, such as the cashmere garment firm Fratelli Piacenza, have moved production to lower-cost countries. In Montebelluna a cluster of companies that produced sports shoes have shifted production to an industrial park in Romania; and in the south of the country, the footwear centre of Barletta, home to some 2,300 shoe companies, is reeling from stiff foreign competition.

Towns and industries such as these have faced competitive threats from overseas on several occasions before and on each occasion they have found ways to outmanoeuvre their rivals, either by moving into higher value-added areas or by emphasising the excellence of their brand or concentrating on new designs. But this time there is no obvious refuge. China is competing in every area of textiles, as well as other manufacturing and artisan industries. At the low-cost end, huge Chinese factories are widely acknowledged to enjoy unassailable advantages. But even in haute couture – the preserve of famous brands such as Givenchy, Yves Saint Laurent, Versace, Valentino, Ungaro, Chanel and others – the influence of China is palpable. It is not that Chinese brands have begun to compete in these areas; that may not happen for many years to come. Rather it is that several brand owners have undertaken large-scale outsourcing to China in an effort to offer good-quality fashion at more affordable prices. The result has been a narrowing of margins at the high end of the fashion industry and a Europe-wide dilemma over whether to follow the outsourcing trend at the risk of diluting brand values.

For a while, some brand owners may think they can have both the outsourcing and the brand. At least one gentleman's tailor on Savile Row in London, for example, measures clients in his premises on the famous street and then promptly outsources the rest of the tailoring process to China. When the customer returns to pick up his new suit a couple of weeks later, he may have no inkling that it was stitched together in a basement somewhere in Wenzhou by a seamstress earning Industrial Revolution-era wages. For obvious reasons, the Savile Row tailor may decide to keep this aspect of his operation discreet. But eventually, the word will get out and Savile Row may lose a little of its aura.

A similar process is under way within many of the big haute couture houses, and the logic behind it is inescapable. If most of the cloth available these days in Prato comes originally from China, then why would a fashion house not go directly to China to buy the same thing for less money? One problem they face, however, is that in the eyes of most of their customers, a large part of a brand's appeal lies in the knowledge that what they are wearing was made by artisans in traditional ways by companies with hundreds of years of history. The other problem with outsourcing is that when work is sent out to China, some key technology and know-how usually follow so that quality can be assured. But to transfer technology is to nurture competitors, and when those competitors reach a critical scale, the pressure for the whole industry to relocate to the cheapest, most efficient production centre becomes intense.[5] Such are the dynamics of global capitalism; the process is the same whether the industry in question is textiles, or autos, or shipbuilding or almost anything else. Only reactions to it vary. Some people are unsentimental about the social capital that is lost when a whole industry shuts down or moves away, but others feel they have lost part of themselves when a community to which they have given their life packs up and disappears.

The beautiful lake town of Como in northern Italy is a case in point. Since Roman times, Como has been a centre of the silk industry. The sensual cloth that flows in liquid harmony with the body's movements was a favourite of Cleopatra, the mistress of Julius Caesar and Mark Antony. The material she wore, which Pliny the Elder, the scholar, believed came from the 'hair of sea sheep' was imported from China both overland and by ship. By the fourth century AD it had become a common accoutrement in all civilised outposts of the Western world and the money spent on it was draining the wealth of a declining empire. In one of the first examples of industrial espionage, the emperor Justinian is said to have commissioned Persian holy men to smuggle the eggs of the bombyx mori, the silkworm, and mulberry seeds into Constantinople in 550. By the end of the sixth century the enigma of sericulture was being unravelled in many parts of Europe and Como flourished as a place that produced silkworm cocoons, spun silk and created finished garments. By 1840 the countryside around the town was given over to more than 3 million mulberry trees, the leaves of which supply the silkworm's only food.

When the Chinese silk industry started to recover about two decades ago, it became obvious that the silk material harvested and spun from Chinese silkworms was cheaper and of similar quality to that made in Como. So the first thing to be outsourced to China was the spinning and weaving work. Then much of the garment-making went too and, later, some companies in the small town of Shengzhou in Zhejiang province got hold of the same computer-controlled looms that gave Como an edge in quality control. Within a few years the Chinese, who run their looms all day and all night, were starting to put Como companies out of business and in the space of just seven years the number of computer-controlled looms in Shengzhou has jumped from eight to 670. The Chinese town single-handedly produces almost half of the world's silk neckties, while Como's industry appears to be in terminal decline. The change has been so swift. To many in the Italian town it seems like only yesterday that Bill Clinton was seen on television around the world taking the oath of the presidency in a silk tie that came from Como.

In one sense, there is a historical symmetry to the rise of Shengzhou and the concurrent decline of Como; it is as if the moth of the bombyx mori has decided after a 1,500-year sojourn in

Europe finally to fly back home. But for Moritz Mantero, whose company makes silk for ties sold by brands such as Ralph Lauren and Brooks Brothers, such observations are abhorrent. He has been to Shengzhou and found the smokestacks, concrete-block buildings and pollution of the place 'horrible'. At home, he has watched as some 20,000 silk industry jobs have disappeared since 2001 and dozens of long-established firms gone under. His company, he is confident, can survive by concentrating on precision manufacturing and excellent design. Walking around the stone mansion that has been the company headquarters since his grandfather's day, Mantero pointed out a room that holds the key to the company's future. Inside were some 10,000 volumes of old design samples, many of them purchased from failed textile mills.[6] He grasped one leather-bound volume, the 1893 spring collection of a defunct French garment maker. The patterns inside still seemed modern; a geometric sequence of ellipses which was at once reiterative and mystic.

But even in design, the Chinese are catching up. When a Como corporate customer of Babei, the largest of Shengzhou's 1,100 tie makers, encountered difficulties in paying for the silk he had imported from China, Jin Yao, Babei's President, took his compensation in the form of the Italian company's design shop. In so doing, he bought access to the only segment of the industry in which the Chinese are not yet dominant. Now, back in Shengzhou, he will be able to marry designs from hundreds of years of Italian creative tradition to his company's ability to churn out 20 million ties a year. That is a combination that might just finish Como off.

I went by train from Prato to Chiasso, a town just over the Italian border in Switzerland. By chance I found myself sitting next to two Chinese, one older, thick-set man in casual clothes and his young, keen colleague in a suit. The older man was the boss of a textile company based in Zhejiang and his associate was the company's representative in France, where they had recently acquired a linen manufacturer, Terre De Lin. The young man had taken it upon himself to be his boss's eyes, ears and cultural compass among the alien corn, offering up an effusion of unsolicited observations in a cloying voice. So when the boss asked him why he had been unable to arrange any business meetings for the next day, the young man went into a discourse on the laziness of Italians. They never wanted to meet because they took so much time off. They were always playing golf or sitting in cafés and leaving their businesses unmanned. Had the boss noticed, the young man wanted to know, how many barbers' shops were closed on Mondays? Imagine that: closed on Monday. In fact, the whole of Europe was similarly affected with sloth, which only went to show that when people had money, they lost enthusiasm for work. 'Their lives are just too comfortable,' said the young man screwing up his mouth as if the thought tasted bitter. The boss nodded silently as he stared out at the Tuscan countryside.

Both men seemed interested by this theme. A while later the boss remarked that they had been travelling for an hour and a half and had hardly seen a single factory. 'Foreigners like looking at scenery,' the young man offered. The boss paused for thought, and then asked: 'Scenery or production. Which is more important?' He then began to leaf through a stack of faxes. Looking up with his reading spectacles still on, he asked his employee to make a call to schedule a meeting at some future point in their itinerary. The young man stood up and excused himself with a little bow and the explanation that only people of 'low quality' made calls in train carriages in Europe. The boss chuntered his objections, but the young man continued to move to the space between the carriages to make his call.

Sometime after he had returned, my mobile rang and I answered it.

'You see, some foreigners can be quite low-quality too,' the young man said to his boss. 'And look at his phone. So old. Yours is so much better than his.'

It was true. My phone, with its scuffed corners and dull grey display, was certainly inferior to the boss's all-beeping, all-flashing, full-colour model. Nevertheless, I found myself unable to resist letting them know that I could understand what had just been said. 'Is that so?' I asked in Chinese.

Disappointingly, the young man did not skip a beat. 'Yes. I was just telling my boss that your phone does not match up to his. How much did you pay for it?' he asked.

As the journey went on, we struck up a lively conversation. The boss's curiosity ranged over many subjects, some familiar, some surprising. Why were foreigners lazy? What was Europe going to do when it did not have much industry left? Could you really run an economy on services alone? Did European cows really consume $2 a day in farm subsidies? Was there any reason for the European Union to exist? Hadn't it come into being because a few French and German politicians had wanted to play political games?

In among the questions, there were statements. China, the boss said, would be finished if it took its eye off economic construction and started to play politics again. Playing politics was the worst thing that could happen to a country. During the Cultural Revolution, playing politics had cost the formal education of millions of people, and the boss had been one of them. Making money was the only objective truth, he said. But foreigners already had enough money, so now they were playing games with politics.

To start with I was not sure whom he meant by the word 'foreigners'. We were travelling through Italy, after all, so by most reckonings the boss and his associate would count as foreigners and the Italians would be locals. But then I remembered an article in the newspaper of the Chinese community in Prato. One front-page story involved 'three foreign thieves' stealing something from Chinatown. It was not until the end of the story that the thieves were identified as having Italian names. I called the newspaper editor on the telephone number provided beneath the masthead to ask if this had not in fact been an error, a misprint, perhaps. She answered that the misapprehension was mine: anyone who was not Chinese was foreign, wherever they were. The same rule seemed to apply in all the Chinese-language newspapers I found. Italians were ubiquitously referred to as foreigners. With this in mind, I asked the boss how he found doing business in an alien culture such as Europe. 'It is better than before. Five years ago, hardly anyone in the textile industry would meet us. Some would not even take our calls,' he said. 'Now, wherever we go, we meet the CEOs. You know what the difference is? Money. It is the only thing that foreigners respect.'

Eventually, the train pulled in at Chiasso. I said goodbye to the boss and his assistant, got off and walked. At the end of a long, empty platform and past some sleepy border guards stood Emilio Camponovo, the person I had come to meet.

The last time we had seen each other was in Shanghai at a large conference on precious metals in a five-star hotel. The audience had just been treated to a tour de force by a Chinese official on the podium; the lines on his powerpoint all aimed skyward, demand was set to soar, and China soon enough would be the largest market for precious metals on earth. Then everyone repaired for lunch. I found Emilio studying his food near a self-service tureen of rice which had drawn a long line of diners. He looked tired. Chinese officials could say what they liked, he said, but the fact was that per capita expenditure on gold in China was a fraction of that in the developed world. Even in India, people spent far more on gold ornaments than the Chinese. It was true that Chinese had a preference for platinum, but that was not much use to Emilio. He was the founder and part-owner of one of the largest gold refineries in Europe. 'All we need is for every Chinese to buy a gold chain,' he said, rolling back his cuff to reveal a chain with the heaviest, thickest links I have seen. I had the sense that he was joking, but when I did not laugh, his eyes lit up. 'You think it is possible? One day they might?' I said I could not tell. 'No, probably not, I suppose,' he said.

At the end of the platform in Chiasso, he looked happier and more relaxed. He was a large man in his sixties, wearing a sports jacket made of silk and an open-necked shirt. The fibres of the jacket scintillated in the sunlight. As we walked to lunch, he told me some local history. The border ran slap through the middle of what was really one town; the south part was Como in Italy and the north was Chiasso in Switzerland, but the dominant ethnicity on both sides was Italian. The separation had made for some interesting arbitrage opportunities, he said. In the 1970s, the Italian government subsidised petrol but sugar was difficult to get hold of. In Switzerland, by contrast, petrol was expensive and sugar plentiful. 'So every day here,' he said pointing at an empty car lot next to the border post. 'You would have a big trading. Sugar that way. Petrol this way. That was how it went.'

At lunch, the conversation was somewhat sombre. The business of gold was in trouble. Northern Italy was home to over 10,000 jewellery manufacturers, most of them small-scale artisan outfits that, taken together, made up the largest gold jewellery industry in the world. But competition from China and Turkey was threatening to wipe them out. You could see the changes already in Italy's demand for refined gold; in the last four or five years it had slumped from over 600 tonnes annually to around 350 tonnes. Camponovo saw little prospect for an improvement. Every year, he said, Chinese entrepreneurs and designers descended on the big jewellery fairs in northern Italian towns such as Vicenza to buy specimens to take home and reproduce at less than one-tenth of the Italian price.

Camponovo appeared resigned that this practice would continue and that Italy's jewellery industry might be heading for a collapse. He did not blame the Chinese, he said. They were willing to work hard and they were smart. What really exercised him during our lunch and later during discussions in his office was how ignorant the Italian and Swiss governments seemed to be of the nature of Chinese competition. From his perspective, the threat came less from China's rise than from the failure of European governments to understand it and formulate policies to deal with it. For instance, he said, corporation tax rates in his canton of Switzerland were effectively over 50 per cent of profits. But in spite of this heavy burden, the canton announced larger budget deficits year after year. The reason for these deficits was not any significant increase in spending on essential infrastructure; Chiasso is one of the wealthiest places in Europe and the roads, railways, schools and hospitals are already excellent. The main cause of the deepening deficit was state payments to individuals for medical treatment. Of some 300,000 people living in the canton, around 90,000 qualified through various loopholes for help in paying their health costs. 'We are killing ourselves with comfort,' he said.

Healthcare was one cost. Unions were another; there were ten different unions represented among the staff who worked in Camponovo's gold refinery. The red tape and the welfare payments were suffocating, he said. In every company and profession it was the same story; the socialist welfare state had turned from a boon to a burden. A couple of years ago, he said, there had been a move to increase the twenty-five-hour working week of school-teachers in the canton by one full hour. But many teachers opposed this, so a public, canton-wide referendum had to be held to resolve the issue. Camponovo shook his head at the memory of it.

I thought of the boss and his assistant on the train and wondered what they would make of a canton-wide referendum on a twenty-five-hour week for teachers.

It is said that in state-to-state diplomacy there is no such thing as friendship, only periods when mutual interests coalesce. So when Jacques Chirac, the French President, struck up a friendship with his Chinese counterpart, Jiang Zemin, that was so attentive it bordered on courtship, some people found it hard to know where to look. The two leaders found time in their schedules to keep up a correspondence on issues of art, poetry and culture. Jiang heard that Chirac admired the poetry of Li Bai, a Tang dynasty poet, and wrote ink-brush calligraphy to the French leader. Chirac repaid the courtesy by showing the Jiang calligraphy scroll to honoured guests and praising the fairness of the Chinese President's hand. Jiang later commended Chirac's knowledge of Chinese culture, remarking once that 'he is more of an expert than me. In Shanghai, he even correctly dated a bronze statue.'[7]

When Jiang and his wife, Wang Yeping, visited France, Chirac invited them to a weekend at Château Bity, the sixteenth-century home in the Corrèze region of central France that Chirac and his wife, Bernadette, usually keep sequestered from their political commitments. Indeed, when Hillary Clinton visited the local town of Sarran, of which Bernadette is deputy mayor, she was given a tour of favourite Chirac haunts in the town but never made it as far as the family château. The special treatment for the Jiangs was extended later to the whole concept of China. The Eiffel Tower was illuminated in the red of the Chinese flag to mark a 'Year of China' in France, and, as part of a reciprocal 'French Culture Year' in China, eight jets from the French airforce swooped over the Great Wall, leaving tricolour trails behind them. Chirac maintained in a speech at Jiang's alma mater in Shanghai that things were getting so close between the two nations that a state of 'brotherly love' had developed.[8]

Was all this merely politics as usual, or did Chirac really harbour special feelings for Jiang and the Chinese people? Certainly, he cannot have been oblivious to the commercial utility of friendship with Beijing; in late 2004 the French companies that accompanied his visit to China garnered contracts for Airbus planes, Alstom trains, water treatment plants, hydroelectric equipment and wheat that were valued at 5 billion euros.[9] But from another perspective, his overtures to Beijing were far from universally popular at home. Alain Madelin, President of the Liberal Democratic Party, likened Jiang to the former Chilean dictator Augusto Pinochet and said there should be a limit to the red-carpet treatment he received in France.[10] Similarly, Wei Jingsheng, China's most famous exiled dissident, poured scorn on Chirac's appreciation of Jiang's calligraphy. 'Everyone in China knows that Jiang writes like a child,' he said. 'Chirac is making a fool of himself.'[11] Perhaps, after all, Chirac's willingness to suffer the slings and arrows of domestic criticism proved that his ardour was genuine.

And then again, perhaps not. Only a few months after he assured Beijing that China's rise was a wonderful thing that offered rare opportunities for French growth and job creation, the French President completely changed his tune. Sitting next to Gerhard Schröder, the German Chancellor, at a meeting to discuss the future of Europe, he said: 'We have a real problem in Europe. The considerable increase in Chinese textile exports to our countries calls into question the jobs of thousands of workers. We cannot accept a death blow to the jobs of a significant number of workers in our countries.'[12] So why the volte-face? The commercial relationship between France and China had not objectively changed and the 'friendship' between the two countries was still nominally intact. What was different was Chirac's perception of his political interests. France was about to vote in a referendum, and the issues of jobs and competitiveness were paramount.

Ostensibly, the subject of that referendum was whether or not to approve a new European Constitution which opened the way for an expansion of the European Union beyond its twenty-five member states. But, in reality, the vote in France was generally about whether people were satisfied with their lot and, more particularly, whether they felt that the previous EU expansion from fifteen to twenty-five members had benefited them. The answer to these questions, first in France and then in the Netherlands, turned out after the vote to be an emphatic 'no'. Various theories have been advanced as to why both countries voted against the adoption of the European Constitution and the further enlargement of the Union. But the dominant concern appears to have been unemployment, and especially the migration of jobs to the new EU members in Eastern Europe. The referendum result was, fundamentally, a conservative cry against the loss of social benefits and a decline in the prevailing quality of life.

The referendum rejection was a painful political blow for Chirac and it threw the whole European project into crisis. Several politicians have since tried to reignite the cause of greater European unity and to point ways out of the current malaise. UK Prime Minister Tony Blair, for instance, warned of 'failure on a grand, strategic scale' if EU member nations were to drift apart, turn their back on globalisation or ignore the need for reform of Europe's institutions.[13] The way to inject new growth and energy into Europe, he said, included investment in knowledge, in active labour market policies, in science parks and innovation, in higher education, in urban regeneration and in help for small businesses. In a speech to mark the UK Presidency of the EU, he added that the Union's social model needed to be modernised and a system of farm subsidies that claims 40 per cent of EU budget revenues gradually overhauled.

But Blair, in common with other Establishment EU politicians who have addressed the subject, has failed to give an accurate accounting of the competitive threat Europe faces. The impact of China's rise is not something that can be mitigated by a few incremental reforms, some reallocation of budgetary resources and the launch of several initiatives to spur innovation. It is a challenge unprecedented in the annals of global capitalism; the product of epoch-making changes under harsh conditions in the world's most populous country. The events unfolding in Prato and Como are merely early soundings of the shape of things to come. One early example of trade friction was the 'bra wars' spat over the entry of super-competitive Chinese textiles to Europe. Tomorrow it will be electronics, motorbikes, steel, chemicals, cars and cartoon animations. The simple, unpalatable truth is this: that in many areas of manufacturing, European companies cannot compete in the longer run – no matter what countermeasures they or the EU may take.

Some examples illustrate this point. An Italian company, Seves SpA, had two factories making heavy glass insulators in Europe, one in Italy and one in St-Yorre, France. It had to decide which one to close after competition from China convinced the management that manufacturing in Europe was not sustainable. It chose to close the French factory because its workers were 57 per cent more expensive than those in Italy and worked 19 per cent fewer hours.[14] What surprised the management were the savings they gained when they built a new plant near Shanghai. The starting salary for a production line worker was 2,600 euros a year, compared to 17,000 euros in St-Yorre. The company offered to rehire any of its French workers willing to make the trip to Shanghai, but none volunteered.

Schiess, a 140-year-old maker of heavy-duty lathes and boring machines based in the East German town of Aschersleben, typifies the 'Mittelstand' machine tool makers who are the backbone of the German economy. But even though Schiess is in the former East Germany, where wages are lower than in the West, the differential between Germany and China is still large. A skilled worker in Aschersleben makes $2,000 to $2,600 a month, while in China a worker of similar ability gets $400 or less. That is why Shenyang Machine Tool decided to shift many of Schiess's jobs back to China after it bought the company in early 2005.[15]

ABB, the Swiss engineering giant, plans to hire 5,000 new employees by 2008 in China and more than half of these will be engineers. They would be in addition to the 7,000 employees currently working for the company in China in different divisions in thirty large cities. During the same time, there are no explicit plans to hire any workers in Europe. 'Our feeling is that we are over-invested in Europe and under-invested in low-cost countries like China,' Jürgen Dormann, the chief executive, said.[16] 'We have too many factories in Europe and buy too many of our raw materials in high-cost countries.' Similarly, IBM has announced a plan to lay off its 13,000 workforce in Europe.

There is no end in sight to the trend that these examples illuminate. Faced with Chinese competition, companies either shift production to places such as the Pearl River or Yangtze Deltas, or move to one of the new members of the EU in Eastern Europe such as Poland, Hungary and the Czech Republic. The deepening of the employment crisis in 'core' European countries that results from these actions represented one of the biggest electoral challenges facing several European politicians such as Schröder and Chirac. Germany is in the grip of its worst employment crisis since before World War Two, with over 12 per cent of its workforce, or around 5 million people, without a job. Throughout the EU, the unemployment rate is around 9 per cent, and real wages in sectors such as manufacturing are falling. A further complication is the relatively low number of those laid off who are able to find new jobs in the service sector. This is partly because jobs in accounting, law, financial and risk management, healthcare, information technology and several other service areas are also in the process of migrating to India and China.

As people fear for their jobs, understandable conservative reflexes – such as those displayed in the French and Dutch referendum votes – can fuel protectionism and jealousy. At this point, it can take all the energy and determination of political leaders to prevent a general regression into chauvinism. The pain inflicted by the type of deep and structural reform that Europe needs can make such reforms difficult to sell to the electorate. The nature of the European malaise so harshly exposed by China's emerging prowess is that the working populations of 'core' Europe are – by many multiples – compensated too generously for producing too little. But, for politicians, it can be tough to sell a promise of downsizing, offshoring, outsourcing and falling real wages to European electorates already saddled with 20 million unemployed. Intellectually, many in Europe may find it distasteful that the EU runs a subsidy under which cows get more than $2 a day – more than the average daily income of 700 million Chinese. But when the consequences of any rapid unravelling of the agricultural subsidy system – the mass bankruptcy of small farms, the decline in land values and the distress of rural communities – are contemplated, the appetite for change may wither.

China was able in the five years from the onset of the Asian financial crisis in 1997 to lay off more than 25 million workers from its inefficient and heavily subsidised state-owned enterprises.[17] The fruits of that stern therapy are now evident in the competitive shock that is hitting Europe and America. But China is not a democracy. The state did not have to seek the permission of its people to 'smash the iron rice bowl' of socialist welfare or turn its back on the ideology of Communism. When workers rioted, protested, petitioned or dissented, it answered with well-honed authoritarian tactics. The result has been that state-financed social welfare has in the space of less than a decade ceased to be a millstone for the corporate sector. The housing, schooling, health-care and pension obligations that over 300,000 state companies used to meet on behalf of their workers have now been eliminated, reduced or privatised. China today is a great deal less socialist than any country in Europe; the 120 million or so migrant workers, for instance, receive no welfare at all.

Not only is the cost of employing a Chinese worker a fraction of that in Germany, France and Italy – and roughly between one-sixth and a quarter of the going rates in Eastern Europe's EU members – but also state expenditure in China is lower as a proportion of gross domestic product than in the countries of Western Europe. That means that the taxes the government levies on its corporations and its people can also be lower. In Germany, for instance, state expenditures came to 47.8 per cent of gross domestic product in 2004. An accurate figure for China is more difficult to calculate because of various categories of quasi-governmental financing, such as funding by state banks for state infrastructure projects, which are not normally included in the official figures. Nevertheless, narrowly defined Chinese state expenditures, as a percentage of gross domestic product, come to less than half of German levels.[18]

These discrepancies define the challenge China presents to the social democratic model that Europe so painstakingly constructed from the ruins of World War Two. But it is far from clear whether, faced with this challenge, Germany and France – and to a lesser extent, the other countries of Western Europe – possess the will or ability to smash their own 'iron rice bowl'. Sometimes, the rhetoric seems to be moving in the opposite direction. Just as Marx and Engels are losing their Far Eastern constituency of 1.3 billion, they may be gaining ground back in their ancestral homeland. Franz Müntefering, Chairman of the ruling Social Democratic Party, told listeners in Berlin in 2005 that 'the growing power of international capital' with its 'unbridled greed for profit' represented a 'threat to democracy'.[19] This was followed a few days later by President Schröder taking issue with the evils of an 'unrestrained neo-liberal system'. Other politicians warned of 'predator capitalists', while Müntefering later lambasted faceless foreign investors who were descending on Germany like 'swarms of locusts'.

From the context of his remarks, he appeared to be pointing the finger at the UK and the US, but he could just as easily have been talking about China.

FIVE

Rockford, Illinois is a low-rise Midwestern town, surrounded by undulating farmland and horizons which, though generally flat, are more eventful than in the prairie country further to the south and west. The straight lines that form where the cornfields and dairy pastures meet the sky are broken by a grain silo here, a clump of trees there and the odd immaculately painted farmhouse. I arrived there from Chicago in late February, when the snow was still in drifts around the kerb at the Greyhound bus stop. A taxi took me down East State Street to the Alpine Inn Motel. My first impressions were of churches, fast-food outlets and waitresses with open faces who said 'mmm, mmm' as they put your food down. Signposts visible from the road offered a flavour of Rockford's character: the Westminster Presbyterian Church, Hometown Buffet, the Church of Christian Fellowship, Pot Bellies Drive-Thru Sandwich Works, the Blackhawk Baptist Association, Don Pablo's Mexican Kitchen, Lutheran Church, Tom and Jerry's Fast Food. Interspersed with these places were shops advertising that everything inside was going for less than a dollar, and glass-fronted booths offering to lend people their monthly income in advance.

Outwardly, it looked like the last place you might expect to uncover evidence of China's global presence. There were no Chinese here that I could see, aside from those working in restaurants such as the Great Wall, and they had been in Rockford for so long that they remembered a visit by George Bush Senior when he was a mere Vice-President. Neither was there any hazy historical connection, unlike in the nearby town of Pekin, Illinois, a place that had long ago borrowed the name of the Chinese capital for reasons that were now forgotten. Rockford appeared to be quintessential middle America, full of practical folk raising wholesome families without too much concern for the world beyond the wheat belt. And yet, through circumstance rather than design, this appearance was somewhat misleading. Though outwardly invisible, the imprint of China was almost everywhere, embedded in the town's past, looming over its future and etched into the contours of its geography.

On the day I arrived, there was a modest traffic jam leading out of town along East State Street to the suburbs. Strangely, almost nothing was travelling in the other direction to the town centre. I asked the receptionist at the Alpine Inn where everyone was going. 'Wal-Mart,' he said. I went against the crowds to the town centre and when I got there I found it was virtually deserted. Only the library, a theatre and a run down Greek restaurant were open. Where was everyone? I asked a librarian. Several years ago, she replied, the town centre had been a focal point. But it had started to die as companies folded and workers moved away. Then, a few years later, Wal-Mart had set up a vast discount store out in the eastern suburbs, inducing a cluster of restaurants, fast-food outlets and other hypermarkets to follow. Soon, Rockford's centre of gravity had shifted.

Behind each stage in the metamorphosis, China's influence was palpable. It had accelerated the loss of manufacturing jobs and then propelled the rise of Wal-Mart, which sourced more and more of its products from Chinese suppliers. Now, the librarian said, the local economy was enmeshed in a kind of Chinese puzzle. Local jobs went out to China and returned in the form of cheap manufactured goods which were bought by the very people who had paid with their jobs in the first place.

Rockford had only recently been laid low. It had in better days risen to considerable prominence from small beginnings as an encampment at the end of the Galena and Chicago Union Railroad. Many of the early settlers were Swedes, hard-working people on the run from pasteurisation. Louis Pasteur's benign discovery of a way to kill the bacteria in milk had had unforeseen side effects: as fathers lived longer, sons despaired of ever being able to take over the family farm and migrated in search of new lives. Like many early immigrants, they had little inkling of where they were heading to; they just rode the railroads west from New York until the track ran out under the looming skies of Illinois. When they got there, they were reminded of home. The area around the beautiful

Rock River was heavily forested and the trees were being felled to feed a construction frenzy in Chicago, the fastest-growing city on earth. The fire that devastated Chicago in 1871 injected impetus into the lumber trade and generated a huge demand for furniture which the Swedes, along with other immigrants from Italy and Germany, moved quickly to fill.

Making fine furniture required precision tools and those tools had to be made by someone. The local carpenters proved more than equal to the task, quickly shifting from woodworking to metalworking and machine tool making. One craftsman, doodling in his spare time, even invented the jigsaw. But Rockford's real rise to prominence in the industry that was to define its development came after an entrepreneur called Winthrop Ingersoll moved his small machine tool factory to the town from Cleveland, Ohio in 1891. Records from those days describe his new plant as 150 feet long and 50 feet wide with nineteen men on the payroll. The town that it inhabited had twenty-seven churches, eight banks, 174 industrial companies and 'six costly bridges' spanning the Rock River. To start with business was quiet, but in the early years of the twentieth century, the automobile industry started to flourish and Ingersoll's reputation for building high-precision tooling and milling machines spread fast. Walter Chrysler, the master mechanic at Buick, bought a complete line-up of machines for milling aluminium crankcases. Henry Ford was also a customer; the key production machinery that made the 'Model-T' was manufactured at Ingersoll. The expertise gleaned from contracts such as these helped the company develop ways to machine parts for nuclear reactors, Boeing aircraft and several generations of military fighters.

One success built on another and, by the middle of the last century, Rockford had become a centre for the American machine tool industry. Although this did not make the town a household name in America, its contributions to the US military-industrial complex won it an unenviable fame in the Kremlin. During the Cold War, this wholesome Midwestern community was near the top of a list of places that the Soviet Union had selected as targets for a nuclear strike. In the event of a showdown, Moscow was set to unleash its intercontinental ballistic missiles at Washington, New

York, Los Angeles and . . . Rockford. Apparently, the motivation for this was similar to that which led to the bombing of Schweinfurt, an unremarkable German town where in World War Two the ball-bearings were made without which the aircraft of the Luftwaffe and the Panzers of the armoured divisions would all have ground to a halt.

Residents of Rockford now laugh at the air raid drills, the fallout shelters and the radios that were tuned to 640 and 1040 on the AM dial, the frequencies for public emergency broadcasts in the event of nuclear attack. But in those days it was serious. Not only was Ingersoll engaged in making equipment crucial to the functioning of the US military, but Sundstrand, a company on 11th Street, was the sole source of an electrical system without which most military aircraft could not fly. At one point of high Cold War tension, the Pentagon grew so concerned at this glaring vulnerability that it ordered Sundstrand to set up a second factory, independent in every aspect – engineering, administration, testing and production – far away in Denver, Colorado.

As things turned out, of course, the Soviet Union was to have no more than a psychological impact on Rockford. It was China, the other Communist behemoth, that was destined to leave a lasting imprint. For about two years before I got there, the town had been caught in a quiet crisis of manufacturing which had stolen across the American Midwest, sweeping away scores of small and medium-sized businesses. Many of those who had gone under were long-established family firms that had weathered wars and economic recessions, as well as the rise of Japan and South Korea. I wanted to acquire an overall reckoning of how many such companies had gone out of business, but comprehensive figures proved difficult to obtain. Many of the closures involved businesses employing tens rather than hundreds of people in towns that rarely made the national newspapers. And yet unofficial surveys offered sobering revelations. In one, Bruce Cain, President of Xcel Mold and Machine in Canton, Ohio, collected the advertisements for equipment sales that followed the closure of companies in the metalworking industry in the ten states in the general area of Ohio. He testified to a hearing conducted by the US Congress that between 1 May 2003 and September 2004 he had collected 180 auction flyers – one, on average, every three days.[1] Behind almost every closure or downsizing was a watershed moment when, apparently out of the blue, a new Chinese competitor had emerged offering prices that were a third or less of the best price the American company could manage.

One industry to be particularly badly hit was machine tools, the bedrock of the manufacturing sector and Rockford's speciality. These are the tools that make the parts that go into machinery. Without the machine tools to make the components of a car engine, there would be no engine; without precision instruments, there would be no high-technology products. The Chinese government, which is overwhelmingly composed of engineering graduates, realised long ago the pivotal role that machine tools have in building a strong industrial base. It made the industry a strategic priority and urged its state companies to scour the world for technologies they could acquire or absorb. At almost all of the closing-down auctions across the Midwest, Chinese buyers were out trying to snap up amortised machinery, technical blueprints and operational know-how. In Rockford, too, the footprints of acquisitive Chinese corporations were everywhere.

I had come to Rockford for a dinner. Not just any dinner, but the Rockford Regional Chamber of Commerce's event of the year. There would be around 600 of the region's leading businesspeople sitting around big tables at the town's premier events venue, a restaurant called Cliffbreakers. The guest of honour was to be Al Frink, the newly appointed 'manufacturing czar' in George W. Bush's administration, the person charged with resuscitating a manufacturing sector that had haemorrhaged nearly 3 million jobs since Bush took his seat in the Oval Office. Don Manzullo, Congressman for the 16th District of Illinois and a campaigner on Capitol Hill for the development of small businesses, would also be there. The official topic of the evening was some anodyne catch-all like 'The state of manufacturing in America'. But what everyone wanted to know was how Washington was going to deal with the challenge from China and, more specifically, whether the town of Rockford was doomed to die.

Cliffbreakers looked a little out of keeping with the strait-laced, God-fearing community in which I had spent a week before the night of the dinner. There was more than a touch of Vegas about it; rhinestone chandeliers, a fountain in the foyer, Greco-Roman plasterwork and a corridor lined with photographs of famous guests – including Frank Sinatra – who had once performed there. I wondered for a while if I had come to the right place, but then I began to see familiar faces. There was a man I had met earlier whose workshops had produced a special gear wheel for the space probe that had gone to Mars. Near him was the young engineer who had made a cog so small that it could fit within Lincoln's nose on a coin. Talking to him was a woman in whose factory I had seen workers welding filaments of wire so fine that they had to be seen with a microscope.

The first person to greet me was Tom McDunn. He was in the same three-piece black suit he had been wearing at his brother-in-law's fiftieth birthday party a few nights earlier. It had been a pleasant, sober evening. We sat at a long table eating slabs of pizza and drinking lemonade. The conversation had been cheery and polite. China was not a topic for a happy gathering, and the only time I remember it being mentioned was when the man next to me leant over and confided that the appetite of Chinese steel mills for scrap was so voracious that some of the manhole covers in his neighbourhood had started to disappear. 'Fancy that,' he said. 'They tell me that local boys lever them up to sell them for scrap. We can sell scrap metal and waste cardboard to China, but our good stuff they can make cheaper than we do.'

McDunn had been a senior executive at Ingersoll, before it ended its illustrious history in bankruptcy in 2003. Even before it went under, Chinese buyers were starting to circle. The first part of the venerable old company to be sold off, the auto machine tools business called Ingersoll Production Systems, was bought by a state-run Chinese giant, Dalian Machine Tool. As soon as the Chinese took over, McDunn said, the stacks of blueprints and engineering specifications from decades of cutting-edge auto-motive innovation were dispatched back to head office in China. Dalian, after all, was one of several Chinese companies seized with climbing the next big technological hurdle: how to build a home-grown, high-performance auto engine.

Having bought Ingersoll Production Systems, Dalian decided to use the US company as a stalking horse for the main prize: Ingersoll Milling Machine. Not only had Milling Machine been an important US military contractor since before World War One, but it was also at the time of its insolvency working on some highly sensitive projects. It made the machinery that honed the wings of America's fighter aircraft and had developed a technology that ensured a more reliable performance from the fuel tanks in rockets. It also produced the equipment that machines the turbines in nuclear power stations and the machines that coated the B-2 stealth bombers with the material that made them invisible to radar. Such secrets would have been invaluable to Beijing, and Dalian came within a hair's breadth of obtaining them. Nobody from the Pentagon, the Department of Defense, the Central Intelligence Agency or the other security arms of the US government had noticed that the Chinese company was bidding for Ingersoll Milling through Ingersoll Production Systems. On paper, such a bid must have appeared a mere family affair. However, some local entrepreneurs tipped off Congressman Manzullo, who alerted Lisa Bronson, Deputy Under Secretary of Defense for Technology, Security Policy and Counterproliferation.[2] The attempted acquisition was blocked and Ingersoll Milling ended up being bought by an Italian company, Camozzi.

McDunn never said so outright, but he exuded a sense that China was a threat. Not everyone in Rockford was ambiguous on that point, however. Shortly before the banquet started, I met Dean Olson, a genial man with grey hair who had taken me around his auto parts factory earlier in the week. His big shock had come a couple of years earlier when Chinese parts at unbelievably low prices started to eat away his market share. 'So,' he said, 'if you can't beat 'em join 'em.' He began to import some Chinese parts and distribute them to his network of customers along with the relatively high-tech parts that he made himself. The quality of the Chinese goods was fine, he said, and business was OK. But he was always waiting for the moment when the Chinese would climb further up the technology ladder and produce the high-end products that kept his machinists employed. When this happened, Olson knew, their price would almost certainly be a fraction of what he charged. Under those circumstances, his only remaining business asset would be his distribution network. I asked him if it was possible that one day he might end up just distributing Chinese products. He looked a little offended. 'That is a big question,' he said.

The last person I met before the speeches started was Eric Anderberg of Dial Machine, a fair-haired man in his thirties with an open face and a quick intellect. He had been to China on a trip led by Manzullo and Dennis Hastert, Speaker of the House of Representatives, and he sat on a committee in Chicago that provided the Federal Reserve Board with feedback on the state of American industry. He saw Rockford's predicament from both a micro and a macro perspective. Dial Machine had had to let go thirty of its seventy staff in the last couple of years and Anderberg seemed deeply affected by the experience.

'How do you tell people who have worked for you for all of their life, people whose families you know, that they no longer have a job? Everyone knows that a skilled, qualified machinist earning $16 to $17 an hour will not find another factory job in Rockford now,' he said. The place his former workers were most likely to end up was behind the counter at the discount end of East State Street working in Lowes, Home Depot, Target, Sam's Club, Menswear House or Wal-Mart itself for $7 an hour without a pension. 'The government says that it is creating jobs for those people leaving the manufacturing sector. But I say what kind of jobs? No wonder real wages were falling across the economy,' Anderberg said.

His view of free trade was that it was fine as long as it was fair. But competition with China was structurally and qualitatively unequal. The Chinese fixed the value of their currency against the US dollar, keeping it undervalued so as to give their exports greater competitiveness. They provided little or no welfare for their workers, so their costs were artificially low. There were no independent unions in China, so the safety standards he had seen in Chinese factories would have been illegal in America. The state banking system provided cheap credit to state companies that could default without consequences. The central government gave generous value added tax rebates to exporters that were not available to US companies. Restrictions on emissions in China were lax, so companies had to pay relatively little to keep the environment clean. Chinese companies routinely stole foreign intellectual property, but it was difficult to prosecute them because their courts were either corrupt or under government control. Finally, the state kept the price of various inputs, such as electricity and water, artificially low, thereby subsidising industry.

By contrast with all these cost advantages, Anderberg said, US companies struggled with a welter of bureaucratic red tape and legislation which, according to official calculations, increased the cost of doing business by over 20 per cent.[3] To Anderberg and many others who had turned up to hear Frink speak, the time had come for America to get tough in its defence of the small and medium enterprises that form the backbone of the US economy and provide around 70 per cent of America's employment. The US manufacturing sector, though declining, is still so large that – taken by itself – it would rank as the sixth or seventh largest economy in the world. In other words, the value created by US manufacturing firms is now only slightly less than that created by the entire Chinese economy. This, then, was Frink's constituency.

As the main course of the dinner arrived, Frink got up to speak. From the start, he was at pains to identify himself with his audience rather than with the bureaucrats he worked for. He began with a brief joke about how he had a full head of hair when he had taken up his job a few months back. But that, as was clear under the stage lights, was no longer the case. 'GTMY,' he said. 'GTMY . . . well, that is government speak for Great To Meet You. Because everything in government is an acronym.'

He gave a brief self-introduction. He had been born south of the border in Mexico, came to the US at the age of four and a half and was raised in California. He started a company from nothing and by the time he sold it off, it had won a national award for industry and employed 400 people. He explained that his position had been created in response to criticism from small and medium-sized manufacturers towards the policies and efficiency of the US Department of Commerce. He did not know why the government had not seen fit to appoint a lead advocate for manufacturing before. After all, agriculture has its own full Secretary even though it contributed about 2 per cent to GDP. Manufacturing makes up 15 per cent of GDP, and with multiplying factors added in, its influence spread to 30 to 40 per cent of the economy. But now, at last, America had its manufacturing czar. 'That is what the papers refer to me as. I am kind of beginning to like that term. I don't know why but . . . you know "czar", it does have a ring to it after a while,' he said.

Anyway, manufacturing now had one of its own in the White House. Someone who could feel its pain. Someone who had 'stared at the ceiling at night wondering how he was going to make that paycheque'. Someone who had made paycheques even in the welfare-obsessed 'people's republic of California'. Not someone who would be seduced by all the protocol and paraphernalia of Washington, but a man who would look political power in the face and tell it how things really were.

Until that point, he had the audience in the palm of his hand. There were deep nods, eruptions of laughter and amused smiles. His 'champion of the little guy' build-up had raised hopes for a piece of good news; a promise, a pledge or a projection that everything was going to be OK. But none came. In fact, he seemed to switch sides. It turned out that he thought outsourcing, a prime cause of Rockford's malaise, was a good thing. 'Eighty years ago, when companies were on the east coast and they moved to California, that looked like outsourcing. Maybe 100 years from now we will be in an intergalactic community where we are out-sourcing to other planets,' he said. 'Who knows where it will lead. But we can't be protectionist.'

He did acknowledge that Washington was too bureaucratic and promised to reduce legal and procedural red tape for businesses. But when it came to China, the audience began to get restless. China was merely a low-cost producer, he claimed. It had no brands. American companies could compete by leveraging the value of their brands, just as he had when he was running his Californian carpet company. He had managed to sell carpets to one of the most 'significant buildings' in China on the strength of the fact that he had carpeted the White House. The Chinese had paid more for that carpet per square metre, he said, than they had for the land the building stood on.

The administration, he said, was working on getting the Chinese to move towards a more flexible exchange rate system. But he could not promise the big revaluation of the renminbi that American manufacturers had been demanding. Yes, he did recognise that intellectual property abuses in China were a problem, but the White House was doing what it could. It had appointed an excellent team of anti-piracy specialists in the US embassy in Beijing and Frink himself had been over to Beijing to reinforce its message. He could not tell if his visit had borne concrete results, but judging by the reaction of his Chinese interlocutors, they had appreciated his candid approach. 'The Chinese told me: "You speak with straight tongue, white man,"' he said.

But this time the laughter was hesitant, muted. And as people filed out of the hall after the dinner was over, there were disappointed murmurs and complaints. How could the so-called champion of US manufacturing support the wave of outsourcing that had decimated small and medium enterprises nationwide and thrown 3 million onto the job market? Manzullo helped me to understand. Missing from the Rockford dinner, were the representatives of the Fortune 500. America's big multinationals were the ones who benefited from outsourcing, and they were also the ones who controlled US political attitudes towards the manufacturing sector. They financed the campaigns of most of the Congressmen on Capitol Hill. If the multinationals said outsourcing was good for America it was good for America until such time as ordinary voters could convince Congressmen otherwise at the ballot box. 'We have lost a lot of market share to China and a lot of guys here have gone out of business because of that,' Manzullo said. 'Nevertheless, Boeing has about a $250 million presence in northern Illinois and the largest purchaser of Boeing aircraft is China. You gotta fight this thing and yet you gotta do it correctly because their economy has to be robust enough to buy the stuff that [companies such as Boeing] are manufacturing.'

The problem was that Boeing, like most multinationals, had worked out that it could save a lot of money by sending some of its manufacturing functions to China and other low-cost countries. It needed to do this to maximise the returns to its shareholders. But in doing so, it threatened to put out of business many of its small, long-term suppliers such as those at the Rockford dinner. The process was self-reinforcing. The more Boeing outsourced, the quicker the machine tool companies that supplied it went bust, providing opportunities for Chinese competitors to buy the technology they needed, better to supply companies like Boeing. Boeing makes money, but ultimately at the expense of the industries and jobs that sustain Middle America. In the opinion of Eric Anderberg, capitalism had lapsed into cannibalism. 'Lenin said that America would tear itself apart from the inside through greed,' he said. 'And you know what? He was right.'

Throughout the 1980s, one of the urban myths about China involved the proverbial state-owned company with more money than sense that had bought a big, sophisticated piece of machinery from a US, Japanese or European company. The prized machine was then put into a corner and never used. The reason for this varied. Sometimes, the story had it, the Chinese were unable to read or understand the instructions. Sometimes it was that the wrong machine had been bought, and sometimes it was merely that the machine was just too advanced for China's backward state. Yet on the many occasions that I heard this story, two things were always constant: the glee on the face of the engineer or technician who told it, and the message that Chinese somehow just did not 'get' technology.

These days that story is no longer heard. But it has been replaced by a new conventional wisdom which states that although China has made giant strides since the 1980s, it is destined to remain nothing more than a mid-technology power. This belief is more sophisticated than the 1980s urban myth and the arguments that support it are reasonable.

One has it that China's abundance of cheap labour reduces the pressure on companies to climb the technology ladder because employing extra workers often costs less than buying new machinery. This, in theory at least, is valid. Another argument points to the large gap in spending on research and development that exists between China and its developed nation competitors. This is also factually correct. Total spending on R&D in the US amounts to 2.7 per cent of gross domestic product, but less than one per cent of China's much smaller GDP is spent in this way. In addition, US spending on R&D is more effective than that in China, adding 22 per cent to the value of the product under development compared to less than 5 per cent in China.[4] A third rationale in support of the 'mid-technology' argument is that the paucity of protection for intellectual property saps the innovative verve of scientists. This too seems to be borne out anecdotally and by the low number of patents per head of population. In the industrialised countries that form the membership of the Organisation for Economic Co-operation and Development, there are on average 150 patents per capita. In China there are only five.

The problem with these arguments is not that they lack merit, but that they miss the point. The observable reality is that China is climbing the technology ladder at a rapid pace and its ascent is neither localised nor specialised, but identifiable almost across the board. The difference between China's technological emergence and that of developed countries is that it is driven not so much by research as by commerce. Chinese companies, by and large, derive their technologies by buying them, by copying them or by encouraging a foreign partner to transfer them as part of the price for access to a large potential market. In this context, it is globalisation rather than R&D that is the main catalyst behind China's re-emergence as a technology power.

The powerful lure of the 1.3 billion-person market, no matter how illusory that may be, has helped China to leapfrog some of the technology barriers that stymied several of the southeast Asian 'Tiger' economies in the 1980s and 1990s. Malaysia, for instance, was unable to build its own car engines, meaning that its national car, the Proton, was never more than a composite of parts imported at considerable cost from Japan and other countries. Neither did Kuala Lumpur, in spite of strenuous efforts, manage to develop a viable industry to fabricate the wafers that go into computer chips. As countries, Malaysia, Thailand, Singapore, Indonesia and the Philippines got stuck trying to clamber over landmark technological barriers, allowing Paul Krugman, the US economist, to remark that the success of the 'Tigers' had been driven more by 'perspiration than inspiration'. China, by contrast, is experiencing little difficulty in transcending these problems and is already more advanced in almost every field of technological endeavour than its southeast Asian counterparts, in spite of being much poorer on a per capita basis. Chinese companies, spurred on by Beijing's policies, are not so much vaulting over the technological hurdles in their path as going around them. The technology of car engines provides a case in point.

The ability to make a high-performance car engine has long been seen as part of the crown jewels of industrial attainment. The state-owned companies that formed joint ventures with GM, Volkswagen, Nissan, Toyota and others have all been applying pressure on their partners for years to transfer enough technology to allow the Chinese side to build its own top-class auto engine. But the foreign partners have refused to budge, knowing that when they lose this technology, they lose not only the product of generations of in-house R&D but also their attractiveness to their Chinese joint venture partner. But while these big Chinese companies chafed, a smaller upstart based in the inland province of Anhui was formulating a new approach. Chery, which had encountered piracy allegations from Volkswagen and GM almost since its inception in 1997, decided there was no time to develop its own engine. Equally, the profit margins on selling cars were too thin to justify the purchase of expensive engines from foreign manufacturers. The only way, according to Yin Tongyao, the President, was to buy engine-building technological expertise. When I visited the company in 2002, Yin had just been to the UK talking to Lotus, the auto engineering firm, about a possible deal. In the end, however, Chery went with AVL, an Austrian engineering specialist that it hired to transfer the technology of engine design and the know-how of how to build one. In March 2005, it unveiled a new engine plant that cost $370 million and will manufacture 150,000 engines a year to start with. Within five years, it hopes the engines will reach the highest European and US environmental standards and production will increase to 500,000 units a year.[5]

The dynamics that drove Chery's technological leap owed little to R&D and much to economies of scale. The reason why Chery, which currently sells cheap cars at a low margin, was able to afford the expensive engine technology was that the banks were willing to finance it. The reason why banks were willing to finance it (aside from some government support) was that the number of people wealthy enough to buy a car in China was due to grow from roughly 60 million in 2005 to an estimated 160 million in 2010. In other words, China was set to be by far the fastest-growing auto market in the world. Having made its technological leap, Chery is starting to export to the US. It has forged an alliance with Malcolm Bricklin, the New Yorker who brought the Subaru minicars from Japan to the US in the 1960s and the ill-fated Yugo from Yugoslavia in the 1980s. But Chery's ambitions are much larger than those of either of these predecessors. It wants to be the next Toyota, exporting one million cars by 2012, all of them priced at a 30 per cent discount to their nearest competitor, Yin said.[6] With the savings that Chinese manufacturers derive from low labour costs, an integrated supply chain and other benefits, Chery is aiming to do for cars what others have done for textiles, shoes and consumer electronics – blow away the competition with prices that can hardly be believed. Already, the company sells a compact car, called QQ, for around $3,600 each in China.

Another big hurdle in the industrial coming-of-age is in the area of semiconductors and computer chips. China has had the ability through purchases of foreign machinery to make chips for about two decades. In the early days, the technology of whatever was being made in China was at least ten years behind the industry leaders. But in recent years, the establishment of a company called Semiconductor Manufacturing International Corporation (SMIC) by Richard Chang in Shanghai has brought China-made chips into closer contention with industry leaders.

As with car engines, this achievement has been procured not by research but by the pull of a burgeoning market. The story of SMIC, one of the most advanced wafer 'fabs' in China, reveals how technology in the global economy cannot but follow the market, no matter how many obstacles governments try to put in the way. The story starts in Taiwan, the breakaway island off China's southeast coast that Beijing insists is part of its territory. By the year 2000, Taiwan had become a world leader, along with the US, in the semiconductor industry. By 2001, it was earning $15.6 billion in selling semiconductors to customers all over the world. But with China booming across the Taiwan Strait, the government in Taipei was facing a considerable dilemma. If it let Taiwanese companies go to the mainland – with its thriving market, cheap building costs and inexpensive engineers – it risked losing one of the island's top industries to its outsize neighbour. But refusing to let them go would mean that competitors, perhaps from Japan, the US or elsewhere, might steal a march on the big Taiwan semiconductor companies, imperilling their prospects in the longer term.[7]

In 2002, Yu Shyi-kun, the Taiwanese Premier, announced a compromise: Taiwan chip companies could invest in the mainland, but only under strict conditions. The most important of these was that the wafers and chips manufactured could be no larger than eight inches and no smaller than 0.25 microns respectively – in other words, at least two generations behind the cutting edge of technology. Such rules, however, were like grass before the wind. Richard Chang, for instance, just registered his company in the Cayman Islands so that he could circumvent Taiwanese restrictions and build up SMIC. When the US government, which also keeps strict rules on the export of high-technology items to China, blocked a purchase of chip-making equipment from Applied Materials, Chang merely looked elsewhere. He got hold of an advanced 0.18 micron process technology from Japan and Singapore and is currently trying to close the gap with Intel's cutting-edge 0.09 micron chips with the help of equipment bought from Europe.

Having cleared these hurdles, SMIC has a firm lead over its competitors in China and plans to build at least six more 'fabs' in the country, some of which will make state-of-the-art 12-inch wafers. Within a few years, the gap between Chinese and US technology in semiconductors may have closed, the only difference being that in China it costs about 15 per cent less to make them than in the US, Chang said. [8]

In other industries, the government has made a strenuous policy out of awarding sales to those multinationals that transfer technology while cold-shouldering those that do not. This trade-off is not unprecedented; post-war Japan demanded the same concessions from US companies who then watched with deepening alarm as their Japanese students metamorphosed first into rivals and then into industry leaders. The size of the Chinese market, however, gives Beijing a special leverage. The most prominent example so far of the pressures in play has been in the rivalry for power equipment contracts in a country that builds enough power stations in a single year to keep a mid-sized European economy supplied with all of its electricity needs. Large companies such as General Electric of the US, Alstom of France, Mitsubishi of Japan, Siemens of Germany and other competitors are all in the race, providing Beijing's industrial planners with ample scope to play one bidder off against another. The stakes are raised still higher for the foreign companies because their home markets are already mature, meaning that a successful bid in China can make the difference between a good or bad year worldwide.

An early goal of the transfer strategy was to wrest from foreign companies the know-how to build coal-fired generators, a natural target given the relative simplicity of the technology and China's overwhelming reliance on coal as a source of power. By 2004, less than a decade after Chinese companies developed the first 'home-grown' 300-megawatt coal-fired generator, Alstom was co-operating with Harbin Power, one of the largest local electricity companies, to make a state-of-the-art 1,000-megawatt machine. But although that was a significant technological achievement, it paled next to Beijing's next ambition – to manufacture top-of-the-range gas-fired generators. It let it be known that any foreign company hoping to win contracts in the gas-fired turbine market had to get serious about transferring technology by forming joint ventures with state companies and handing over the advanced manufacturing specifications.

This presented the multinationals with an agonising decision. The technology embedded in gas turbines is close to that of the engines which power commercial airliners. But for the sake of the market, GE decided to play ball. It would hand over some of the details of how to make its '9F' gas turbine, one of a series of generators that had been created by its aircraft engine and power systems divisions in conjunction with the US Department of Energy. The '9F' alone had cost around half a billion dollars to develop. In the three months of negotiations with potential Chinese partners, GE's approach as always was to offer just enough technology to win the contract but not enough to allow the Chinese side to build a rival turbine immediately. The Chinese, for their part, wanted the drawings for the entire turbine; the modelling and mathematics behind the shape of the turbine's blades, how the blades were cooled while rotating and the chemistry of the blades' make-up.[9] A GE spokesman declined to comment on the details of the deal it reached, but it did eventually win an order for thirteen of its '9F' turbines worth some $900 million. Nobody is under any illusions, however, that when the next big contract comes up for grabs, the Chinese will be driving an even harder bargain.

In other industries, market penetration is linked in a less direct fashion to technology transfer, but the two are nevertheless connected. Most large technology companies have been prevailed upon to set up R&D centres in Beijing, Shanghai or elsewhere as a precondition, either explicit or implicit, for the award of contracts from state companies. Motorola has poured more than $300 million into nineteen technology research centres in the country. A Microsoft Corp centre in Beijing employs well over 200 researchers. Siemens says it has spent more than $200 million since 1998 working with a Chinese scientific institute to develop a third-generation mobile phone standard, TD-SCDMA, to challenge two competing standards being promoted by European and US companies. Such research centres are not merely efforts by multinationals to ingratiate themselves with Chinese authorities; they are also becoming useful and cost-effective parts of the global research effort. But for Beijing, their main attraction is that they are educating Chinese scientists in some of the world's latest theories and technologies. And given the promiscuity of ideas, it is beyond doubt that a degree of cross-pollination between the foreign laboratories and their Chinese counterparts will occur.

Thus, for reasons that have little to do with indigenous research, China is leaping up the technology ladder. As every year passes, the conventional wisdom that the country will languish for years in the domain of mid-technology looks more and more like wishful thinking. And although domestic R&D spending is limited, some national science programmes have been strikingly successful. The most famous is the space programme, following the cosmonaut Yang Liwei's successful space orbit in 2004. In supercomputing, the construction of super-powerful computers to help in complicated scientific research, the progress has also been impressive. A decade ago China did not have a single supercomputer ranked among the top 500 in the world. But by the end of 2003, it had nine and its fastest, DeepComp 6800 built by Lenovo, was ranked fourteenth. Its biotechnology is also world-class in some areas. Its scientists are developing a safe 'pebble bed' technology for nuclear power stations and a 'clean coal' technology that may allow China to derive energy with vastly reduced carbon emissions. It is, in fact, difficult to think of an area of technology in which China does not have credible ambitions to lead the world.

It is said that when Zhou Enlai, Chairman Mao's urbane Premier who was educated in France, was asked his opinion of whether the French Revolution had been a success, he answered without irony that it was too early to tell. Like many sayings attributed to Chinese leaders, that one may be apocryphal. But its longevity springs from the validity of the insight that it offers: fortune in China has often waxed and waned according to cycles that are measured in centuries. One way to identify these cycles was in the accumulation and dissipation of dynastic energy, or the time it took for heaven to withdraw its imperial mandate. Another way to order the long passage of Chinese history is through the integrity of trends and ideas. And it is in this regard that 2005 was a very rare year indeed. Although it did not make any of the world's newspapers or websites, it was in 2005 that an idea which has done more than anything else to condition China's fate in the last 200 years finally came full-circle.

To understand this cycle, it is necessary to return to its beginning: the arrival of Lord George Macartney, envoy of the British King George III, at the court of the Qing dynasty emperor Qianlong in 1793. Macartney was a veteran diplomat who had served British interests in the court of Catherine the Great in Russia, as Governor of Grenada in the Caribbean and administrator in Madras, India. He had come to China with unusual luggage: telescopes, a planetarium, celestial and terrestrial globes, a great lens, barometers, lustres, clocks, airguns, fine swords, Derbyshire vases, porcelain figures and a carriage were just some of the items that made it intact to Beijing after a long voyage over sea and land. His aim was to use these items to impress the court of Qianlong and secure the undertaking of the emperor to open the vast Chinese market to trade. He had also brought with him George Staunton, a twelve-year-old pageboy, who had spent the journey learning the Chinese language with a tutor so that he could make a short speech to the emperor in his own tongue.

Qianlong, who was in his eighties, was impressed with Staunton and plucked an embroidered pouch from his own belt to give him in recognition of his linguistic efforts. But there was no such warmth towards Macartney, who first refused to kowtow in the way that was customary and then proceeded to make a tiresome list of demands. The emperor instructed his mandarins to send Macartney back home with a note to inform King George that China had not the 'slightest need of your country's manufactures'.

That much of the story is commonly cited, but it is less well known what Macartney confided in his diary on a melancholy voyage back home. It was 'futile', he wrote, for the Chinese to resist British goals of opening up China for trade because that was tantamount to trying to 'arrest the progress of human knowledge'.

Futile or not, Qianlong and subsequent emperors resisted the trading ambitions of the British and other European powers in almost every way they could. For nearly the next two centuries the interplay of foreign covetousness and Chinese reluctance was the ordering force behind events. At times this conflict of desires escalated into warfare and at others it subsided into brooding inaction. The British, having failed to open the door through diplomacy, resorted to the evil gambit of selling opium to an increasingly addicted population. In 1790, some 4,000 chests of opium entered China, but by the 1830s there was almost ten times that amount. When the Chinese emperor of the day banned the drug, the British sent a fleet from India to pound the Chinese into submission in the first Opium War. Another Opium War followed a couple of decades later when Beijing again tried to limit the inflow of narcotics. These periods of partial openness followed by phases of atavistic reclusion set the tone of relations with the outside world up until the 1949 Communist revolution, when foreign missionaries were thrown out, treaty ports closed and trade with capitalist countries limited. But Westerners never lost their lust for the China market.

Almost always, then, from the time that Qianlong met Macartney, the West had been clamouring at a door that was sometimes kept ajar but never unreservedly open. In the first few years of the twenty-first century, however, the lingering reservations toward free trade began to fall away. When China joined the World Trade Organisation in late 2001, it was for the first time in its history agreeing voluntarily to open its markets according to a set of rules and principles set down by an extraterritorial body. Then, at the first full ministerial meeting of the WTO China attended, it showed free-trade credentials that were in no way inferior to those of the industrialised West. And the pendulum of centuries began to swing. As China's prowess in manufacturing showed itself ever more clearly, so the countries of the developed world found an ever greater number of ways to keep Chinese goods out of their domestic markets. Anti-dumping clauses were invoked, import surge safeguards dusted off and political reasons cited.

By the time of the textiles trade dispute which simultaneously brought the EU and the US to loggerheads with Beijing in 2005, it had become clear that when it came to manufactured products, China was for the first time since Macartney's trade mission more open to the world than the world was towards China. Bo Xilai, the Chinese Minister of Commerce, caught the irony of this tectonic shift in an interview with the BBC in Beijing. [10]

I think the doctrine of free trade is an outstanding one. The free trade doctrine has propelled the economies of Europe and the US to a soaring path of development over the past 200 years. It has also been a doctrine that Europe and America have propagated as a glorious doctrine. They have brandished the banner of free trade and gone around the world doing commerce and making money, and becoming developed countries. But now that a developing country that is quite poor and has a GDP per capita of only one-thirtieth of theirs has found a few textile companies that can finally compete with European counterparts, they want to close their doors and engage in protectionism. This, in fact, is a double standard. When they had a comparative advantage, they encouraged the whole world to open their doors, but when they discover that one developing country is becoming more competitive, they say, 'OK, enough. Let's close the door now.'

One day, as the textile spat was raging, I was writing at home when my phone rang. It was Jane Macartney, a friend who works as the London *Times*'s Bureau Chief in Beijing and who also happens to be a direct descendant of Lord George Macartney. We chatted for a while about this and that, and then our conversation turned to textiles. Her view was adamant. It was pointless for Europe or America to resist Chinese exports if China had the comparative advantage. What was Europe doing still making textiles anyway? she asked.

That view is certainly valid from a theoretical perspective, but if past is prologue, theory may prove inadequate in foreshadowing actual events. Qianlong and other Chinese leaders spent roughly 200 years testing the futility of their country's resistance to free trade, and the reason they did so was simple. They knew they could not compete. The superiority of Europe and, later, America in the production of 'manufactures' was unassailable. Now, though, the shoe is on the other foot. It is increasingly clear to companies, industries and governments in the developed world that in manufacturing they cannot match China's might. The big question for the future, therefore, is whether the world's door will remain open.

That question may take years or decades to be answered. Nobody can tell what the final outcome will be, but one thing seems certain. The competitive strain that is visible in the artisan communities of Italy and in the industrial heartlands of America, Germany and France is spreading. Yet China's impact on these developed world economies is uneven. Not everyone is being adversely affected. Broadly, the powerful, the international and the wealthy are reaping huge benefits, while those in the middle are suffering in either relative or absolute terms. Middle-class people in medium-sized enterprises in industrial heartlands comprise the group most likely to be laid off, downsized or offered wages that do not keep pace with inflation. In Germany it is the 'Mittelstand', the medium-sized firms forming the backbone of the industrial base, that is being decimated. In the US, the Midwest – including states such as Ohio and Illinois – is hardest hit. In France, Italy, Spain and, to a lesser extent, the UK (which lost much of its industry in the 1970s and 1980s) it is also companies occupying the centre of the spectrum that are – on average – finding life increasingly tough.

This dichotomy of influence springs from globalisation's great failing: that although goods, services and capital are mobile across borders, jobs are much less so. Even if workers wanted to move their lives and families to different countries to work in unfamiliar conditions, the restrictions on such types of movement are legion. This means that, by and large, people cannot move to the companies that need them, so companies must move to the workers. But upping sticks and shifting to a place like China, with its welter of regulations and customs, represents a cost and a risk that most medium-sized and family-run businesses are unable or unwilling to absorb. The result is that the beneficiaries of the cheap, diligent and often skilled labour available in China are overwhelmingly the multinationals. And the benefits they have reaped have been handsome. According to a recent study, about 25 per cent of the profits that American multinationals make these days derive from their foreign subsidiaries. Or, to put it another way, 25 per cent of the market value of these companies – a whopping $2.7 trillion – is built on profits earned by overseas arms. But, ultimately, these profits come at the expense of the industries and jobs that sustain Middle America.

On an individual level too, the impact of this type of outsourcing also seems to be hitting employees of the middle and lower echelons of a company disproportionately hard. The managers who make the decisions to outsource or offshore their production processes rarely move overseas themselves; they continue to direct the operations from head office. Those who lose their jobs are more likely to be on the factory floor or in engineering or in the lower levels of management. But while it is staff from the middle and lower ranks of a company who will find themselves on the job market – almost always looking for a lower-paid position – the managers who orchestrated the outsourcing programmes often benefit twice over from the initiative they have taken. If their bonuses are linked to profit performance, as they almost always are, then they benefit directly from the cost savings they achieve.

They are also likely to see the value of their shareholdings and stock options rise as the company's financial performance improves.

Obviously, life looks very different for those whose jobs were outsourced. As in Rockford, Illinois, and other declining centres of manufacturing, people who lose $20-an-hour jobs in high-end manufacturing companies are unlikely to find similar employment. They normally end up taking a part-time position in the service sector which pays less than half their former salary. The impact of this, writ large, is that the American middle class is shrinking. The wealthy segment of society is growing, as is the impoverished segment – but the middle-income bracket is starting to hollow out. According to the US Census Bureau, the number of employed Americans who earned between $25,000 and $75,000 fell in 2003, while the number of people earning both more and less than that increased. The number living below the official poverty line climbed by 1.3 million in 2003 to 35.9 million Americans. Overall, real wages – that is, wages less inflation – have been either stagnant or falling across the US economy, while in some areas of manufacturing the decline has been striking.

So far, the trend to outsource has been concerned mainly with manufacturing industries, but over time the number of service jobs moving to China and India could eclipse those that have moved from manufacturing. The McKinsey Global Institute, in a global study on outsourcing, has calculated that 9.6 million US service jobs could theoretically be sent offshore today.[12] If that was actually to happen, the US unemployment rate would rise to 11.4 per cent from 5 per cent in mid 2005. A similar potential exists in the large European economies.

These trends taken together foreshadow a political crisis. Although many multinationals are benefiting from trade and investment with China, those companies represent only a narrow, albeit politically powerful, cross-section of opinion in the US and Europe. They are no match, ultimately, for the middle-class voters who determine the future of Western democracies at the ballot. If these voters turn against free trade with China in large numbers, then there may be little that politicians can do to prevent the West's door to the Middle Kingdom from creaking shut. Of course, such a course would be inimical to the interests of free trade and, quite possibly, inimical to the interests of the middle-class voters themselves. But, as Qianlong showed at the end of the eighteenth century, national leaders can and have acted against the economic interests of their people. It may well happen again.

But, notwithstanding that scenario, not everything for the US and Europe is gloom and doom. This is because, in spite of its impressive performance over the past two and a half decades, the graphs that track China's trajectory do not all point upward. In fact, the country is riven with weaknesses that, to a significant degree but not entirely, are the by-products of its success or the alter ego of its competitiveness. China may be a burgeoning economic force, but it cannot rewrite the rules of comparative advantage. What the theory of David Ricardo, the eighteenth-century economist, described is that no country can enjoy a competitive edge over everywhere else in everything that it does and makes. That insight is fundamental to China's situation today because much of the country's prowess in manufacturing has been caused by a strenuous, state-sponsored skewing of domestic economic inputs. The aim of this orchestration of advantage has been to resolve China's most fundamental problem – the creation of jobs. The government has set out deliberately to ensure that its manufacturing sector will be a world-beater. Thus, it keeps the cost of electricity artificially low, prices water at a huge knockdown to its real value, puts a cap on the price of some categories of coal, subsidises oil to make it cheaper to industry and transport, ensures that workers cannot form independent unions so that they have little power to bargain wages upward, barely implements its own environmental laws so as not to hobble industry with extra costs, orchestrates savings patterns so that its banks are always flush with capital to lend and provides generous tax rebates to any company that exports its goods.

All this has helped create a manufacturing sector that is undoubtedly earth shaking but at what cost? That, broadly, is the subject of the final four chapters of this book. The sacrifices made in the service of manufacturing have created shortcomings, frailties and deficits that have to be compensated for somehow. And, already, in the quest to make up for its deficiencies, China has started to affect the world in a way that is no less profound than the impact caused by its strengths. In many cases, these deficiencies are the source of an appetite – not for jobs, capital, technology and trade surpluses – but for energy, resources, education and respect – that the Chinese are obliged to buy from other parts of the planet.

SIX

The Anyuan coal mine is known throughout China because it was one of the places in which Mao Zedong cut his revolutionary teeth. When he worked there in the 1920s fomenting disaffection among workers towards their German bosses, the mine was one of the main sources of fuel for the Yangtze River Basin and an early industrial base in the poor interior province of Jiangxi. By the time I got there, though, most of the coal reserves, along with the ideological poignancy of the revolution, had been exhausted. The place had a desiccated feel to it, as if it had been plundered and left with little but memories. A cavernous museum to Mao and the glory of the revolution stood on top of a hill, but the city of Pingxiang, which stretched out beneath it, was anything but resplendent. Its streets were dirty, thronging with unemployed miners and full of brothels masquerading as hairdressing salons. But that was not the worst of it. Large urban precincts had begun to sink into the disused pits and mineshafts that had provided the town with its livelihood for a century. In some areas, the thin slivers of land that had concealed gaping subterranean holes had suddenly given way, causing the buildings they had supported to tumble into them. In other areas, schools, hospitals and houses were slowly and unevenly subsiding into the earth like ships listing at anchor.

I climbed up the hill where the coal mine's first mineshaft had been sunk, passing through an old arched gateway as I went. On each gatepost, large red characters urged 'Carry forward the revolutionary tradition. Strive for greater glory.' I went on up the hill and at the top I met an old woman selling 'white rabbit' sweets from the front window of her home. While we talked, three or four children from the neighbourhood came running up the mud path, each clutching enough money to buy a single white rabbit wrapped in rice paper. The woman reached into a plastic jar, took out the sweets one at a time and handed them to each child with a smile and a few kind words. From where we stood by her jar of white rabbits, you could see the hall where Mao and his comrades had organised unions and worker revolts. In the other direction, on top of another muddy hill, the engines that winched miners up and down the mineshafts were silhouetted against the horizon. One of those shafts, she said, ran right underneath her home and it had claimed more from her family than the miners had ever taken out of it.

Her eldest son was the first to be swallowed by the hill on which she lived. In 1990, at the age of twenty-seven, he was trapped in the shaft that ran beneath her home after some equipment malfunctioned. He died below ground. A few years later, her husband succumbed to lung cancer brought on by breathing coal dust without respiratory filters. Photographs of her son and husband, both in black and white, hung above an alcove that abutted the house's only room. The alcove seemed to have taken on the roles of shrine and living room simultaneously. It had a clean white tile floor which made a contrast with the muddy concrete of the rest of the house, and a big television in the corner with an embroidered cloth hung over its screen. The old woman pointed to the alcove and the TV. They had been paid for by her late husband using the compensation award from their first son's death and they represented something tangible that had emerged from the transience of two lives. But the sense of solidity the old woman saw in them was itself only relative. Long, jagged cracks an inch or two wide had opened in the house's main wall. The place where the woman stood as she sold sweets was sinking perceptibly into the hillside. The wooden front door, upon which the character for 'prosperity' was stuck, stood in a doorframe that had once been rectangular and upright but was now slipping into the shape of a rhombus. 'The hill beneath these walls is completely hollow. It has all been mined away,' she said. 'All the houses on top of it will probably end up in the mineshaft one day. But it is OK for now. There is nothing to worry about until the cracks get to about six inches wide.'

The era of Communism in China, as in the former Soviet Union, has not been kind to the environment. A combination of neglect, overpopulation, careless industrialisation and the inability of a planned economy – in which prices are fixed by state fiat – to put an accurate value on nature's gifts has contributed to an environmental crisis that is unparalleled in its severity. Everywhere there are signs of distress. The deserts of the north are marching towards the towns and cities on their fringe. Waterways that just ten years ago were gushing torrents have slowed to a trickle or disappeared altogether. Food is often contaminated with illegal and alarming levels of animal hormones and agricultural chemicals. Strange new diseases such as Sars and bird flu appear with regularity. Air pollution is so bad that some 380,000 people may be dying prematurely each year by 2010 because of respiratory ailments.[1] Several animal and bird species face extinction or loss of habitat as wetlands and forests vanish. Several towns and cities like Pingxiang are sinking into underground holes that have been burrowed by miners or emptied of the groundwater they used to hold.

These problems, or their antecedents, have been around for decades. It is no revelation to assert that the edifice of Chinese statehood rests on frail ecological foundations. But what is new – and world-shaking – is the projection of this environmental exhaustion into the international arena. Extraordinary though it now seems, the famine that followed Mao's 'Great Leap Forward' in the early 1960s took place for the most part without the outside world's knowledge. More than 30 million people died of starvation while 'China watchers' debated whether hunger was, in fact, widespread at all. Now, though, the appetites unleashed by the rise of the world's most populous nation are felt even in the most remote corners of the earth. The forests of Indonesia and Papua New Guinea, the fish of the Pacific Ocean, the iron ore extracted from mines in Australia and Brazil, the soybeans grown in Latin America and the United States, the freshwater that flows into the Mekong River, the oil underground in the Middle East, the gas from Russian Siberia, cashmere from goats on the Mongolian steppe and hundreds of other resources and commodities from places all over the globe are subject to voracious demand from a burgeoning China.

It may seem obvious that the rise of a great nation will result in great appetites and that those appetites would, in their turn, drive up the international prices of the commodities in demand. But history also provides alternative precedents. The prices of grain and meat actually fell during the emergence of the United States in the last three decades of the nineteenth century because the commissioning of more and more virgin territory for agriculture raised the supply of food. China, however, is not blessed with excess farmland. Around half of its land mass is uninhabited, so one-fifth of humanity is crowded onto just 7 per cent of the world's cultivatable land. Not only do domestic producers find it difficult to keep up with the surge in domestic demand, but the ongoing degradation of the environment and the exploitation of natural resources also means that the ability of producers to respond to demand signals is actually regressing with time.

China's growing appetite, complemented by that of India, is helping to create profound shifts in the global terms of trade. Prices of commodities began to pull out of a twenty-year slump in late 2001 which, not entirely by coincidence, was also exactly the time that China joined the World Trade Organisation, cementing the links of 1.3 billion people to the world economy. It was difficult in the year 2000 – the bottom of the twenty-year cycle for most commodities – to imagine the boom in oil, base metals and many agricultural commodity prices that has since unfolded. In the same way, in 1969–70, on the eve of a roughly ten-year commodity boom, it was hard to believe that crude oil prices would shift much from their prevailing level of around $1.70 a barrel. Now, though, the global surge in prices of almost everything that humans need to run their factories, feed themselves and build homes is easier to understand. Hundreds of millions of Chinese have begun to seek a new life and many of the things they demand – fuel, metals, food, materials and a certain quality of life – are simply not available in sufficient quantities within the boundaries of their environmentally exhausted nation.

Indeed, China's endowments are deeply lopsided. The extreme frailty of its physical environment contrasts with the prodigious strength of its human capital. The disequilibrium that results from this mismatch explains, in a nutshell, both the intensity and polarity of the influence China exerts on the world. At one extreme, the world has never had to deal with such a large, cheap and versatile workforce joining the globalised economy in such a short period of time. At the other, never before has so large a country emerged so quickly from so eviscerated a natural base. These starkly different characteristics explain why China can drive down the average level of working wages and the prices of manufactured products worldwide, while propelling the prices of most sources of energy and commodities through the roof. The cleavage between these areas of influence falls neatly between the things China makes and the things it needs.

At the top of the list of needs is oil. The US during the twentieth century was able to fuel its development with oil drawn from deposits in Alaska, the Gulf Coast states, Oklahoma, offshore Louisiana, California and Illinois. But China's geology is less fecund. It made a few large discoveries in the 1960s and 1970s, but in the last two decades its production has fallen far behind domestic demand. Twenty years ago, it was the largest oil exporter in east Asia. Now it is the second-largest oil importer in the world. In 2004, it accounted for 31 per cent of the global growth in oil demand, suggesting that the rise in the price of oil to above $60 a barrel in mid 2005 was to a significant degree due to the influence of Chinese demand.[2] China's appetite is growing at a pace that makes a mockery even of expert predictions; in 2005 it was consuming almost as much oil as the US Energy Information Administration thought it would need a full five years later. And, as always, from a per capita perspective, the potential was mind-boggling. In 2001, Americans were using more than eleven times more oil per person than Chinese. Indeed, if Chinese were ever to consume at the American levels of 2001, they would need to guzzle three times the world's total consumption.

The main catalyst behind China's appetite is the mismatch in the size of its population and its resource base. But that is not the only cause; another is the decades of wasteful exploitation and disrespect for the environment that characterised the era of Communism. Mao, who was frank in his hostility towards nature, set the tone for subsequent leaders. In 1940, at the inaugural meeting of the Natural Science Research Society, he articulated his vision. 'For the purpose of attaining freedom in the world of nature,' Mao said then, 'man must use natural science to understand, conquer and change nature and thus attain freedom from nature.'[3] Those comments had in them the seeds of the disasters and damage that followed; the famine, desertification, pollution, erosion, water shortages and disease. They also acted as a basic mantra for the heroes of the age – men such as Wang Jinxi, the 'Iron Man' who discovered oil in Daqing, the country's largest oilfield in the far northeast near Russia.

Iron Man Wang, who died in 1970 but is regarded as an icon of socialist reconstruction to this day, came to Daqing from a small oil rig in the northwestern province of Gansu, a place where, as he put it, 'no grass grew and when the wind blew, the pebbles rolled'. He had been a child labourer before the revolution and had only a rudimentary education. But he possessed an uncanny facility for saying and doing the right thing at the right time. When he went to Beijing as a 'model worker' and had a brief meeting with Mao, he capitalised on the moment by staying up all night to write a panegyric to the Great Helmsman. When he saw that Beijing buses ran on coal gas stored in large, unsightly bladders on their roofs, he announced that this was a national humiliation that could only be rectified by the discovery of more oil. A year later, when his soon-to-be-famous No. 1205 drilling team did strike oil in Daqing, he was ready with just the right turn of phrase. China, he said, was about to 'take off its oil-poor hat and cast it into the Pacific Ocean' – the inference being that America would have to learn some respect for a new China powered by the vast oilfield of Daqing.

Yet these rhetorical triumphs were mere preparations for the Iron Man's defining moment. A few years after finding the first oil, his team was drilling at another rig in the big-sky wilderness next to Siberia at well No. 2589.[4] They had been there for weeks, with no result. Wang's shin had been half crushed in an accident with a piece of machinery, but he refused more than a brief visit to hospital. Within days, he was back at the derrick, barking orders as he hobbled about on crutches. Then, suddenly and unexpectedly, the rig struck oil at a depth of 700 metres, sending a gusher 10 metres into the air. The workers rushed to cap the spouting crude by dumping tonnes of cement mix on top of it. But the pump that was used to mix the cement with sand in a slurry pit near the derrick failed to function. Unless something was done, the oil would all go to waste. Iron Man leapt into action. He tossed away his crutches, jumped into the slurry pit and began twisting his body to and fro, using his torso as a surrogate cement mixer. Other workers followed his example and, as they stood there gyrating back and forth, one of the most famous photographs of Mao's era was taken. It was published in newspapers and hung in public places as the whole country was exhorted to learn from the spirit of the Iron Man. The black and white photo now hangs on the wall in the 'Iron Man Wang Museum' in Daqing. It shows Wang with his posture twisted, the slurry splashing above his waist and his face creased into an exhilarated roar.

If these events seem a little too perfect really to have happened, that is a feature they share with the broad body of China's propaganda mythology. Some might wonder, for instance, how come a news photographer happened to be waiting near a lonely drilling rig in the wilderness just at the moment it unexpectedly struck oil. Nevertheless, the story of the Iron Man and the slurry pit has stuck in the national consciousness. An attendant at the Iron Man Museum told me I was a 'backward element' after I questioned whether it was possible to mix tonnes of cement just by twisting your torso. But scepticism is a minority view. Even the Premier, Wen Jiabao, is a fan of the Wang Jinxi legend; he noted a couple of years ago that if you placed all the wells his team had sunk on top of each other, they would reach to the peak of Mount Everest.

What has attracted quiet scrutiny, however, has been the effectiveness of the oil extraction techniques during the first thirty years of the oilfield's life. Statistics on the recovery rates of oil from underground deposits are, like much else about Daqing, still a state secret. But geologists and experts told me that in the first two decades of drilling, as much as 90 per cent of the oil was wasted – either left unrecovered underground or spent in gushers that coloured the pastures around the wells black. This was partly the result of old, inadequate machinery and drilling techniques and partly because the focus of the teams which followed the Iron Man's shining example was to find as much oil as quickly as possible so as to win propaganda plaudits. Little attention was paid to the technical task of ensuring that deposits were not wasted. Indeed, the use of technology itself was antithetical to the

Iron Man spirit that human will could overcome anything nature could throw at it.

Nobody is yet ready to admit that China's current dependence on imports of foreign oil is due, at least in some part, to the wasteful exploitation of an oilfield that was in its day a symbol of self-reliance. But Daqing today is a study in how things have changed. The nodding donkey rigs which stand by bus stops and in hotel forecourts still rock rhythmically up and down, and the cloying smell of crude still pervades the atmosphere. But production is falling year after year and the city's mayor speaks at length about the need to diversify into new industries. The most famous resident there these days is another man named Wang, an intense, slightly built geologist who talks non-stop in acronyms, jargon and scientific terms. His job is to find ways of squeezing more oil out of the ageing and increasingly complex field. For this, he has earned the nickname 'Iron Man of a New Era'.

We met in a hall belonging to PetroChina, the state oil giant that owns and runs Daqing, and sat in two chairs at the end of the room looking at each other over a small table furnished with teacups on paper mats. A line of officials and oil company executives sat behind Wang on his side of the room, in the usual manner adopted for formal meetings. But Wang's enthusiasm for his subject meant that any formality was short-lived. Within a few minutes, he was on all fours on the soft pile carpet poring over large detailed geological maps, pointing out the fissures and stratas in cross-sections of rock which, to the trained eye, were tell-tale signs that a river had changed its course at some point in the Jurassic era. He also spent some time explaining the method he had pioneered to bring abandoned oil deposits to the surface by first pumping groundwater down their disused well-shafts to flood the underground caverns that used to contain oil. When the pressure had built up sufficiently, pumping could resume, he said, and the mixture of oil and water that came to the surface could be turned back into pure crude in a treatment plant.

It all seemed rather convoluted and as I listened to the flow of his explanations, I began to wonder what Wang felt about the contribution of the man whose nickname he had partially appropriated. The answer was singularly lacking in the type of praise that is customary for a national Communist icon. 'Our work is not the same. He was the leader of a well-drilling team. I am responsible for the development of the oilfield. I graduated from university and he came over from Gansu,' he said. 'He basically relied on brute strength, whereas we rose up through bitter struggle using our brains. In those days we did not have any experience of oil extraction.' My curiosity deepened at this response, and I asked another question. But I got my nicknames in a jumble and ended up calling him the 'Second Generation Iron Man'. Suddenly, the effervescent explanations stopped and he gazed at me steadily over his spectacles. 'The name is New Era Iron Man,' he said. 'But if you can't manage that, just call me "New Era".'

I wondered whether his disinclination to share an identity with the Iron Man of an earlier generation derived from vanity, or from the fact that his whole career had been dedicated to cleaning up the mess that Wang Jinxi and his pioneering comrades had caused.

China knows from experience the way in which a lack of available resources can hold back the development of the nation. One of the main reasons why the country fell so far behind Europe in the nineteenth century was that a surging demand for wood from a burgeoning Chinese population pushed prices to levels that inhibited economic activity. The cost of building a sea-going ship in 1820, for example, was seven times that in 1550 so trading vessels were increasingly constructed in southeast Asian shipyards, where sources of wood were plentiful. The type of 7,000-ton vessel that Zheng He, the famous mariner of the Ming dynasty, used to explore much of the known world would have been prohibitively expensive for most of the 300 years before the current era – a fact that may help explain why China turned in on itself. Voracious deforestation continued throughout the nineteenth century and in some places the shortage of wood was so acute that families burned little but dung, roots and the husks of crops for fuel.[5] In provinces such as Henan and Shandong, where population densities were among the heaviest, forest cover dwindled to between two and six per cent of the total land area – or to between one-twelfth and one-quarter of the prevailing levels in European countries such as France at that time. With fuel so expensive and so scarce at times during the eighteenth and nineteenth centuries, the chances that an industrial revolution could have taken place in China as it did in Great Britain were remote. By the 1930s, by which time the population had increased by between 150 million and 225 million people since 1800, the general level of forest cover on the central plains was so thin that even trees in protected areas could not be saved from illegal felling by people desperate for firewood.

These precedents have bred a visceral aversion in Beijing to the notion that it might run out of the things it needs to progress. And history is not the only guide. Since Deng Xiaoping's ascent to power in the late 1970s, the Communist Party has defined its legitimacy in terms of delivering economic growth and using its economic power as a lever to attain greater international prominence. It cannot achieve either of these things without oil, but, fortunately, it can import enough to make up the shortfall. However, this dependence on a foreign commodity for 40 per cent of its needs has put Beijing in an acutely uncomfortable position. Its growth and legitimacy depend squarely on the supply of a fuel source controlled in the main by regimes that are either unstable, unfriendly or within the sphere of influence of its strategic competitor, the US. Driven by this discomfort, Beijing and its large state oil companies have tried with increasing urgency since the country became a net importer of oil in 1992 to shore up supply lines and reduce their vulnerability in virtually any way possible.

The three large state oil companies had invested in nearly thirty overseas oil and gas development projects and had committed more than $5 billion by the end of 2002. But the short history of these deals has been chequered. Obviously in a hurry and clearly in need, the Chinese side almost always paid a significant premium to the market price for the reserves it was able to buy. In some cases, the deals that were arranged politically fell apart later and, in others, foreign oil companies manoeuvred deftly to block the overtures of their Chinese competitors.[6] Nevertheless, the China National Petroleum Corporation, the largest state oil company, has managed to purchase assets in Sudan, Iraq and Kazakhstan. Other companies such as China National Offshore Oil Corporation (CNOOC) have secured long-term supply contracts from places such as Australia. But, all told, the volume of oil imports that are either owned or are under long-term supply contracts amounts to a small proportion of the country's total requirement. If Beijing was to enjoy anything approaching real security of supply, it needed to do deals of a different magnitude, something that would make its companies real players. But as it tried to do these deals in the outside world it bumped up against barriers which, though invisible, were nevertheless more stubborn than the most complicated subterranean geology.

One case in point was the attempted acquisition by CNOOC of a large US counterpart, Unocal. It was clear from the beginning that this bid was going to be about a lot more than oil and dollars. The nickname it went by within CNOOC and its team of advisors from Goldman Sachs and J.P. Morgan suggested something of a grand design. They called it 'Operation Treasure Ship' after the vessel that Zheng He used to 'sail the western oceans' and in which, according to the UK historian Gavin Menzies,[7] he may well have discovered America long before Columbus. Zheng He was a tall, dashing man who distinguished himself at court through his ability, and the advisory team's use of the 'treasure ship' allusion signified a journey of discovery, a voyage with uncertain endings into alien waters. It was to be potentially perilous but ultimately rewarding – certainly for the bankers who stood to earn some $300 million in advisory fees.

The man leading CNOOC's bid, Fu Chengyu, the company's CEO, was as close to a corporate Zheng He as can be imagined. Tall and square-jawed, the fifty-four-year-old had also risen through his ability. Unable to finish his university studies because of the chaos of the Cultural Revolution, he was assigned at the age of twenty to Daqing in 1972, a time when the oilfield was still in thrall to the legend of the Iron Man who had died only two years earlier. But from those nationalistic beginnings, Fu's career took a more cosmopolitan turn. By the early 1980s, he became one of the few young people selected by the government to study abroad and earned a Master's degree at the University of Southern California. Following his return to China, he became a rising star in a strategic industry that was one of the first to open to foreign investment. CNOOC had a monopoly in those days on offshore exploration and was therefore the only joint venture partner available for the world's oil majors who poured hundreds of millions of dollars into the dream of striking it rich in the seas off China's south and east coasts. Fu, therefore, had developed his expertise working alongside or for the world's oil majors.

By the time he launched the bid for Unocal, he ranked as one of China's most credible corporate ambassadors. Urbane and sophisticated, he could claim to understand the ways of the West better than virtually any other head of a Chinese state enterprise. If anyone was going to lead China to 'go out', as the former President Jiang Zemin was fond of describing the process of outward investment, it was he. But it was clear from the image that his public relations advisers had started to make for him that Fu also had his qualms. He knew his plan was audacious; it was the largest attempted overseas acquisition by a Chinese company. It was also an attempt to buy a strategic asset at a time when the US's national security guard was heightened by the war in Iraq. So, in his first few interviews, Fu was at pains to stress his cosmopolitan credentials. He emphasised his background in California, and his experience with Western oil firms and even his unusually Western adoration for coffee. 'People in China think I am strange because I do not drink tea,' he told one interviewer.[8]

But this amounted to little more than a manicure. The problem that 'operation treasure ship' faced was nothing less than a gale-force clash of political economies. First of all, insistent questions were asked about how closely CNOOC was related to the Communist Party. After all, it was true, as commentators pointed out, that Fu – in common with all the bosses of large, strategic Chinese state companies – was first and foremost a civil servant. He had been appointed by the Party's personnel department and if there was any doubt about where his true loyalties lay, then one had only to think of his predecessor, Wei Liucheng. Wei had been running the company one day and then the next was appointed to the senior government post of Governor on the southern island of Hainan. Also revealing was that Fu, in addition to his job as head of CNOOC, the listed company, was head of the wholly government-owned state parent which held 70.6 per cent of the listed company's shares. Such an ownership structure put it beyond doubt that CNOOC would – if push came to shove – put the interests of the Party above anything else.

Indeed, tell-tale signs of a dual agenda had already surfaced in the way that the bid was conceived. Fu had first met with Charles Williamson, CEO of Unocal, on Boxing Day in 2004 and began canvassing support for a bid among the upper echelons of the Communist Party in February. Having secured the go-ahead from the government, CNOOC appointed Goldman Sachs and J.P. Morgan as advisers on the deal and on 7 March 2005 submitted a first bid that valued Unocal at between $16 billion and $18 billion. All that was fine, but the problem was that the company's board had not been formally informed of any of these plans until after the company's financial results were released on 30 March.[9] The response was predictable. The board's four non-executive directors – a former Shell senior executive, a former Swiss ambassador to China, a Goldman Sachs banker and an Australian solicitor – were taken aback. They were told matter-of-factly that there was an auction going on for a company valued at nearly as much as CNOOC itself and that their support would be appreciated so that the financing could be locked in. In effect they were being asked to agree to an $18 billion deal on the back of an envelope. They refused.

One director, Erwin Schurtenberger, the former Swiss ambassador who had warned of a backlash in US public opinion, resigned.[10] For several weeks after the board bust-up, there was a stalemate. Valuable time was lost to Chevron, a US oil company, which had already made a bid that had been recommended by Unocal's board. But CNOOC had not given up, and it later raised its original offer considerably, valuing Unocal at more than Chevron had. But it was not a knock-out blow, allowing Chevron just enough space to mount a counter-attack. The company picked the straight-talking veteran Vice-President Peter Robertson, who pulled no punches. He went straight for CNOOC's most vulnerable characteristic. 'We are not competing with this company. We are competing with the Chinese government,' he said. 'I think it is wrong.'[11]

Robertson's point was not solely political. He was also pointing out that because of its close relationship with the Chinese authorities, CNOOC could call on financing at concessionary terms that were unavailable to Chevron. But as the media coverage around the bid swelled in its intensity – and given time by CNOOC's boardroom conflicts – the focus of attention in America switched more and more to issues of national security. To counter this, CNOOC paid top dollar, hiring the law firm Akin Gump – and its attorney Daniel Spiegel, a former Permanent Representative to the United Nations under Bill Clinton – to help it face the political storm. But eventually it was all in vain. A vote in the House of Representatives went against CNOOC's interests, referring the bid to President George W. Bush on the grounds that its implications for national security needed to be reviewed. When Fu heard that, he knew the game was up and withdrew from the competition.

How bruised CNOOC was can be gauged by the reaction of the company's chief financial officer, Yang Hua. He said the use of political prejudice to deny China access to the energy it needed amounted to a violation of human rights. 'What are human rights?' he asked at a news conference in Hong Kong. 'I'll tell you what it means. It means having guaranteed access to energy. It means having petroleum to run your car.'[12]

But whatever the lessons of CNOOC's failure, one thing was clear. The influence of the Party – so critical in the creation of China's manufacturing prowess – had been an unambiguous impediment when it came to the cause of acquiring key American corporate assets. Firstly, Fu had to get the permission of Party elders for the bid, a process that put him in breach of his company's rules on corporate governance and then fomented a crisis of confidence on his own board. Then the subsidised lending that CNOOC had lined up from state banks gave Chevron a legitimate target upon which to concentrate its efforts. And lastly, as media attention around CNOOC's links to the Party intensified, Fu was unable to distance himself from his political bosses – meaning that his arguments never quite addressed what American opinion saw as the main issue.

My student days in China in 1982 were spent at Shandong University in Jinan, the capital of a province that lies midway between Beijing and Shanghai. The officials in charge of my intake took it upon themselves to introduce us to aspects of China's history and culture. They organised trips for us to the beautiful port city of Qingdao, to the birthplace of Confucius in Qufu and even to the far northwestern frontier region of Xinjiang, where Turkic Muslims live alongside Han Chinese. The officials were generous and indefatigable hosts and we, for the most part, were not as grateful as we should have been. But of all the trips we went on, the one that sticks most clearly in my memory was also the shortest distance away from Jinan. We were put in a bus and driven out to the Yellow River. As we travelled, I was full of imaginings of the raging, gurgling torrents of treacherous water that we would see when we got there. A university official fed these images by standing at the front of the bus and talking excitedly about the river's significance. It was known both as 'China's pride' for the fertility it bestowed on the land around it and as 'China's sorrow' for the floods that destroyed what it nurtured. The reason why Jinan had not been built along its banks, in the manner of many cities which line the Yangtze and Pearl Rivers, he said, was that the Yellow River was simply too tempestuous.

As we approached the river, an empty flood plain opened out on either side of the road. Soon, a newly built suspension bridge loomed into view. Its thick iron cables looked from a distance like the rigging on a tall ship. We drove halfway across it and stopped. When we got off, I ran to the railings on one side of the bridge and leant over them to get a better view of the mother of Chinese civilisation. But what I saw was profoundly disappointing. Instead of the angry, churning waterway of my imagination, there was a dark brown, narrow channel which resembled nothing so much as a mudslide in flow. My fellow students and I found it hard to believe that this was the fearsome watercourse that over the millennia had probably caused more deaths than any other single geographical feature in the world.

Records of the carnage are so old they marked the start of Chinese history itself. One flood in 2297 BC was said to have led to a horrific loss of life; and since 602 BC, when meticulous records began to be kept, the river has burst its banks more than 1,500 times and changed its course twenty-six times. In recent centuries the human toll from the regular deluges has risen along with population densities. In 1887 the river tore through its banks at a point in the province of Henan, inundating eleven cities and putting an area of 50,000 square miles under water for two months. Between 900,000 and 2 million people are thought to have died. In 1943 some 3 million peasants in Henan died from starvation after their crops were destroyed.

But the most infamous disaster came on 9 June 1938 during the second Sino-Japanese war when a retreating Chiang Kai-shek, the leader of the Nationalist government, broke the dykes at Huayuan-kou in Henan province at a time when the river's flood waters were close to their peak. The aim of this desperate action was to stall the Japanese advance but the results were catastrophic: up to 900,000 died as the flood swept over 9,000 square miles of the north China plain and another 12 million were made homeless. As a military strategy it was disastrous. The Japanese vanguard did have to wait a few weeks before resuming its southern progress, but as news of the action spread, Chiang's popular standing plummeted.

As my classmates and I looked down on the muddy flow below us, it seemed hardly credible that it had been responsible for so many harrowing pages of history. I think the administrator must have noticed our scoffing, superior reaction. He walked over to us and said, 'Do not look down on the Yellow River because if you do, you are looking down on the Chinese people themselves.' I did not know it at the time that this was a quotation from Chairman Mao. Its inference was based on the accurate observation that although the Yellow River may not seem impressive for much of the year, its power is deceptive. Its salient feature, the one that gives it its name, is that it is the most silt-laden river in the world. It carries up to sixty times the load of the Mississippi-Missouri, which is itself often called 'big muddy'. As the river's velocity slows along its lower course, the silt in the water is deposited on the river bed. This deposit builds up until the bed stands above the flood plain around it and the only things that prevent a flood are the dykes holding the water in. In some parts of Henan, for instance, the river is 'suspended' some 11 or 12 metres above the flood plain. All it takes is a sudden flood crest, caused by heavy rain in the upper reaches, and the pressure can become unbearable.

The challenge over 4,000 years and more to control the floods became the story of Chinese history. China was one of the great hydraulic societies such as those that grew up along the banks of the Sumer, the Nile and the Indus. The connection in all of these places between civilisation and rivers flowing through arid but fertile areas is irrigation. The political structure needed to organise people for digging canals and fair use of water resources also lends itself to other types of construction, city planning, state religion, education and a class with leisure who can pursue mathematics, science and philosophy. It is not down to chance, therefore, that some of the earliest scientists also blossomed in such areas. A premium was put on historical records because through these, rulers could study how their ancestors had dealt with floods and consider how they themselves might be able to guard against them. There was, in addition, something deeper than this: the methods used to combat floods have also influenced political philosophies that remain prevalent to this day. One school of thought, that of the Taoists, was relatively laissez-faire. It maintained that it was better not to build up huge dykes because, although these would reduce flooding in average years, they were liable to burst when flood waters were really ferocious – thereby exacerbating the death toll when disasters occurred. This philosophical approach recommended keeping human habitation off the floodplains, so that when the river spilled from its bed, the damage was relatively mild. The other school of thought, the Confucian way, aimed to control nature. It required the construction of strong dykes, the regimentation of society and strict hierarchies.

Both philosophies have been used, often simultaneously, on different parts of the river. But the Confucian approach has been prevalent, not only on the Yellow River but also on others such as the Yangtze. In fact, the word for political control in Chinese – 'zhi' – shows three drops of water next to a dyke or platform.

There are other examples of the political efficacy of irrigation. The construction of the Zhengguo Canal, the first to be built in China, laid the foundations for the rise to power of the state of Qin. It was completed by the Qin in 246 BC and irrigated about 200,000 acres in the Wei Valley north of Xian and led to such prosperity and population increase that the state of Qin became the first to unify China after a long period of internecine strife. The power of that state – and its ability to organise – can be seen at the tomb of the Quin emperor near the central city of Xian today. It is guarded by a life-size army of terracotta warriors – some 8,000 of them. However, both the canal and the Qin empire were short-lived. The canal silted up and became useless about 150 years after it was built. Furthermore, the Qin population pressure caused farming to expand out into the loess plateau.

Thus the link between hydraulic control and political power is ancient. In recent years, though, it has taken on a symbolism that is extremely uncomfortable for Beijing's rulers. The river known as 'China's sorrow' for its power and ferocity now elicits pathos for an entirely different reason. It is running dry. In almost every year since 1985 it has failed at times to reach the sea. In 1997 it was dry in Shandong for a full 226 days. The problem is entirely man-made. Since the founding of the People's Republic, the area of irrigated land along the river has grown twenty-fold. Well over half the water in the river is taken for industry, agriculture and residential use, but it is estimated that as little as one-third of the water taken for agricultural irrigation actually reaches the crops. The rest spills out of irrigation ditches or sinks into the soil beneath the eight large dams and thousands of small ones that have been built to control the river's fury. Farmers are virtually heedless of the need to conserve water which costs as little as one bottle of mineral water for 10 cubic metres.

Conservation in general appears to be a blind spot. Perhaps it is that after thousands of years of political organisation to control the consequences of too much water, the machinery of the state has not had enough time to readjust to the reality of too little. This might explain why the officials in charge of the Yellow River Conservancy in Jinan were, as late as 2004, still using the first twenty minutes of their briefings to journalists to explain the measures they were taking to control flooding from a river that was by then little more than a trickle.[13] There may, however, be a more telling explanation for China's ineptitude in conservation: that the authoritarian political system that was born on the banks of the Yellow River, grew up through thousands of years of dynastic despotism and was refined by five decades of Communism, is simply not configured for the niceties of tending to nature. Behind virtually every environmental disaster lurks a failure of politics or policy. Elizabeth Economy in *The River Runs Black* tells the story of how the basin of the Huai River, an area the size of England which covers parts of Henan, Anhui and Jiangsu provinces, became a toxic hazard for the 150 million people who live there.

The problem started in the 1980s when tens of thousands of small companies, including pulp and paper mills, chemical factories, dyeing and tanning plants, sprang up along the river and dumped their toxic waste into it. By the early 1990s there were clear signs of distress. The water in many areas was unfit to drink, cancer rates were twice the national average and, according to one report, for years none of the boys from certain villages in the Huai River area were healthy enough to pass the physical examination required to enter the armed forces. But when Beijing resolved to address the problem, things merely got worse. When local authorities were ordered by Beijing to resolve the problem they released the polluted water that had been building up in their reservoirs and tanks, and in so doing, unleashed a tide of black liquid which killed almost everything it touched as it flowed downstream. Some 26 million pounds of fish died and thousands of people were treated for dysentery, diarrhoea and vomiting. At this point no less an official than Li Peng, the then Premier, got involved – ordering the closure or relocation of thousands of factories to halt all waste pollution by 1997 and have the river run clear by 2000. Several hundred factories were indeed closed, but they opened up again almost as quickly. By 1998 and 1999 it was clear that the campaign was going to fail; reports of people dying from being exposed to the noxious gases and chemicals in urban trenches were regularly reported in the newspapers and in 1999 the Huai ran dry for the first time in twenty years, ruining crops and killing thousands of tonnes of fish. Nevertheless, Xie Zhenhua, head of the State Environmental Protection Agency, stepped forward to proclaim that the campaign had been successful and the Huai water was now drinkable again.

There was a time when such a barefaced lie would have become a propaganda truth, but by the late 1990s some newspapers were bold enough to report the real situation. It emerged that the waters of the Huai, far from being clean, were so toxic that, by the government's own classification standards, they could not even be used for irrigation.

On the Yellow River, as on the Huai, the root cause of the crisis is the lack of political accountability. Local officials in China's top-down hierarchical system can only be supervised from above, not from below. Thus the people who live in cities, towns and villages cannot choose their leaders or criticise them if they do a bad job. The partial exception to this is in the country's 900,000 villages where, under an experiment with democracy, local people can directly elect their village chief but not the more powerful local Communist Party boss. The vertical nature of the system has predictable results. Local officials strive to fulfil the criteria upon which they are judged by their superiors. These include boosting local industrial output, providing employment and raising tax revenues. Compared to these considerations, environmental protection is a secondary concern, an issue that may have to be dealt with at some point but can usually be postponed until the next batch of officials take their posts. In any case, as long as a local official keeps his superiors happy, it matters little what the people whom he governs think of his tenure. Similarly, the pyramidal structure of the system means that, more often than not, neighbouring towns, cities and provinces will have a competitive rather than a co-operative relationship – an alignment that helps to explain why the Yellow River's upstream provinces routinely use more than their allocation of water and cut down many more trees than they should.

Conservation in any part of the world happens best within stakeholder communities where citizens have the responsibility and the right to hold local officials accountable to their promises. But in China, notwithstanding the growing role of some embryonic non-governmental organisations, these conditions do not exist. Problems therefore deteriorate until they are so grave that they can no longer be hidden from central authorities. But by the time central authorities are called in, it is often too late for conservational solutions and Beijing resorts to sweeping, revolutionary policies. In the case of the Huai, this amounted to the over-ambitious and ultimately unsuccessful decree to halt all industrial waste pollution by closing down thousands of local factories. In the case of the Yellow River, it was to commission the largest civil engineering project since the Great Wall: a $60 billion project to transport a river-load of water from the Yangtze and its tributaries to the Yellow River Basin and to parched northern cities such as Beijing and Tianjin. The project, which was already under way in 2005, envisages digging three canals of over 1,000 kilometres in length and pumping the water northward.[14] But even before the scheme had started operating, environmentalists were questioning the efficacy of the Herculean efforts required. For one thing, some of the water to be pumped was expected to come from heavily polluted sources, including the Huai. For another, when the price of water is increased – as it must be – the incentive for theft by the communities through which the canals pass is set to rise.

The costs of patching up China's wounded nature are only just starting to be realised. Beijing had until recently tended to act as if it could postpone payment for its environmental deficit by refusing to acknowledge it. But now, as it faces up to reality, it is clear that repairing the devastation it has suffered is a task so onerous that it could slow down, or even derail, its stellar economic trajectory. When a researcher in a state think-tank in the northern province of Shaanxi, the country's coal-producing heartland, attempted to calculate a Green GDP for the province (that is, the economic growth rate minus its cost in resource depletion and environmental degradation), he estimated that Shaanxi had hardly grown at all in the past twenty years. Regardless of whether such estimates are accurate, they hint at the magnitude of a concealed debt. Streams and rivers are drying up all over the northern half of the country and water-tables are falling precipitously as wells, many of them illegally dug, are sunk ever deeper into dwindling reserves of groundwater. Altogether some 400 out of 668 large Chinese cities are short of water and the incidence of rationing is growing. But still the pressures of population, the demands of a burgeoning industrial expansion and the inability of the political system to inculcate a conservation mentality are taking their toll. China uses between seven and twenty times more water to generate a unit of GDP than the developed countries of the world.

Of course, the crisis extends beyond water and beyond national borders. On the World Bank's list of the twenty most polluted cities in the world, sixteen are in China. Acid rain falls over 30 per cent of its territory. Although some large showcase cities such as Shanghai and Beijing are being cleaned up, rural areas are becoming a dumping ground for toxic waste. Chinese environmentalists tend to see the problem as at least partly imported. The factories that multinational companies have set up have turned China into the workshop of the world but have also made it the 'rubbish tip of the world',[15] one senior official once told me. But this view is at variance with how much of Europe, America and the rest of Asia regards the international impact of China's environmental failure. In an increasing number of ways Beijing is catching the censure of overseas non-governmental organisations, green pressure groups and even governments.

Air pollution, once considered a local affliction, is increasingly being viewed as an intercontinental problem. A study by Daniel Jacob, a Harvard professor of atmospheric chemistry, traced a plume of dirty air to a point over New England, where samples revealed that it had come from China.[16] Concern centres on mercury, a highly toxic pollutant given off by the combustion of coal. The US Environmental Protection Agency recently reported that a third of the country's lakes and nearly a quarter of its rivers are now so polluted with mercury that children and pregnant women are advised to limit or avoid eating fish caught there. Scientists estimate that around one-third of the mercury settling into the soil and waterways in the US comes from other countries, in particular China. Josef Pacyna, director of the Center for Ecological Economics at the Norwegian Institute for Air Research, calculates that China spews around 600 tonnes of mercury into the air each year, accounting for nearly one-quarter of the world's non-natural emissions.[17]

The effect on the world's forests of China's rise is still more palpable. In 1998, in response to grievous flooding along the Yangtze that was caused partly by chronic deforestation around the headwaters of the river, Beijing placed strict restrictions on logging. In the meantime, the world's largest furniture and paper-making industries have grown up. The result of these two developments is that China has become by far the fastest-growing market for timber products and paper pulp in the world. From 1997 to 2003 China's timber product imports surged from 12.6 million cubic metres to 40.2 million cubic metres, while imports of paper and pulp soared from the equivalent of 27.6 million cubic metres of wood to 66.5 million cubic metres. The impact of this voracious appetite, which shows no sign of abating, has been increasingly ruinous for the world's primary forests. The rainforests in Indonesia, Myanmar and central Africa and the boreal woodlands of Siberia, places known as the 'lungs of the planet' for their role in turning carbon dioxide into oxygen, are disappearing at unprecedented rates to satisfy Chinese demand.

In both places, logging restrictions are circumvented by various underhand and illegal methods. In Russia, licences to log virgin boreal woodlands are very difficult to obtain but not if the area in question has been damaged by fire. So the criminals who supply Chinese logging syndicates first set fire to large areas and then obtain permits to fell the timber there. In 2003 some 22 million hectares of spruce, fir, scots pine and oak were destroyed or in some way affected by fire.[18] US satellite photographs recorded 157 fires across almost 11 million hectares, sending up a plume of smoke that reached Kyoto in Japan 5,000 kilometres away. The felled trees are a non-renewable resource that may have taken 400 to 500 years to grow in frigid tundra temperatures.

In Indonesia, an area the size of Switzerland is illegally logged each year and although reserves of teak, ramin and meranti hardwoods have been virtually exhausted, vast tracts of protected merbau trees in remote provinces such as Papua have become the latest focus for illegal logging syndicates. A complicated network involving Malaysian logging companies working with falsified documents, Singaporean warehouses, Hong Kong middlemen and merchant ships from the Middle East ensures that loads of merbau are delivered to secondary ports such as Zhangjiagang on the lower Yangtze every week. Most of the merbau felled is used as flooring for the millions of new middle-class houses being built in Shanghai, Beijing and other large cities. The size of the illegal trade is considerable: in 2002 China cleared the import of 2.6 million cubic metres more Indonesian timber than Indonesian authorities cleared for export. The International Tropical Timber

Organisation, a United Nations-backed intergovernmental organisation, estimates that five out of every ten tropical logs shipped worldwide are bound for China; and the Worldwide Fund for Nature reckons that 44 per cent of the timber imported into China has been illegally felled.[19]

But in terms of potential damage to the global environment, China's demand for soybeans may be having an impact at least as deleterious as its requirement for timber. The shortage of water in northern provinces, where most domestic soybeans have been grown, has led to a decline in output even as demand for beans from an increasingly affluent population has shot up. The inevitable result of this is that imports have surged and in the space of a decade, China has gone from being a marginal presence in international markets to its current position as the world's biggest importer by some margin. Brazilian farmers have moved quickly to satisfy China's hunger, felling swaths of the Amazon rainforest to plant new fields of soy. In 2004, the rate of clearance of the Amazon was the second highest on record. An area of 25,900 square kilometres – nearly the size of Belgium – was cut down during the year, which is to say that the forest was disappearing at the rate of six football fields every minute.[20] Environmentalist groups say that the deforestation is a national shame. The Amazon, which sprawls over 4.1 million square kilometres, is home to 30 per cent of the world's animal and plant species. The trees are also a vital source of oxygen for the world, but this supply is being undermined by forest fires which release hundreds of millions of tonnes of carbon dioxide and other greenhouse gases into the atmosphere every year.

Greenhouse gases, mainly carbon dioxide, are so called because they accelerate global warming, melting the polar ice caps and possibly triggering all kinds of unforeseen weather phenomena. China is both a culprit and a victim in the planet's warming trend. It is now the second-largest producer of greenhouse gases after the United States, following a 33 per cent increase in emissions of carbon dioxide between 1990 and 2002 to 3.05 billion tonnes.[21] Changes in the domestic climate have been observable. The 1990s was the warmest decade for more than 100 years and since 1950 there has been a gradual reduction in precipitation nationwide.

This has contributed to the falling volume of water in the six major rivers since the 1960s; and an unpredictable cycle of droughts and flash floods is becoming more pronounced. On the coast, sea levels are rising and inland vegetation is moving to higher altitudes. But the glaciers in the Himalayas and other high mountain ranges are melting at an alarming rate.[22] At the current pace of deterioration, two-thirds of China's high-altitude ice fields, which account for 15 per cent of the planet's ice, will have melted by 2050, environmentalists estimate.

In an interconnected world, the environmental stresses of a country China's size cannot be regarded as peculiarly a domestic problem. Yet curbing the waste and appetite that are exacerbating some profound global climate trends is not going to be easy. The country has only just embarked upon a developmental journey that has so far faithfully followed the path blazed by the United States in its ascent to wealth and prestige. An American-style communications infrastructure is being built. Chinese dream of buying a car, a house, a first-class education for their children and a range of consumer goods conferring status and convenience, just as they do to middle-class families in Europe and America. As disposable incomes rise, people are eating more protein and using more electricity to run their computers, televisions and household appliances. But in spite of the resemblance China bears to America in an earlier stage of its development, the chances that the Chinese will one day be able to consume at the same rate as Americans do today are close to zero. It is not that they will choose to be more frugal. It is simply that the world does not have the resources to cater for 1.3 billion Chinese behaving like Americans.

Perhaps, in the end, the lack of alternatives will force China to adopt a whole new approach to resources that is based on recycling, conservation and clean fuels. But the cost of implementing such a strategy would seriously erode the country's industrial competitiveness, so progress is unlikely to be rapid. And in the years that it takes to reach that hazy goal of environmental responsibility, the international tensions released by China's appetite for foreign resources and the abuse of its own environment may escalate sharply.

SEVEN

Mencius looks stern and pinched about the mouth in portraits purporting to show his likeness, but his teachings are among the most gentle to have issued from the golden age of Chinese philosophy that spanned the few centuries before the birth of Christ. Much in the same way as his contemporary Plato, who he would not have known about, he was concerned with the most crucial and vexing of questions: how men could be good and how society could prosper. His teachings revolve around 'ren', a word often translated as 'benevolence' but which also has the wider, more general sense of 'goodness'. The most important property of 'ren' was compassion, or not being able to bear that others should suffer. It meant a feeling of responsibility for the suffering of others, such as was felt by the legendary ruler Yu, the subduer of primeval floods: 'If anyone were drowned, Yu felt as though it were he himself that had drowned him,' Mencius wrote. Another mythical leader, the counsellor I Yin was also said to have possessed 'ren', for if he knew of a single man or woman anywhere under Heaven who was not enjoying the benefits of wise rule 'it was as though he had pushed them into a ditch with his own hand; so heavy was the responsibility that he put upon himself for everything that happened under Heaven'[1].

Empathetic feelings such as these, the sage said, are the natural birthright of everyone. But just as in modern times our best intentions at the start of the day can be diverted by the complications of living, so 'ren' can be worn away, leaving a mean spirit where there was once a natural magnanimity. Education, however, can temper such regressions and keep people from having their charitable feelings pared to the nub by competition for scarce resources. Mencius described what he meant in the allegory of Bull Mountain:

The Bull Mountain was once covered with lovely trees. But it is near the capital of a great state. People came with their axes and choppers; they cut the woods down and the mountain lost its beauty. Yet even so, the day air and the night air came to it, rain and dew moistened it till here and there fresh sprouts began to grow. But soon cattle and sheep came along and browsed on them and in the end the mountain became gaunt and bare, as it is now. And seeing it thus gaunt and bare, people imagine that it was woodless from the start. But just as the natural state of the mountain was quite different from what now appears, so too in every man (little though they may be apparent) there assuredly were once feelings of decency and kindness; and if those feelings are no longer there, it is that they have been tampered with, hewn down with axe and bill. As each day dawns, they are assailed anew. What chance then has our nature, any more than that mountain, of keeping its beauty?.[2]

The link between man and nature that Mencius made is as valid today as it was more than 2,000 years ago. His home town, a place called Zoucheng in a corner of Shandong province, wears the strain of population upon its sleeve. Large areas of land are sinking into exhausted coal mines underground, just as in the city of Pingxiang far away to the south. The low hills surrounding the town have lost most of the trees that in Mencius's day would have covered them. Slag heaps stand next to industrial plants spewing dust and smoke into the air. And, if the experience of Qi Yuling, a slight woman in her late twenties with bright eyes and hair scratched tightly into a bun, is anything to go by, the degradations of nature are mirrored in society.

Qi was in her seventeenth year when her life altered course. Her brother came running back from her school, swung open the wooden door of their home and with an expression of sheer joy announced that Qi had won a place to study in a technical college in the nearby city of Jining. He had just spoken to her teacher, who said it was so. Qi then hurried to the school but as she approached her teacher, she noticed the shadows in his face. He told her that her brother must have been mistaken. There was no notice from the Jining college of her acceptance. She followed her feet back home, reflecting that her education was over. The single-plank bridge that spanned a chasm between those who would use their brains to make a living and those who would use their brawn was no longer there for her to cross. The life that seemed to stretch out before her would be the one her parents had known: tilling the fields near their home in a village near Zoucheng. The money her parents had invested in her schooling had been wasted and her horizons would be as limited as theirs had been. Mencius's mother was legendary for moving house three times so that her son could sit at the feet of the best teachers. But Qi had had only one chance, and she had blown it.

Those among her school friends who had passed the exam drifted away, first to college and then to city jobs. When they returned to the village they wore the bright fashions of the city and some came in black cars which they parked incongruously outside their parents' ramshackle homes so that the whole village could take note. They barely acknowledged the friend with whom they used to walk hand-in-hand to the school gate and play hopscotch on the cement forecourt. To them, Qi had become the embodiment of everything they had striven to leave behind. At first the nonchalance of her former school friends was hard to bear, but as the years went by Qi's exam failure passed into memory and life found familiar rhythms. Only occasionally did things happen that gave her pause for thought.

One of those times was when she applied to leave the village and go to Zoucheng to get a factory job. To do this, she needed to move her 'hukou', or residence permit. But when she went to the authority in charge of keeping everyone's hukou, she was told that her permit could not be found. A few days later, it reappeared. A hukou is probably the most vital document that a Chinese person owns, and so Qi did wonder for a while how the village authorities could have been so bumbling and forgetful.

But it was not until eight years after her exam failure that she began to realise that something really was amiss. One day, when she was in Zoucheng city, there was a knock at her parents' door back in the village. A young woman stood in the doorway clutching bags full of gifts. She said she had come to congratulate Qi on the birth of her newborn baby. Qi's parents were flummoxed. They had not heard that their daughter was pregnant, and there had been no mention of a baby. In any case, they told the visitor, she did not live in the village these days; she had moved to the city and she had not been back for a while. Perhaps the gifts were intended for someone else, maybe another young mother in the village, the parents suggested. The well-wisher stood her ground, however, and became a little petulant. She had come to see Qi Yuling from this very village, a colleague of hers at the Bank of China branch in Tengzhou city. People had informed her that this house was where she lived. Well, the parents answered, their daughter was indeed called Qi Yuling but she did not work in any bank and not in Tengzhou. She was in Zoucheng and, having been made redundant from a ferro-alloy plant there, she was now doing odd jobs to make ends meet. The visitor took her presents and returned to her car.

When Qi heard of the perplexing visit to her parents' house, she decided to go to the Bank of China branch in Tengzhou to satisfy her curiosity. She asked at the counter if she could speak to Qi Yuling but the service assistant told her that 'director Qi' was away on maternity leave and would not be back for a few weeks. As she turned to leave, she was confronted with a billboard pasted with photographs of the bank's key personnel. In the bottom right-hand corner was a face that was instantly familiar. It was Chen Xiaoqi, a former classmate. The two had not met since Chen had passed the exams to the Jining Business College. The photograph showed a slightly changed appearance; her hair was styled with ringlets and waves and her expression had grown quite serious, but there was no mistaking her old friend. Beneath the picture, a nameplate read 'Qi Yuling, director of the savings department'.

The realisation that not only her identity and but also her life had been stolen came slowly to Qi. Chen had been a rather lazy pupil at school but nobody doubted that she would do well in life; her father was Party secretary, the highest-ranking official in their village. He tapped into a power network which threaded from the village to the county and then to the city of Tengzhou itself; there was not much in this small corner of Shandong province that he could not make happen. When Chen got a place at Jining College, therefore, nobody was surprised. It was not until the evening of the day she had visited the bank that Qi began to suspect Chen had somehow taken the college place that should have been hers. It was a bewildering feeling as she awoke to the realisation not that she was someone else but that someone else was her.

Over the next weeks, she pieced the details together. Chen's father had intercepted her exam certificate (though not before a teacher had let slip to Qi's brother that she had passed). Then he had bribed or threatened several school officials into silence. He arranged for his daughter to take all of Qi's personal files to the Jining college, so the matriculation officials would not notice anything untoward. Chen had then embarked upon the accountancy course that Qi had wanted to study, and passed. Of course, her assumed name was on her diploma certificate and it was, therefore, the basis upon which she won her job at the Bank of China, the most prestigious of the country's 'big four' state banks. The lie had to be sustained. When she wanted to transfer her 'hukou', or residence permit, from the village to Tengzhou city where she worked, she had to borrow Qi's. When she got married, she again had to use Qi's documents and when her baby was born, its mother's name was registered as Qi. So complete was the deception that it was unclear, when the case eventually went to court, whether even her husband had known who she really was.

But when Qi first approached Chen's father with a question over why his daughter was using her name, the Party secretary did not attempt to deny it. He said it was nothing that should concern her. Chen was only 'borrowing' it for a while. She had been inclined to take his advice, perhaps it was not such a big deal. But as the investigations continued and she discovered the examination slip showing that she had passed, it became more and more difficult to let the issue rest. Then, one day, Chen sent a representative to Qi's parents' house with 5,000 renminbi ($617) as a 'token of respect' which would be theirs if they would agree just to drop their concerns about the name. 'He just kept saying that it was only a name. What was the difference? We should just forget about it, take the 5,000 and move on,' Qi said as we talked in a hotel room in Zoucheng. 'The arrogance of it was unbearable. As if 5,000 was the value of a stolen life.' When Qi and her parents refused to

152

accept the money and declined to drop their investigations, Chen sent some thugs round to beat the family up. That only increased their determination and, after a long legal wrangle, a court found in Qi's favour. Chen was ordered to pay out 98,000 renminbi ($12,098) in damages.

When Qi and I met it was just before the lunar New Year of the Wooden Cockerel. She had parked her moped outside the hotel in which we met, and, as I saw her back to it, I gave her some white sorghum spirit and a two-litre flagon of sunflower oil that the shop had given away free as an inducement to buy the spirit. She refused both gifts at first, saying that she had not told me her story in order to receive anything in return. But after a while she agreed to accept the gifts, and we spent several minutes as dusk was falling shifting the tub of oil this way and that to make it fit in the basket on the front of her motorbike. Eventually, we managed it and said 'good-bye'. She drove off in the direction of the temple to Mencius that stood in a suburb of town. I was too full of thoughts to return to my hotel room and so I wandered in that direction too. When I got to the temple, the moon had risen over the old cedar trees that stood in front of the main hall, creating a scene of haunting beauty. I got out a small booklet of Mencius's quotations I had bought earlier in the day and read: 'If beans and millet were as plentiful as fire and water, such a thing as a bad man would not exist among the people.'

The story of Qi Yuling presents a microcosm of the breakdown of trust that bedevils the whole of Chinese society. In saying this, I do not mean to give the impression that everyone is untrustworthy or unreliable. That would be far too black. Most people whom I have come across have been decent and honest, and some have shown kindness and hospitality that would be rare in the West. Neither would it be true to say that Chinese culture fails to value integrity. History is replete with reverence to people who were upright, loyal and altruistic. The great philosophers, Confucius, Mencius, Zhuang Zi, Lao Zi and Mo Zi, to name but a few, were all concerned with virtue in its crucial manifestations. Nevertheless, trust is a commodity constantly under siege. Poverty and the competition for scarce resources impinge upon it. The ideological

that replaced Communism undermines it. The daily diet
aganda disorientates it. The venality of officials devalues it.
endancy of a value system dominated by money hollows
What is left is a society in which describing someone as
'honest' can just as easily be a gentle criticism as a compliment.
Even offical newspapers have highlighted the problem, rating a
'crisis of trust' as one of the top ten ills ailing the country.

The vast industry for counterfeit products and the violation of
intellectual property rights, described in earlier chapters, are part
of the general crisis. But the problem delves much deeper than
that. The influence of artifice is almost omnipresent and identity
is an item to be bought and sold. In Beijing and other cities, the
mobile phone numbers scrawled with spray paint on walls and
under overpasses have been put there by scam artists advertising
fake papers – residence permits, work permits, university degrees,
identity cards; you name it – a whole identity makeover with a
Ph.D. in rocket science can be bought for less than $100. People
use these to assume new identities, launder a dubious past and
secure city jobs. But they are by no means the only people masquerading as someone else. The media regularly report cases of
criminals who have gone around the country pretending to be
some senior official and enjoying the pampering of sycophants
before finally being exposed. In a country where a uniform bestows
unquestioning respect, the numbers of people impersonating
police and military officers is astonishing. Beijing authorities said
that in the five years to 2002, they had apprehended more than
10,000 phoney police officers in the capital along with 320,000
fake uniforms, badges and weapons.[3]

In the media, a practice called 'you chang xin wen' (news with
bonus) has become a staple of the newspaper business. Many, if not
most, Chinese journalists these days expect to find several hundred
renminbi tucked in an envelope along with their press release when
they attend a news conference on a corporate announcement.
Similarly, many will not agree to write an article on a company
unless they get paid in advance. The practice is so blatant that the
PR companies which organise news conferences inform their
corporate clients airily that 'everybody does it' and advise them on
how much money to insert into the envelopes.[4] The few news

organisations that have a strict no-bonus policy, such as *Caijing Magazine*, are regarded as heroic trailblazers for an impartial media and, indeed, the quality of the reporting in the no-bonus newspapers and magazines is on a different level from the rest. But the 'news with bonus' mentality has spread to many fields of endeavour, including football. Referees have often accepted bribes to swing matches with a few deft dubious decisions. Such people are called 'black whistles' and every time a black whistle is uncovered, the media is up in arms.

One of the most intriguing identity subterfuges comes with the number plates on officials' cars. It has long been the habit of the Beijing traffic police (the real ones, that is) to turn a blind eye to the driving infringements of cars with official number plates so as to avoid incurring the wrath of the powerful people inside. The immunity the plates offer give them a value on the black market and the more senior the official rank denoted by the licence number, the greater that value is. At the bottom of the pyramid of privilege are the black plates reserved for foreign residents, which, although not official, still afford a measure of protection, probably because many traffic cops dread the linguistic hassle that stopping a foreign driver can entail. On the next level up, there are plates for officials from outlying provinces. Above them are those that indicate a mandarin from the Beijing city government is travelling inside, and, one up from that, are those reserved for central government officials. But the apogee in this motoring hierarchy is with the plates of the Central Military Commission (CMC), the second most powerful body in the land after the Communist Party politburo (which does not have its own dedicated plates). The CMC plates, until recently, bore the character 'Jia', meaning 'Armour', and the immunity these bestowed from speeding tickets, parking fines, and spot checks by traffic police was iron-clad.

All of these activities contribute towards a large and growing underground economy which is not captured in the official figures and is therefore ignored except in special studies. Neither the World Bank, the International Monetary Fund nor the brokerage houses that analyse the ups and downs of China's growing global influence make allowance for the size of the underground economy. This is clearly a significant oversight. In some provinces, such as Zhejiang on the east coast, the underground economy is almost institutionalised. Scores of underground banks provide finance for private companies that still find the traditional state-owned lenders reluctant to co-operate. In Guangdong, especially around the cities of Shenzhen and Guangzhou, there are hundreds of thousands of unlicensed factories operating in the twilight of symbiotic relationships with local officials. Tax evasion is endemic all over the country, as is shown by the regularity of scandals involving fake VAT tax receipts. The size of the underground economy is by its nature difficult to estimate, but a Chinese scholar, Yao Jianfu, who has spent years studying it, says it could amount to about one-third of the size of the official economy.[5] This impression was reinforced by an intriguing encounter with Li Ruogu, deputy governor of the People's Bank of China, the central bank, who told me in late 2004 that nearly one-third of the growth in money supply could be attributed to the informal economy.

The grey area in economics, therefore, may be huge. And in personal relationships too. The incidence of extramarital affairs, paternity tests, prenuptial agreements and divorce rates is surging in the cities along the east coast. Private detectives, a job description that did not exist just over a decade ago, now number in their hundreds of thousands and are employed increasingly by one lover to trail another, or by wives to check up on their husbands. In the southwestern city of Chengdu, a chambermaid walking into a hotel room was intrigued to find the following note written in a female hand in an opened letter on the bed:

Dear Mr Song,
Please excuse my deception. It was due to my job. I'm a love detective and I was hired by your lover to test your love. I have now got your ID card and underwear as proof. You have loved each other for three years and are now preparing to wed. Please go back to your lover's side.

At the end of the letter was written the name of the detective agency, 'Hunting Fox', its address and the signature, 'Xiao Qing', the assumed name of the young female detective who had lured

Song to the edge of seduction and then left with his underpants when he was in the shower.

Xiao Qing was the epitome of Chinese beauty. She was twenty-seven years old, 1.65 metres tall, slim with curves and white skin. Her face was an oval that drew to a gentle point at her chin and her almond eyes were dark and shining. When she smiled, a shallow dimple formed in one cheek. Although she looked innocent, she was accomplished in make-up and male psychology. Her employer in this assignment was Ms Yun, a plain-looking twenty-five-year-old who worked as an accountant in a foreign company and earned 6,000 renminbi a month. The cost of hiring Xiao Qing to lure her fiancé was just 1,000 renminbi. Not much more, observed Yun, than the price of a Burberry shirt. It was nearly Christmas and there was barely three weeks to go before she was to marry Song, who worked in a private trading company. He was wealthy and in many ways a good catch but Yun was fretting that he had grown cold of late and their relationship was turning stale. She had to fathom the depth of his love.

Xiao Qing waited by the lift in the building where Song worked. As he entered, she asked him to hold it for her and then thanked him with a charming smile as she took her place close to him. Song walked towards the coffee shop across the street and she followed. As he passed her in the shop, she nudged her bag onto the floor. He picked it up and Xiao Qing said, 'You work in that building. I work there too. I came here only a week ago by myself. I don't have any friends here.' They exchanged name cards and began to meet from time to time. On Christmas Eve, Yun called Song to ask if he was free to go out that night. They were not Christian but Christmas Eve is nevertheless an occasion, a time when friends and lovers get together to eat. But Song had already agreed to see Xiao Qing so he told Yun he was very busy at work. That evening they danced and drank and Xiao Qing pretended to lose her bag. Inside were the keys to her house and her cash, so when Song offered to take her to a hotel, it seemed as if fate had had a hand in the decision. She suggested he take a shower first. But when he emerged from the bathroom, he found her gone and the letter lying on the bed.

Yun felt the money had been well spent and, even though Song apologised several times, she decided to take time out of the relationship to reconsider.

In the end, no more than feelings were hurt. But at other times the breakdown in morality has descended into pure evil. Two of the most shocking cases in recent years have both involved commercial activities – the sale of fake baby milk powder to unknowing parents and the transfusion of HIV-contaminated blood to villagers in the northern province of Henan. In both cases, local governments were implicated in crimes that caused death.

The milk powder tragedy began when some forty companies in several provinces hit on the idea of selling powder that looked like the real thing but was in fact a cheaper, less nutritious substance inserted into packages bearing counterfeit brands. It contained just enough protein to keep a baby alive for about six to eight months but not enough to promote growth and development. Instead of dried, fortified milk, the powder contained a mixture of sugar, flour and gluten. The companies that sold it reasoned that the more sickly and malnourished the babies began to look, the more of the fake powder their parents would feed them – which would be good for sales. In the event, it turned out almost as the companies had hoped, though with one variation that also worked to the companies' advantage. The powder made the heads of babies swell up and their cheeks grow chubby, even though their bones remained small and brittle and their internal organs underdeveloped. The big heads convinced many parents that all was well, and so they delayed taking the babies to hospital. Some thirteen are known to have died of malnutrition in and around the city of Fuyang in Anhui province, where the scam was most prevalent.[6] Many hundreds more are thought to be in poor physical and mental health and will probably be affected for the rest of their lives. When the case was cracked in 2004, several Fuyang officials were fired or put in prison for complicity with the milk powder companies. But this has had little effect. Within months of the sentences being handed down, new fake milk powders were on the market in Fuyang and elsewhere.

Children were also among the victims of the HIV scandal that has been unfolding in villages in Henan since the mid 1990s. Back then there was a shortage of blood in local hospitals and a society that was not accustomed to giving it. Local officials set up blood collection centres and offered payment to donors of around $5 a donation, a significant sum for a peasant in one of China's poorest areas. Indeed, the main limitation to what became a roaring trade was anaemia, which set in when a person had given too much blood. So the collectors switched to taking just plasma – that way they could extract the blood, pool it with that from other donors with the same blood type, skim off all the plasma at once and then return the remaining blood back to the donors. The arrangement seemed to suit everyone, though it was also a sure way to spread diseases throughout the donor community. Nobody is quite sure how or when HIV-tainted blood entered the blood bank, but it travelled rapidly. AIDS, the disease that is brought on by the HIV virus, is estimated by health workers to have infected a million Henan peasants. Around 100,000 children have become orphans. Local governments, who profited from the blood collection centres in the first place, have tried to cover up the scandal, arresting AIDS activists, closing down orphanages and conducting a strenuous campaign to keep the issue out of the national media. It seems unlikely, however, that they will be successful over the longer term. Pierre Haski, China correspondent of *Libération*, the French newspaper, has obtained official documents showing that branches of the Henan government knew that HIV was being spread through the contaminated blood long before they did anything to stop the blood trade.[7]

The horrific nature of such cases provides a bleak commentary on contemporary society. They also detract from the national image. To some people, that may seem a mere inconvenience. But the reputation of a country, like that of an individual, is of inestimable value. China has much going for it in this regard: an ancient culture, sparkling traditions in literature and the arts, the accumulated wisdom of thinkers over thousands of years, the size of its potential power, the taste of its cuisine, kung-fu and other martial arts, the diligence and intelligence of its people, the gleaming skyscrapers in cool new cities such as Shanghai and, of course, the cuddly giant panda. But against these positive associations is a raft of less alluring images: shabby products, counterfeit goods, rip-offs of intellectual property, exploited labour, human rights abuses, the

1989 Tiananmen massacre, official nepotism and corruption, the persecution of religion and other forms of spirituality, a sick environment, outbursts of angry nationalism and its opposition towards the Dalai Lama in exile. All or any of these impressions – plus others too numerous to mention – can coalesce to shape the attitudes of people in the West when they read the label 'Made in China' on products. The resultant image, or 'brand', is often far from positive, and Chinese companies pay handsomely every year for the poor perceptions that are formed.

The cost incurred flows mainly from the way in which global capitalism is configured. When a consumer item is sold in a shop, most of the money paid goes to the owner of the brand, the distributors, the advertisers and the retailers. The manufacturer, which in more and more cases is a separate company contracted by the brand owner, gets a relative pittance for its work. China, as is obvious from even a brief trip around the Pearl River Delta, is firmly at the manufacturing end of this value hierarchy. The girls and young women labouring away at their tables making shoes in one of the world's largest shoe factories, the Taiwanese-owned Pao Chen in the city of Zhuhai near Hong Kong, get around one or two per cent of the price paid by customers in the US and Europe for the famous brand-named shoes that they make.[8] The same is true at Galanz, which single-handedly makes around 40 per cent of the world's microwave ovens on contract for foreign brand owners. And it is the same story for almost every manufactured product that Chinese companies make. Seventy per cent of the world's photocopiers, 70 per cent of its computer motherboards, 55 per cent of its DVD players, 30 per cent of its personal computers, 25 per cent of its TV sets and 20 per cent of its car audios – to name but a handful – are made in largely brand-less factories by workers who get no more than a few percentage points of the final sale price. In fact, all of the work done in China – the sourcing, manufacturing, transportation and export – rarely qualifies for a return of more than 10 or 15 per cent from a product's sales revenue.

This may seem unfair. Certainly, the effort expended by a typical migrant worker who is far from her village, working fifteen-hour days without welfare or union protection under a management regime that may use fines as a motivational strategy is not inconsiderable. But the harsh truth is that this effort is valued less by the consumer than some of the other functions that go into bringing the product to market. It is the advertising, marketing and sales work – which are almost always performed in the country where a product is sold – that command most of the sales value of the product the migrant workers create. There is no doubt that the brand holders sometimes feel uneasy about this arrangement; the most common plea I have heard during scores of visits to contract manufacturers has been, 'you can write anything you like, but please don't report the names of the brands for whom we manufacture.' It may be that brand holders wish to shield their customers from the discomfort of knowing the torment under which their products were made. Or it may be that they feel that any association with China could undermine the image they are trying to project. Whatever the reason, the reality is that world trade is arranged in this way. The customer is the ultimate arbiter, and if customers in the US and Europe think that the greatest portion of a product's value derives from its logo, then most of the commercial rewards will continue to accrue to those who build and sustain the brand.

Chinese companies who try to build their own brands, meanwhile, bump up against a series of barriers, not least of which are the associations that come with their national identity. It is not easy to create an aura of quality, consistency or 'cool' among overseas consumers if the news coverage from your country centres on repression, corruption scandals, worker exploitation, and, for many people, a vague and menacing presence called Communism. Thus Chinese firms are condemned to surrender the lion's share of the value that comes from making and selling things to foreign companies. This disequilibrium has not escaped the notice of Beijing's leadership. Wen Jiabao, the Premier, speaks regularly about the requirement for companies to concentrate on creating and building their brands, and events such as the Olympic Games, to be held in Beijing in 2008, are being viewed as a rare opportunity to launder the country's reputation in the eyes of the world. But until that reputation is overhauled (and it will take more than an Olympics to do it), Chinese corporations are likely to find other ways to build their brands. Near the top of the preferred strategies in evidence so far is the acquisition of foreign brands.

The outward investment of Chinese companies has become an identifiable trend. Lenovo, the Chinese computer company, paid $1.75 billion for the personal computer unit of IBM, the American icon. TCL, an electronics company, bought Thomson, the French TV maker, and its German counterpart, Schneider, and took a majority stake in a mobile handset joint venture with France's Alcatel. BOE Technology bought the liquid crystal display unit of South Korea's Hynix Semiconductor for $380 million. Haier, the consumer electronics manufacturer, launched an aggressive but ultimately unsuccessful bid for Maytag, an American household name. Such sorties have prompted comparisons with the outward extension of Japanese corporate might at the end of the 1980s, when Mitsubishi Corporation bought the Rockefeller Center in New York and Honda, Toyota and Sony made investments in other arenas. But there are important differences between the internationalisation of Japan Inc. and the first faltering foreign footsteps of Chinese companies. The main difference is that Chinese manufacturers (the energy and resource companies are in a very different category) are being pushed overseas through weakness rather than strength. In the case of Lenovo, for instance, the acquisition of IBM was motivated not by pretensions to the US market but by the need to defend itself at home, where it is being squeezed by competition from giants such as Dell and Hewlett-Packard.

Another difference is that many of the Japanese acquisitions followed inroads that their formidable brands had already opened up. They had real corporate clout. By the end of the 1980s, Japan had been an emerging Asian powerhouse for nearly four decades and brands such as Sony, Hitachi, Sharp, Sanyo, Nissan, Toyota, Honda and many others were already household names. But Chinese brands, perhaps because of the speed of China's rise, have been given very little time to establish themselves. Thus, when TCL bought Schneider and Thomson, it decided to keep selling products under European brand names rather than substitute them with its own. This was not the only expression of relative weakness. The CEO, Li Dongsheng, also acknowledged that his company was being *driven* overseas by the paucity of profit at home.[9] The problem of oversupply was endemic in China, he said, and profit margins were therefore perennially thin. The only answer was to build a bulwark in offshore markets where decent margins could be collected to reinforce the home front. This amounts to a reversal of usual business logic, but it is surprising how many Chinese bosses employ it.

The big exception to this tendency are those Chinese companies that enjoy monopoly or near-monopoly conditions at home. These firms, such as the oil giants PetroChina, Sinopec and CNOOC, the telecoms operators China Telecom, China Mobile and China Unicom and some of the financial institutions, are flush with cash and intent on snapping up opportunities overseas for rather different reasons. Nevertheless, the magnitude of the task facing Chinese manufacturers in building their brands abroad and in acquiring foreign counterparts is sizeable – though that is unlikely to stop many from trying. Indeed, a deluge of outward-bound Chinese investment may be about to wash up on foreign shores. As the trend unfolds, heroes, villains and legends seem certain to be created.

Legend, in fact, was the English name of Lenovo before the company found out that others abroad were already using it, and had to change. That is unfortunate because no word describes the ascent of Liu Chuanzhi – the man who started his career as an IBM sales agent in a borrowed suit and twenty years later bought the company – more accurately than the one he gave to his corporation. His experience could not have been more different from those of Bill Gates, Larry Ellison, Steve Jobs and other luminaries in the global information technology industry, and in certain respects his curriculum vitae appears a little lacking. He can hardly speak a sentence of English, has almost no experience in operating in markets beyond China and is by no means a technological visionary. Yet, like several other Chinese entrepreneurs over the age of fifty-five, he has come through a school of hard knocks *summa cum laude*.

Liu was born in 1944 into a family without a single revolutionary credential to its name. On his father's side there were bankers, which is to say capitalists. His mother's father had been the finance minister to a famous warlord, which is to say both capitalist and of suspect loyalties. As a boy, he dreamed of being a pilot but was prevented by his background from even applying. A gifted scholar at university, he wanted to join the Party but was prevented from doing so because of a perceived lack of feeling towards the workers and peasants. With these disadvantages, he had to turn himself into a 'needle wrapped in cotton'; someone who could do things that he disliked and yet appear cheerful. One of his first moves was to volunteer to collect excrement from the public toilets on one street to prove he was not aloof from the masses. He shovelled out the nightsoil, put it into a cart and then hauled it away to be used as agricultural manure.[10]

His efforts paid off. By the time he had graduated in radar technology, he had found favour with his teachers and fellow students. He was also known as a good public debater, a skill much in demand in the early years of the Cultural Revolution. In 1968, he graduated and was assigned to a good job in a research institute in Chengdu, a city in the southwestern province of Sichuan. But only a few months after he got there, Mao had come up with a new idea: all young intellectuals should be sent to the countryside to learn from peasants. Liu was dispatched first to till paddy fields on a farm near Macao and then to another farm in Hunan which used to be a labour camp for criminals. In 1970, however, his luck changed and he was transferred to Beijing to work as an engineer in the prestigious Academy of Sciences' Institute of Computing Technology. Even though the Cultural Revolution was still in full swing in that year and most 'intellectual' institutions had been disbanded, the Institute of Computing was allowed to continue with its work because it was designated as a military unit: 'Army BJ 116'.

By the early 1980s, however, China had stood down from its war footing and military budgets were being cut. The Institute of Computing Technology had over 1,000 scientists and 500 workers on its payroll when suddenly its funding was slashed. For Liu, as it turned out, that was to be the luckiest break of all. The institute could no longer afford to keep so many intellectuals in its suffocating embrace and encouraged several young scientists to find an income by themselves. In December 1984 a group of them set up the cumbersomely named New Technology Development Company of the Institute of Computing Technology of the Chinese Academy of Sciences. Its headquarters was a 20-square-metre breeze-block bungalow that served as the institute's gatehouse. It had a cement floor, no sofa, no armchairs and no computers; just two benches and two desks with three drawers each. From the outside, it was about as unprepossessing as could be imagined. But that was where Lenovo got its start, and the timing could not have been more auspicious. In the same month as the scientists moved into their brick gatehouse, the government of Deng Xiaoping approved a document that stated, famously, that some people would be allowed to get rich first.

Rich would not have described Liu then. Like forty other scientists' families at the institute, he lived in a room of around 12 square metres that he built with his own hands in the institute's bicycle parking lot. He and his colleague Li Qin, who was later to become a vice-president of Legend, used to go together to fetch sand from a nearby construction site to make the mortar between the bricks. The two of them built the kitchen together and Liu then plastered newspapers on the walls and put a reed mat on the ceiling. These cramped quarters were to be home for Liu, his wife and son as he embarked on his illustrious corporate career. One day, when Liu's wife was washing a lot of clothes, a sock dropped unnoticed into a cooking pot and nearly became soup. At that time Liu's salary was just over $13 a month, a wage on which a family had to save patiently for months just to buy a pair of cotton long johns.

But things were changing. The institute gave him 200,000 renminbi in seed money to get his company started, along with the authority to spend the money how he wished, employ whom he liked and decide business strategy by himself. Unlike other entrepreneurs at this time who branched off by themselves, Liu saw the value in maintaining strong links with the institute. He gained the respect that the institute's name offered, the close relationship with the government that it signified and access to its research and expertise. But in spite of this, his first business ventures ended in failure. He and his colleagues lost their bearings and started to trade all manner of things, looking for quick profits. They bought and sold electronic watches, sneakers, tracksuits and refrigerators, and managed to lose two-thirds of the seed capital to a swindler in Jiangxi who had promised to sell them TVs. That could have been the end of Liu's business career had it not been for the decision of the Academy of Sciences just at that time to buy 500 IBM computers. Liu and his team landed the contract to maintain those computers and earned back their losses. As he got to know the computer business better, he could not help noticing the mark-up that retailers were making by selling imported products such as those from IBM. The import price for the IBM PC 286 was 20,000 renminbi, but retailers sold them for 40,000. Liu had an idea what he was going to do next.

Later, he remembered his first meeting as an IBM agent. 'I was sitting in the last row in my father's old suit and for the whole day I didn't get a chance to talk,' said Liu, a powerfully built man with a broad face. 'It was all new and startling. Even in my dreams I never imagined that one day we could buy the IBM PC business. It was unthinkable. Impossible.'

Those early days after he jumped into the sea of business were difficult and unpredictable. He had to swallow his pride on many occasions, drawing on the resilience that he had built up during his turbulent student times. Once, when he was angling to secure a licence, a young man still in his twenties cursed him to his face, but Liu still invited him out to dinner and flattered him enough to achieve his aim. On another occasion, he and his associates spent 25,570 renminbi to buy ten TV sets, two refrigerators and ten bottles of Maotai wine as 'gifts' for officials who needed to be kept sweet. Yet another time, he waited all night with bricks in his hands by the door of a business associate who had defaulted on a payment, and gave him such a shock on his return that he found a way to pay up. But although he could be tough on outsiders, he lavished attention on those who worked for him. In 1989, food was hard to come by in Beijing and inflation was galloping ahead. So Liu went to Shandong and lent peasants there 100,000 renminbi, telling them that they did not need to repay with money, only with vegetables and pork.

That is what doing business in the 1980s was like. But as his employees were eating the pork and vegetables that came by train from Shandong, they were working on a project of global significance: building the first Legend computer. As soon as the prototype was cobbled together out of smuggled parts intended for the computers of other companies, Liu began to harbour dreams for the future. The company's name was changed to Legend, and a strict – not to say militaristic – corporate culture, which Liu fondly called the 'Spartacus matrix', was adopted. All employees had to go for a morning run, then sing the Legend song and then study. If managers were late for a meeting, they had to stand in a corner as the meeting progressed.

It was around this time, too, that the company developed its breakthrough product – a circuit board that would allow IBM PCs to process Chinese characters. The Chinese language system helped them sell imported PCs, which gave them distribution experience and an understanding of consumer needs. In 1990, they started to assemble PCs under their own brand name as well as sell printers for Hewlett-Packard and computers for AST, a now defunct US manufacturer. Following that, business took off and in 1994 Legend floated its shares on the Hong Kong stock market. The company copied Hewlett-Packard's sales management system and applied it to the network it was increasingly using to sell its own branded products in China. It also copied HP's employee ID card. Liu acknowledged once that Legend was the rising brand, but HP was Legend's teacher.

In the late 1990s and in the first two years of this century, things seemed to go swimmingly. Legend computers became the market leader and then extended their lead over IBM, HP, Compaq and others. At its zenith, the market share of Legend computers hit 30 per cent. But after China's accession to the World Trade Organisation, which dispensed with many of the restrictions hobbling the foreign competitors, Legend's rivals began to make up lost territory. Liu described the dynamic like this: 'In the past Chinese enterprises competed with foreign counterparts rather as in a race between a turtle and a rabbit in a swamp. The foreigners, the rabbits, complained that the race was unfair but after China's WTO accession, we are now competing on a racetrack.'

Things began to go awry. The company, by now called Lenovo,

saw its share of the domestic computer market slip to around 27 per cent in late 2004 and early 2005. Hundreds of young Chinese companies sprang up copying exactly what Liu had begun twenty years earlier: cobbling together cheap, serviceable computers from a lucky dip of different parts and selling them at knock-down prices. Various attempts by Lenovo to diversify into other businesses failed. A fervent hope that making mobile phone handsets would deliver much needed profits proved misguided after the industry was savaged by the old afflictions of oversupply and price wars. A much trumpeted initiative to set up an internet portal, FM365, with AOL Time Warner and a planned investment of $200 million foundered on a lack of chemistry between the two companies. And the rabbits – especially one called Dell – were starting to move so quickly in the China market that the turtle was for the first time in eight years fearing that it might surrender its position as market leader. All these problems in the domestic market led Liu to look for a dramatic solution. He found it in IBM.

After buying the American icon, he explained his reasoning. 'What we did was to let the turtle ride on top of the rabbit and let the rabbit run. IBM is the rabbit, and Lenovo is the turtle on the rabbit's back. Let it take us forward.' There could be no doubt after that comment that Lenovo saw the IBM acquisition as an answer in part to its domestic troubles. But Liu, who was due to retire from his day-to-day involvement with the company after the deal was done, also saw IBM as a route into unfamiliar foreign markets. 'What do we want from this deal?' Liu asked. 'We want brand. Can we build up our own brand? It is tough. We want teams of internationalised talents. IBM already has such teams. We want market, distribution and sales networks. IBM has them. We want technology. IBM has it.'

Acquisitions such as the ones by Lenovo and TCL are attempts to enrich China's impoverished repertoire of corporate brands. On a human level, the same impulse for respect and invisible capital motivates a vast demand for overseas education. Although Beijing's record in improving the availability and quality of the education it provides for its people has been impressive, there is an insatiable thirst for more. And the branding that comes with a degree from a good foreign university, such as Harvard and MIT or Oxford and Cambridge, is valued at least as much by Chinese society as the knowledge that may have been acquired from studying there. It is difficult to comprehend quite the size of potential demand in this area. In the past, for instance, the flow of qualified Chinese applicants to such universities was circumscribed by a lack of financial resources, substandard teaching in some Chinese schools and an imperfect mastery of the English required for the entrance examination. But now that China's 'middle class' has swelled to include roughly 150 million people, and education loans secured against property are available from state banks, the potential increase in applications is enormous. English is becoming less of a barrier now that an estimated 200 million people are studying it across the nation. Teaching standards are shooting up and hundreds of thousands of gifted children, who just a decade ago would have been denied anything but a rudimentary education, are now thriving under competent tuition. What this portends for the world can be seen in the 2004 participation numbers at the annual international Science and Engineering Fair run by Intel, the US semiconductor company. In the US, 65,000 students participated in local fairs to select finalists. In China, six million did.[11]

The reverence of Chinese society for education has remained undimmed since the days of Mencius, and some schools and universities around the world have begun to get ready for what that may mean. In Dulwich, a leafy suburb of London, I met a secondary school headmaster who was under no illusions as to what China's rise meant for education worldwide.

Headmasters' studies, for those who can recall their schooldays, are places that can elicit an involuntary spasm of angst. But the office of Graham Able, Master of Dulwich College in south London, was not designed to evoke awe. There are soft cushions on a pea-green sofa, a snug woollen carpet underfoot and a window through which the vague sounds of England are audible: groundsmen mowing lawns, the shouts of boys playing cricket and airliners on their way to distant lands. Nor is Able himself a particularly daunting figure. His middle-aged face has a kindly ruddiness to it, with just a dusting of grey at the temples. He sits attentively, leaning slightly forward in his chair, fixing me with a look that is enquiring but devoid of animosity. Yet as I sink into the sofa I somehow feel flustered, forget the items of small talk customary on these occasions and plunge straight into the reason for my visit.

Dulwich was the first English public school to reach out to China. It set up a campus in Shanghai and another in Beijing. Harrow, the alma mater of Winston Churchill, has also set up shop in China. Eton, the most famous of all elite British schools, is also represented in Beijing but it is not the genuine article, just a gambit by a local pirate who has appropriated its august name. Aside from these moves into China, British schools back in the UK have become preferred establishments for wealthy Chinese to send their boys and girls. Able is seizing this opportunity. He devotes considerable efforts to finding the right kind of student in places such as Shanghai and Beijing. It is a project that is still in its infancy, but Able feels it may have a considerable bearing on the school's prospects in the longer term.

As we spoke about the boys from mainland China who had already attended Dulwich, it dawned on me that Able kept lengthy biographical details on each one stored in his head. Achievements, affiliations, successes after leaving, examination statistics and snatches of conversations recalled from years ago all came tumbling out. He was delighted, for instance, that Robin Tang, who came from the Shanghai Modern Foreign Language School and had left a year earlier to go to Yale, was soon to be coming back to perform as second tenor in a Yale choir. Robin had learned to sing at Dulwich and also to play the saxophone from zero to Grade Seven with distinction in fourteen months. Most of the boys who come from China are from relatively wealthy families, Able explained, and the fees for some of them – Robin being one – were paid only after the boy's parents and grandparents had pooled their savings.

Only two boys a year came from poor backgrounds and they were financed by scholarships from HSBC, the Hong Kong-based British bank. One of these boys had just turned down a place at Oxford with a pledge of funding of £20,000 a year from a financial firm in London that would have required him to work holidays in the City. He also forfeited a chance to compete in the final of the British Maths Olympiad because he went home to China during the Easter holidays, and he decided to take up a place at Columbia University in New York. That dismayed Able somewhat. The Oxford offer plus the City funding was the equivalent of a top internship, he said. Nevertheless, he understood why Chinese boys make such decisions; they get advice back in China from family and friends who generally believe that America is best. 'I am not cross with the boy but I am with the advisers,' he said. 'He is a lovely boy. And he writes brilliant English too. In the written SATs [Standard Aptitude Tests], a good English candidate would get 750 out of 800. He got 785 and he is Chinese. When he got here his English was pretty reasonable but not great.'

A boy whose English name was Harrison, another HSBC scholar from the south-western city of Chengdu, got a pre-Christmas place at Harvard before he had taken his A-level exams and then 'oddly for a Chinese boy, very odd, he stopped working'. In the end he got two As and two Bs at A-level and Harvard were a 'little bit pissed off with him' but they took him anyway. The reason they took him in the first place, though, was that he has a great personality. He was a senior prefect after being here two terms and was very good at looking after the younger kids and organising things. Harvard often look for people who are not only academically sharp but also show leadership qualities in some way. They show more imagination than Oxford and Cambridge in that respect, Able said. Not every boy, however, gets the university place he is hoping for. One lad, whose English name was David, did not get a place at either Cambridge or the top American universities in spite of the fact that he was brighter than some who did. Able thinks that may have been because he was a bit disorganised. In the end, though, he was taken by Imperial, the UK's top science college. 'He will do well. He will get a first at Imperial,' Able said.

The boys who make it to Dulwich are taken only from 'key' middle schools, meaning they belong to the most gifted 3 per cent of China's huge school intake. Many are the best or near the best in their class. They are then subjected to Dulwich's rigorous selection criteria and because there are only thirty-four boarding places at the school each year, the Chinese applicants have to compete with Poles, Russians, Germans, Nigerians, Indians and boys from the

Persian Gulf. Although Able finds he could fill 95 per cent of his boarding places with gifted boys from China every year, he tries to be fair and awards a considerable number of places to the other nationalities. Thus the Chinese boys who do eventually make it to Dulwich have been whittled down from an already excellent group of gifted pupils to a few truly exceptional people.

Able makes no apology for the elitism that underpins the process. In fact he relishes the memory of how he once tried to explain the UK comprehensive school ideology – that pupils are admitted in state schools without selection or streaming – to the Principal of the East China University Number Two High School in Shanghai. 'She was like, "Surely not! You're joking! You are pulling my leg! This cannot work!"' Able remembers with a chuckle. The problem in the UK schooling system, he adds, is not that it is too elitist but that it is not elitist enough. 'If you look for underachievement in the lower socio-economic groups in the UK, you can actually map that, sadly, onto the demise of the grammar schools. Sorry, but I do believe that very strongly. All the arguments for comprehensives are eyewash. No argument whatsoever.'

The benefit to Dulwich from accepting several clever Chinese students each year is that their performance bolsters the school's reputation. Parents who send their children to fee-paying schools in the UK make their choices increasingly on the basis of their rank in 'league tables' of exam result achievers. Good students, therefore, boost a school's exam result average, while brilliant pupils – such as those who win scholarships to top US or UK universities – give their headmasters something to boast about when prospective parents come to look around on open day. The elitism, in other words, has become self-perpetuating. The best schools lure the best potential students, who then improve their school's performance and so on. This dynamic, though pervasive, is far from universally popular. In the UK, just as in China, some teachers and parents bemoan an intensifying culture of competition that can place unbearable strain on pupils while depriving them of time to play sport and indulge in the cherished aimlessness of childhood. But no matter what misgivings parents may have, the root cause of the trend is clear; just as today's world is global to an extent unprecedented in history, the world of tomorrow will be more so.

The current generation of Dulwich College students, if they choose when they are adults to work in an international business, will have to compete for their jobs with many more candidates than do their predecessors today. Faced with this hyper-competitive vista, the reaction of many may be to opt out of the globalised market place and take up locally focused jobs that may pay less but offer a more sane existence.

But Able is in no doubt about where he is heading. The world is becoming more global and education has to follow. This conviction drives his school's overseas expansion. By most reckonings, Dulwich is already the world's most internationalised secondary school, with a campus in Phuket, Thailand as well as Shanghai and Beijing. There are now plans for six more franchised international schools in China and negotiations are well advanced to set up three joint ventures as well. A search for an opening in India is also drawing to a close and Able is sure that Dulwich will have a school there in the not-too-distant future. There could also be one in the Gulf, he adds. The rationale for all this activity turns out to be surprisingly familiar. The income from the franchise fees and a per-pupil fee in all of its overseas branches will return to Dulwich in London, where it will fund bursaries for clever boys from the UK and elsewhere in the world. The final aim, Able explains, is to expand the Dulwich financial endowment to a size at which the school becomes 'needs blind at the point of entry'. In other words, so wealthy that it can offer scholarships to anyone, regardless of their circumstances, whose presence will enhance the school's brand. The hope is, Able says, that in a few decades' time Dulwich will be to secondary schools what Harvard is now to universities.

The future of such ambitions will ultimately depend on China and boys like Ricky, who at the end of my allotted time with the headmaster stood hesitantly in the doorway in a blue striped blazer. Able had arranged for the eighteen-year-old from Xian to show me around. Ricky is friendly and willing and laughs a little nervously when the headmaster tells him to include his study-bedroom in the tour. 'I think Ricky's room should be relatively tidy?' he asks. As we walk around the school, Ricky reveals that he is acutely aware of the privilege that he has been given. His mother, a teacher, and his father, a wealthy entrepreneur, were both deprived of a formal education by the Cultural Revolution. Xian, though a large city, is in a relatively backward central province of China and although he was top of his class in secondary school (with marks of 98 per cent in maths, physics and chemistry and 'only' 85 per cent in Chinese), he has found that Dulwich teaches things his old school did not. One is economics. That is, modern, capitalist economics of a type his father says will set him up nicely to make money in stocks and shares. Another is how to think. But when I ask him to explain how it teaches him to think, he cannot quite find the words and we stand in silence for a while in a quad beneath the school's towering, red-brick Victorian buildings. In the end, we leave the subject aside, agreeing that Chinese and English employ different ways to analyse issues.

Later, in his study-bedroom he observes that in a Chinese university a place the size of his room would be a dormitory for six students. That is one of the many good things about England, he says. There is not much population density. And the bad things? I ask. 'I think mostly there are too many foreigners in England. That really disappointed me. The reason I came to a foreign country is to feel a foreign culture but I can say half of the people here are foreigners and mostly they come from Hong Kong. There are many yellow ones but not many white ones. I think that is the big problem that the British government will have to deal with or the whole country will lose its culture and that would be really terrible.'

'Oh, and the food,' he added before we said goodbye near a monumental horse chestnut tree in the grounds. White blossoms stood upright like candelabra among the expanse of leaves. 'I do not understand what the British do with their vegetables,' he said.

EIGHT

Many of the weaknesses and deficiencies described in the last two chapters can be traced back to China's overarching contradiction: that it tries to run an increasingly sophisticated, capitalist economy with a political system that was designed to issue crisp commands from a single source of authority, and to be obeyed. This observation is not controversial, nor it is insightful; political scientists have been pointing out as much throughout the era of reform since 1978. Indeed, it is widely accepted that China's crisis of trust, environmental malaise, rampant piracy and official corruption derive at least in part from systemic inadequacies thrown up by the country's transition. For much of the last two and a half decades, though, these problems have mainly been the concern of the Chinese themselves and a limited circle of sinologists abroad. The intricacies that surrounded the dichotomy between Communism and capitalism were primarily the preserve of academic political scientists. But since China has become an inescapable global force, the glaring mismatch between its political and economic polities has become an issue not just for Beijing but also for Washington, Tokyo, Brussels, London and other national capitals.

That is because the influences that China has on the world are all external expressions of internal affairs. Just as the decisions of the White House invite international scrutiny from the governments and people affected by them, so China's trade partners increasingly feel the need to address the systemic sources of the issues they are confronting. Signs of this trend are already in evidence. The reasons that the bid by CNOOC, the Chinese oil company, for its US counterpart, Unocal, foundered all had to do with American misgivings over China's political economy. Similarly, protectionist sentiment welling up within the US Congress, industry associations and trade unions derives much of its impetus from arguments that the Chinese *system* puts US competitors at an unfair disadvantage. Thus the spotlight is falling ever more unsparingly on a number of sensitive issues: Beijing's insistence on keeping the renminbi's value fixed at what US critics think is an unjustifiably low rate; the government's ban on independent unions for migrant workers so they have little power to campaign for more pay; the domestic prices of water, electricity and oil, which are kept low by administrative fiat or state subsidies; the heavy restrictions on capital flows which act as a mechanism to support Chinese banks; the many industries in which foreign investment is limited; the incapacity of the state to bring counterfeit pirates to book; the export of pollution to neighbours because of ineffective environmental safeguards and the illegal felling of rainforests overseas by China-based syndicates.

Thus China's vulnerability to international censure – and therefore to the protectionism and obstructionism that threaten to frustrate its economic ascent – flows in almost every case from the unevenness of its political and economic transition. But, if so much is at stake, then why is it that Beijing does not accelerate its political reforms and adopt the type of law-based, multi-party democratic system that has proven itself as an effective regulator of capitalist economies all over the world? That is a 64 million renminbi question, and one upon which there may be no consensus or answer for a long time to come. One way, however, of elucidating the issues in play is to consider the life and career of Cao Siyuan, one of China's most brilliant and dogged advocates of reform.

Cao is a short, rotund man with thick spectacles and unruly hair. His face, with its gentle folds and bunched-up cheeks, looks as if it has been moulded by laughter. And, as you get to know him, this impression is reinforced. He laughs frequently, often at his own jokes, and with differing seismic intensities. The lowest gradation is a good-natured chuckle which either peters out into conversation or rises into a more generous eruption that can escalate to the highest pitch of hilarity: a wheezing, body-reverberating guffaw. In conversation he can be lyrical or blunt, but is rarely bashful about letting his audience know of the role he has played in some of China's pivotal moments. He dramatises his speech by slipping from time to time into the third person. Devices such as 'And what do you think Cao Siyuan did next?' or 'When Cao Siyuan heard that, he . . .' are deployed as he gets closer to the point he wants to make. Yet he can also be self-effacing. Even though he spent six years working in Zhongnanhai, the exclusive compound that houses the ruling elite in central Beijing, he says his own role there never amounted to more than that of a 'seventh-grade, sesame seed-sized official'. He also enjoys poking gentle fun at his roly-poly physical appearance. After making observations such as 'in those days I was a mere slip of a thing, no more than a bag of skin and bones', he pauses mischievously to watch for his listeners' reaction. If he senses a flicker of incredulity, the reverberating laugh may follow.

In China he is not well known by his real name, but if you mention the words 'Cao Pochan', 'Bankruptcy Cao', to someone, the nods of recognition may follow. The international media, to which he sometimes makes himself available, often call him on second reference simply: 'Mr Bankruptcy'. His nickname comes from the fact that he was the architect of China's first bankruptcy law. That may not sound like much. But in the late 1980s, bankruptcy was at the cutting edge of the ideological transition from communism to capitalism. It was the Rubicon which, once crossed, rendered hollow any lingering pretence that Beijing was trying to build an economy along communist lines. Communism was all about production, not profit and loss. But bankruptcy not only recognised financial performance, it also made it the key criterion for corporate survival. Once bankruptcy had insinuated itself into the code of commerce, other expressions of capitalism were sure to follow. Companies would have to cut costs, improve productivity and put a value on their assets. The 'iron rice bowl' notion that factories existed to provide lifetime employment for the proletariat and production for the masses was doomed to dereliction.

On one of the first occasions that I met Cao, we had dinner in the St Regis Hotel with the Editor of the *Financial Times* and other colleagues from London. The St Regis is a self-styled 'six star hotel', and the restaurant we had chosen offered some of the most upscale Chinese cuisine in town. As we arrived, we were shown past a painted lacquer screen to a table in a discreet corner where

Cao, settling into his chair, called over the waitress and made an impromptu order. A few minutes later it arrived on top of a bed of ice in a boat made of woven rattan, beneath a mainsail carved out of a white radish and placed artfully around a carrot mast. Over the boat's prow sat the sculpted head of a dragon, hewn from a sizeable block of pink turnip. We all stared as the waitress lowered the boat and placed it diagonally across the centre of our table. We peered in to see what she had brought. It was Long Xia, 'dragon prawn', more commonly known as lobster. The dinner passed convivially with Cao in an ebullient mood, charming us with his wit and insights. At the end, after we bade him a fond farewell, the Editor called over the waitress again and took the bill. As he looked at it, I could not tell whether the expression that formed on his face was a grin or a grimace. 'No wonder they call him Mr Bankruptcy,' he said. The lobster we had consumed had turned out to be of Australian-reared, air-freighted, $300-a-pop variety.

During the dinner, though, Cao said something which to me, at least, was well worth the price of a lobster. I was to keep it with me throughout my seven-year reporting assignment and came to see it as a basic formula for understanding the twists and turns and ups and downs of China's political economy. 'Gaige tai kuai, jiu luan. Gaige tai man, jiu si' or 'When reform is too fast there is chaos. When reform is too slow there is stagnation.' To put it another way, it meant that without the liberalisation of controls on the economy, growth would slow and eventually stop. But when the pace of liberalisation was too fast, the rapid growth that resulted could spill over into disorder. On the face of it, this was straightforward enough, but there was an added, paradoxical twist: the legitimacy of the Communist Party sprang from both growth *and* control. Yet in order to get more of one, it had to sacrifice part of the other.

Without fast growth, Beijing has no chance of meeting its job creation targets and too few jobs could mean social instability. But surrendering administrative control to the invisible hand of the market saps the essential power that sustains a single-party state. Therefore, the Party is a reluctant reformer and, in areas where control is critical to the maintenance of its rule, it has tended to resist liberalisations that go beyond the superficial. The reluctance also means that when things are going well and the economy is riding high, reform generally decelerates only to pick up again when the tide of growth ebbs away. The waves of activity created by this interplay of government fear and covetousness define the economy's momentum. Some call it the 'business cycle' but that does not quite capture it. It is, like a lot of things in China these days, more of a mixture, a sort of a yin and yang amalgam of business and politics. And Cao, by the nature of his work as a leading advocate of reform, has found himself bound up with its undulations. Typically, he would be busiest during the cycle's troughs when the government was receptive to ideas of how it might generate growth. During the booms, however, his services were less in official demand.

His ebullience during the St Regis dinner was partly down to the fact that in 1999 China was weathering the aftermath of the Asian crisis and the government was receptive to ideas. But his mood that night was in strong contrast with the torment he had been through. His troubles had begun in 1989, the year that a boom created by the first decade of reforms overheated, kindling the grievances that fuelled anti-government demonstrations in central Beijing's Tiananmen Square. When those protests were eventually crushed by the tanks and troops of the People's Liberation Army, Cao was rounded up and thrown into jail. He had not been a leader of the disturbances or one of a number of so-called 'black hands' whom the government accused of inciting students to complain against the nepotism, corruption and despotism of the Communist Party and, later, to demand an all-out shift to Western-style democracy.

Nevertheless, he had been involved in the drama in a different way – one that reveals a tantalising missed opportunity for political reform. In addition to being the author of the bankruptcy law, Cao at that time was also a policy adviser to Zhao Ziyang, the then head of the Communist Party. Zhao was not exactly a democratiser but he was part of a minority of Chinese leaders who seemed to believe that economic and political reform were two sides of the same coin. He had suggested a number of mainly technical ways to make the bureaucracy more accountable to the people that they ruled, but before any of them could be implemented, he became embroiled in the maelstrom that would be his and Cao's undoing. He argued against using military force to quell the protests in Tiananmen Square, fielding fierce opposition from his hardline colleagues. When they prevailed and imposed military law about two weeks before the troops were called in, Zhao was put under house arrest and remained there until his death in early 2005. Cao, though, made a desperate attempt to save his boss and prevent the army crackdown.

Audaciously, he treated the institutions of the state as if they were part of a democracy. The plan was to turn the National People's Congress (NPC), the toothless legislature that is used to rubber stamp Party directives, into a political tiger. Working with Li Shuguang, another Beijing academic, he cited Article 29 of the Constitution – the statutes of which are often neglected – to argue that the imposition of martial law against a peaceful people's demonstration was in violation of the principle that the People's Liberation Army 'belongs to the people'. It was clear, Cao and Li went on, that the only way forward was for the NPC to impeach Li Peng, the Premier, for imposing martial law in the first place. Given that an impeachment of this type had never before been attempted and that the NPC had never been used to check Party power, it was surprising that Cao's initiative made any headway at all. Yet he and Li managed to collect fifty-seven signatures, all from people on the NPC's top committee, in support of impeachment. In the end, of course, Premier Li crushed the attempt to unseat him and ordered the military crackdown that began on the evening of 3 June, when Cao was also arrested. Nevertheless, if his attempt to use the NPC to impeach a Premier had succeeded, China's future might have been radically different from the one we know today.

Cao was released from jail just under one year after his arrest at a vegetable market near his office. He was freed along with another 210 people who were, according to the official Xinhua news agency, being given 'lenient treatment' but would be severely punished if they failed to repent of their 'criminal activities' and began doing 'evil' all over again.[1] In common with almost all of those arrested following the massacre, he was not charged with any crime or offered an apology when he was released. As far as he was concerned, he had acted entirely in accordance with the rights afforded him by the Constitution. Nevertheless, he kept a low profile for most of the rest of the 1990s, declining media interviews and concentrating on a new career as an adviser for his own company, the Siyuan Bankruptcy and Merger Consultancy.

So it was with some relish that, with the economy faltering in 1998 and 1999, he returned to his role as an activist. He was forthright in his opinions and sometimes mischievous in his turn of phrase. When I asked him what was meant by the term 'the collective leadership', the way that newspapers then described the pinnacle of party power, he replied: 'Collective leadership means never knowing which bottom should be spanked.' Later, he had the following to say about being critical of the government:

Often when I am making speeches, people ask me, 'Cao Siyuan, will the central government be able to accept your points of view?' I say: 'Why do you always ask whether the central government will be willing to accept them or not?' What is the central government? They are servants. They are the servants of the people. You cannot use acceptance as a standard to judge servants. For example, if at home I hire a maid to do the cooking, I do not try to do everything the maid wants. The maid should ask me what I like to eat. The relationship between citizens and public servants should not be transposed.

But in spite of his daring, he was not a dissident and if you asked him to describe his role in life, he would say:

I think that on the dramatic stage there should be different types of actor. There should be those with red faces, those with white faces, clowns, beauties, sages. In the same way, on the stage of history there should also be different roles. If you said that red faces are good, then I ask, is it good to have a whole stage full of red faces? Nobody is able to be everything, so what should Cao Siyuan be? The result of my research is that I should be a student of the people. As a student of the people, how do I define my job? I define it by making suggestions. I am a 'suggestive student of the people'. I suggested making a bankruptcy law. I suggested having people in to listen to the National People's Congress. I suggested privatisation etc. I specialise in suggestions and I don't complain. Is it that there are no complaints at the pit of my stomach? No! My whole belly is full of complaints. The problem is that complaining does not solve problems. In my articles I never slate people, never complain, I only write prescriptions. If someone is ill, I never say 'they should die, they should have died long ago'. I say 'they still can be saved' and the prescription is as follows.

As 1999 wore on with urban unemployment surging and outbreaks of social unrest proliferating nationwide, the prescription Cao had in mind was privatisation. He could see that private companies were far more dynamic than their state cousins and that they could provide the jobs the country badly needed. He could also see that the central government was reluctant to give a free rein to private enterprises because, by their nature, they represented a dilution of state control. Although the NPC had passed an amendment to the Constitution in 1998 saying that private enterprise should be regarded as a 'component part' of the economy, it left no doubt that state enterprises should remain dominant. Another indication that Beijing was ambivalent about the rise of the private sector, Jiang Zemin, the President, was travelling around the country making speeches pledging that the government would never promote the privatisation of state enterprises. Cao, meanwhile, was also travelling the country, urging the exact opposite. It was highly unlikely that their paths would cross; it is easier, as they say, to climb a tree to catch a fish than it is for an ordinary citizen to gain an audience with the General Secretary of the Communist Party.

But then, out of the blue, an opportunity presented itself. Cao was invited to speak at a forum organised by *Fortune* magazine in Shanghai. When he looked at the programme, he saw that he would be on stage in the auditorium just a few hours before Jiang himself. Prior to leaving Beijing, he called me excitedly. He told me I should be ready for some news. I asked what sort of news, but he would only say that he was going to drop a bombshell. Later, in a speech he made to overseas Chinese in New York, he described what happened at the Shanghai forum:[2]

Where do you think Cao Siyuan was when Jiang was giving his speech? [he asked]. Sitting about thirty metres away! When he finished and returned to his seat, I put books in both of my hands and waltzed over to him. Some people say the head of state is closely protected by guards, so how can you get near him? When I gave a speech at Columbia University, someone asked me if I could have been shot walking over to him. So how was it that I was able to march up to Jiang Zemin while keeping life and limb intact? Well, because when I worked in Zhongnanhai for six years, I was able to ingest deeply the code of the secret service. That code, however, I regret I am unable to share with you today.

Anyway, Jiang was just sitting there with his gaze directed forward when this fattypuff lumbers into his field of vision from the right. He turns to look and suddenly our lines of sight cross. He is staring at me and I am staring at him. I meet his gaze and walk over to face him. I discover that Jiang Zemin's eyes are glistening. Maybe he is thinking, who is this guy? I don't do the normal thing and say who I am, I just put one of my books into his hand. He sees the book title: *The Wind and Clouds of Bankruptcy* and at the bottom it says: 'Author: Cao Siyuan'.

He says: 'So you are Cao Siyuan' and I say: 'At your service.' Then I give him thirty seconds to remember how our paths once crossed by saying: 'Thank you Chairman Jiang for your generous support when you were Mayor of Shanghai and I came to do an investigation on matters related to the bankruptcy law. I have written about your support in this book on page 111.' When he heard this he was, of course, happy. A smile spread across his face and it was during his delight that I served him with the second book. The second book was *Society's Righteous Path Toward Privatisation*. He has just been on the podium saying, 'we are absolutely not doing privatisation' and here am I not only doing it but doing it right under his nose. If Jiang had thrown a wobbly and slapped the table and said, 'Take him away!' I would have been finished. But I calculated that there would be another outcome. Maybe he would not only keep his temper, but he might also think, 'Why is Cao Siyuan so audacious? Why is he calling it *Society's Righteous Path Toward Privatisation?* Maybe I should find out for myself by reading the book.'

But there was no way I was going to leave it at that; just giving the books and leaving. So I filched out a name card and gave it to him, saying 'if you need anything, call me'.

Jiang did not call, and it is not known whether Cao's bombshell had any impact on the course of privatisation. What is true, though, is that at the 16th Congress of the Communist Party in late 2002, the Constitution was amended to put private business on an equal footing with state corporations. In addition, private entrepreneurs were allowed to join the Party and a small handful were even given unprecedented invitations to attend the congress itself in the Great Hall of the People. But then, unfortunately for the cause of privatisation, and for Cao's well-being, the economy began to take off again. Growth in 2003 surged ahead and the pressure on the government to create jobs abated. The Communist Party had had to surrender considerable control to deliver the growth it needed; since 1998 it had privatised almost all of the country's urban housing stock, made redundant more than 25 million workers from state companies, allowed hundreds of thousands of state companies to free themselves from the burden of providing medical care for employees and free schooling for their children, and promulgated new freedoms allowing tens of millions of people to travel from the countryside to cities in search of work.

But since the growth spurt that followed those liberalisations kicked in, Beijing has taken the opportunity to consolidate its power. It has conspicuously failed to follow through on the 16th Party Congress promise to put private enterprises on an equal footing with state corporations. Private companies are still restricted from 'strategic sectors', such as retail banking, investment banking, basic telecom services, newspapers, television, publishing, oil and gas extraction, power generation, railways, ports and petrochemicals. In addition, private companies still find it difficult to get permission to list on the stock market, and only 40 out of the 1,600 listed companies are private. They also run into obstacles securing financing from an overwhelmingly state-run banking system, receiving as little as 10 per cent of total bank loans annually. As the Harvard University academic Yasheng Huang notes, private companies, far from being accorded equal

184

status with their state brethren, are actually treated worse than foreign companies.[3] The latest example of this was in the sale of several multi-billion dollar equity stakes in state banks in 2005. Foreign financial institutions have shelled out more than $20 billion to buy the various minority stakes on offer, but private Chinese company participation has been barred.

In fact, the first two years of the tenure of Hu Jintao, who took over from Jiang Zemin as Party chief in late 2002, have been marked by a distinct emphasis on the primacy of large, efficient state-owned companies. Corporations such as the oil giants Petro-China, Sinopec and CNOOC, all of which are rising up the rankings of the world's largest companies, are considered models of state capitalism. But as Hu and his administration promote the interests of large state firms, the non-state reform agenda has slipped and Cao's situation has also taken a turn for the worst. Following a conference he organised in the eastern seaboard port city of Qingdao in mid 2003, during which he called for a major overhaul of the Constitution, his phone has been tapped, he has been followed, banned from public speeches and his clients have been warned away from him.

These days, he is back living the low-profile type of life that he remembers from the last boom in the mid 1990s. He maintains contact with his circle of friends, finds work here and there and continues to write essays and books. But there is at least one difference between now and then: technology has allowed him a wider audience for the short poems that he writes in a classical meter and sends out from his mobile phone. Those that I have received have been elegantly written and melancholy. Many allude to unappreciated service, a theme that is almost as old as China itself. One recalled Qu Yuan, a brilliant and upright adviser to an emperor in ancient times who hung himself after he could not be loyal to his monarch and to the interests of his country at the same time. Another one, received at the time of the mid-autumn festival, when Chinese admire the moon and think existential thoughts, went like this:

Year after year, when the autumn wind picks up,
We say goodbye to summer and welcome the frost,

If you plant melon, melons grow. Beans yield beans.
Sweet or bitter, who can dictate which?
Eating melon, gazing at the moon,
The world is multipolar yet singular, love is universal yet in one
  heart.

But the last line, read another way, could also have meant 'The world is multipolar yet singular, charity resides with the central government'.

The main problem with China's political system is that it does not permit the checks and balances necessary to supervise and regulate a capitalist economy in an efficient manner. In a democracy, this is achieved by configuring the system so that each organ of government and each economic entity is regulated or overseen by another external and independent body. The whole edifice is then supervised by the will of the voting public. But a Communist political system is engineered to venerate and sustain a single source of authority. Thus, the Chinese Communist Party is officially held to reside above everything, including the law. There are no direct, public elections for Party posts (some experimental village-level elections that have been permitted are for the non-Party post of village chief), so there is no mechanism to allow political renewal through a popular mandate. Each level of the bureaucracy reports to and takes orders from officials on the next rung up, creating a giant pyramidal structure in which the chain of command is mostly vertical. No organisation engaged in governance is permitted to exist independently of the Party. Even non-governmental organisations, of which there are an increasing number, are supposed to maintain an affiliation with a Party body and to support its work. Religions, too, are free to practise as long as they accept – at least nominally – that the Party, which is atheist, is a higher authority than their own spiritual leader.

Such a system does not lend itself to supervision from external forces because it recognises no authority greater than its own. That does not matter in a centrally planned economy, where the Party is master of all it surveys. But it is far from adequate in a capitalist system animated by the antagonism of competition. It has become clear in recent years that the Party is fully aware of this mismatch and has poured enormous energy into attempting to create the impossible: a system of self-regulation in politics, law and the economy under which all parties are equal but the Party is more equal than the others.

The waste generated by this grand project of political engineering is evident in many places, but nowhere is it more pronounced than in the most democratic of all capitalist institutions, the stock market. In the West, stock markets function by allowing the investor public to supervise the actions of corporate decision makers. If investors do not like the strategy of a CEO, they can 'vote' against it by selling their shares. But in China the system has been turned on its head, so that the bosses of listed companies do not have to suffer the indignity of listening to the opinions of minority shareholders. In fact, every aspect of the system has been designed to extract a maximum of public money while surrendering a minimum of accountability. Companies typically float less than one-third of their share capital, so that even if minority shareholders banded together, they would still be unable to influence the decisions of the board. Lax disclosure rules mean that listed companies are required to divulge a bare minimum of financial information, and even that, it has transpired, is often false. The decision as to which companies may list is made not on the basis of financial health but by Party officials, with the predictable result that only a small minority of listed companies are private and the rest are the corporate offspring of the Party and the state.

With so many of the state's interests at stake, the market regulator, the China Securities and Regulatory Commission (CSRC), does not even pretend to be independent. Shang Fulin, the CSRC boss, takes his orders from a 'leading group' of Party officials who dictate what should happen in the financial sector. He regularly makes public statements about how he is taking steps to boost share prices and drive the index upward. And when prices edge down, other Party branches can be called upon to join a chorus of bulls. The starkest example of this was in 1999 when, in the aftermath of the Asian financial typhoon, the *People's Daily*, the official mouthpiece of the Party, tried to lift a soggy market by declaring on its front page that securities markets were facing 'uncommon opportunities for development' and that the Party had 'firm confidence' on behalf of investors.[4]

But as the years have passed, the costs to China from its regulatory laxity have been expressed in a legion of corporate corruption scandals. One of these involved a department store and distribution company based in Zhengzhou, the provincial capital of Henan, China's largest province. The company, Zhengzhou Baiwen,[5] was run by Li Fuqian, a former soldier who had started in the shop as a counter assistant in the mid 1970s after leaving the army. In those days, that was a dream job because people who worked in shops had access to rationed commodities before anyone else. Baiwen was owned by the Zhengzhou branch of the Communist Party, so it was naturally one of the first chosen for listing, even though it did not meet a requirement that it had to be profitable. A small lie was required, but Li and his associates decided to tell a big one – they claimed that the company's profits had increased by thirty-six-fold in the ten years before its flotation in 1996. When those numbers were announced, the investing public took note, and Baiwen's share price soared.

In 1997, the company was named a 'red flag', a rare official distinction that denoted it was a model from which others should learn. Li was also selected as a 'model worker' at a Party ceremony in Beijing and when he got home, he manoeuvred himself into the posts of chairman and Party secretary of Baiwen in addition to the position of president that he already held. From then on, he made all decisions single-handedly. A few months after that, he issued the order that the company should attain 'double 8' – reaching 8 billion renminbi in sales and 80 million in profits, even though he knew these figures bore no relation to the company's actual performance. They were in fact double the numbers the company was then publicly announcing, and those were already wild exaggerations. In reality, Baiwen was losing millions. But on the strength of the falsified figures, it managed to raise another large dollop from the stock market, which Li poured into a dizzying array of schemes run by people to whom he owed political debts.

When the company toppled, Li was fined and thrown in jail. But the most extraordinary passage in the story was yet to come. The

CSRC, or the shadowy Party officials from which it takes its orders, decided that even though Baiwen was insolvent several times over, it should not be declared bankrupt or have its stock market listing revoked. The government, which still owned most of Baiwen's shares, ordered the state to arrange a bailout and, after some restructuring, the company just carried on trading.

But the malignancy that Baiwen represented has spread, and the stock market has been rocked by one scandal after another. In 2001, the CSRC found forty instances of companies faking their results, including one called Yinguangxia which fabricated almost $100 million in profits.[6] Around the same time, several stock price manipulation scandals were also making headlines. The worst involved Yorkpoint, a science and technology company based in the southern boomtown of Shenzhen, which managed to enlist the help of around 120 financial institutions, mostly securities companies, in twenty provinces and municipalities to spend more than half a billion US dollars to push up the company's share price before taking profits and letting it crash.[7] In 2004, one of China's most respected companies, the car-parts-to-tomato-ketchup conglomerate D'Long, was also caught in fraudulent dealings worth an estimated $3.6 billion.[8] Later in the same year, Huayin Trust and Dalian Securities were dragged down after it came to light that the chairman of both companies had engaged in a $3.2 billion fraud.[9] Southern Securities, an industry pioneer with impeccable connections to the Communist Party, also succumbed in a $2.4 billion scandal that mainly involved executive theft.[10] In 2005, the chairman and chief financial officer at Yili Corp, a dairy company of nationwide renown, were arrested on suspicion of embezzling $50 million.

Similar problems, and others, afflict the banking sector and there, too, the lack of regulatory independence is a root cause. The 'big four' banks, which control more than half of the country's deposits and loans, are all owned by the state. Their presidents dress like bankers and talk like bankers, but they are, in fact, high-ranking Party officials who are appointed to their posts by the Party's personnel department. Having served their term, they are rotated back to positions at the top of the People's Bank of China, the central bank. While in their jobs at the 'big four', the presidents all insist that their banks are 'commercial'. What they mean is that the decisions the banks take on whether to lend money to companies are based solely on the judgement of whether that company will be able to repay its debts plus interest. Following several years of reform, this claim may be more true than it used to be, but the reality is still that if an important state company needs a loan, or a big state project needs funding, the 'big four' can be counted on to oblige, regardless of commercial considerations. In return, they can feel secure in the knowledge that they will never be allowed to fail, no matter how many bad debts pile up on their balance sheets. The central bank, which regulates the banking industry alongside the recently established China Banking Regulatory Commission, has a track record of bailing out the 'big four' every time they need it.

The cost to China of this system shows up in the money that the central bank has spent on bailing out the 'big four' and other financial institutions. If the various cash infusions and bad debt relief for the state banks over the last five years are added together, it transpires that China has allocated nearly $250 billion to clean up its banking system. And the task is far from over. Standard and Poor's,[11] the rating agency, estimates that it may cost the government another $190 billion to clean up the balance sheets of the two worst-performing members of the 'big four', the Industrial and Commercial Bank of China and the Agricultural Bank. Further money will be needed to rehabilitate the tens of thousands of Rural Credit Co-operatives, which are thought to be mostly insolvent, and scores of City Commerical Banks, another weak pillar in the financial architecture. It is quite possible, then, that the total bill for returning the financial system to health could come to over $500 billion – or, to put it another way, enough money to build twenty 'Three Gorges' hydropower dams across the Yangtze River. Even after that money is spent, the governance deficiencies that contributed to the bad debt problem in the first place may remain. The probability is that until state banks are divorced from government influence and subjected to the discipline of knowing they may fail, the incidence of reckless, corrupt and state-guided lending may continue.

In the natural environment, too, similar shortcomings are evident. According to Pan Yue, the outspoken deputy head of the State Environmental Protection Agency (SEPA), the degradation of the environment is exacerbated by the absence of an independent system of supervision. Local authorities, all too often, own the companies that they regulate and are therefore often unwilling to make them abide by costly environmental safeguards. Meanwhile, the local branches of SEPA are dependent on funding from local authorities, so they have little power to enforce any measure that is unpopular with their mayor's office or, for that matter, with local state companies that may have strong links to the mayor's office.

The legal system is also beset by channel conflicts. The funding of local law courts and the appointment of judges and other legal officials is performed by local governments, so the mayor's office can be confident that any ruling it deems important will not go against its interests. Some courts are more compliant than others; a few in Beijing, Shanghai and other large cities are staffed by highly trained legal officers and are relatively independent, but most provincial and municipal systems lack legally trained staff. When asked, most local officials will claim that their courts are independent and impartial, but sometimes this façade slips. The vice-mayor of Wuhu, the second city in Anhui province famous for the local car company, Chery, which is owned by the mayor's office, once told me that if Volkswagen was worried that Chery might have violated its intellectual property rights, then they were welcome to come to Wuhu to settle the issue in court. 'Let's see who wins,' said the vice-mayor. Volkswagen decided, in the end, that it would not pursue the issue through the courts.

In other places, such as the northeastern city of Shenyang, the legal system has at times suffered a near total breakdown. In 2001, it transpired that the Shenyang procurator's office, a key legal agency, was in thrall to a local mafia boss called Liu Yong who swaggered about town shooting rival gang leaders with his pistol, ordering the local police force to torture people who disobeyed him and engaging in corrupt commercial schemes with the mayor, the taxation bureau and several other parts of the local government. Liu even used his connections to get himself a post in the local branch of the National People's Congress, before he, the mayor and several others were arrested and thrown into jail.[12]

It is difficult to put a figure on how much corruption has cost China over the years. But there is no doubt that the bending of rules and massaging of accounts that helped to facilitate economic activity in the early stages of the reform era no longer describes the problem. The abuse of power has now become a debilitating, multi-billion dollar annual scam that is eroding the efficiency of almost every organ of the Party and state. The Organisation for Economic Co-operation and Development, a grouping of wealthy nations, estimated in a report that in 2004 corruption accounted for between 3 and 5 per cent of that year's £1.4 trillion in gross domestic product, or between $50 and $84 billion. Such estimates are necessarily based on imperfect data, and may well be conservative. Indeed, an audit of government accounts by Li Jinhua, the auditor-general, in 2004 suggested that corruption is uniformly present throughout the government – all of the thirty-eight central government ministries and organisations that he investigated were discovered to be cooking their books or using their influence to extract illegal fees.[13] Another audit in the southern province of Guangdong, one of the country's most economically advanced areas, showed a similarly high incidence of malfeasance. It found that no fewer than 400 officials were corrupt. Jiang Zemin, the former President and Party boss, said towards the end of his term in office that official corruption had become so injurious that it was jeopardising 'the very existence of the Party and the state'.

If that is the case, then why does the Party decline to launch the political reforms necessary to save itself? And why does it continue to preside over a system of governance that is inadequate in serving its burgeoning, increasingly sophisticated economy? There is unlikely to be a single answer. One part of the issue might be that the economic reforms of the past twenty-seven years have generated so much wealth that Beijing feels able to bankroll its systemic inefficiencies. Another could be that, contrary to the aura of confidence that it strives to project, the Party is so neurotic about the erosion of its executive power that it is in no mood for political liberalisation. But, in my view, the most powerful inhibitor of political reform is corruption itself. Local governments in many parts of the country have been hijacked by special interest syndicates that typically consist of government officials and the most influential among local business leaders. These secret syndicates exist to enrich their members, often at the expense of the public, and they are therefore implacably opposed to any reform that could unravel the web of relationships that boost their bank balances.

There is no research on how prevalent these syndicates may be, but a surge in the number of public protests directed at local governments suggests a sharp deterioration in the problem. The number of so-called 'mass incidents', the Ministry of Public Security's catch-all term for sit-ins, strikes, group petitions, rallies, demonstrations, marches, traffic-blocking, building seizures and other forms of unrest, reached 74,000 in 2004, an all-time high, and involved 3.7 million individuals. In 1994, by comparison, there were about 10,000 such incidents with just 730,000 participants.[14] In 2005, the numbers continued to rise. Although none have escalated into co-ordinated, nationwide movements, the sharp increase in localised protests shows that material enrichment alone does not guarantee greater public contentment. In fact, the outbreaks of 'mass incidents' have grown in recent years at roughly the same rate as the economy; that is to say, around 9 per cent. In the overwhelming majority of cases, the flare-ups have been sparked by the arbitrary behaviour of local government officials who seize land and other assets from ordinary citizens but offer little or no compensation.

There are any number of case studies that demonstrate how local officials abuse their administrative powers to enrich themselves and their cronies. But in 2003, I began to follow a saga that was played out in the wilds of the northern province of Shaanxi, in towns and villages on the dusty Loess plateau, but nevertheless held relevance for the outside world. That is because if incidents such as this come to define the modus operandi of local Chinese governments, then the chances of Beijing being able to bring its political economy into line with international norms may be slim.

The first time I met Feng Bingxian was on one of those rare summer days in Beijing when the hills beyond the western suburbs were visible from Tiananmen Square beneath a fathomless blue sky. I found him sitting in the coffee lounge of the VIP section of the Beijing Hotel, next to the banquet hall where Mao had once hosted Nikita Khrushchev, the former Soviet leader. He was a thin, wiry man with a cheerful, animated face and he sat, dressed all in black, behind a glass of kiwi juice. Next to the juice was a Nokia mobile telephone and the key to a suite costing more than $100 a night.

He had called me to say that he was petitioning the government to take action against the wrongs that he had suffered. Foreign journalists regularly received such calls and were frequently reluctant to follow them up because they usually led to hurried, furtive encounters with desperate people in back alleys near the premises of the State Petitions Office, a holdover from imperial times when people of conscience wrote memorials to a supposedly benevolent emperor. It was not the inconvenience of such assignments that made them unpopular, but their hopelessness. Only two in one thousand petitions actually led to a resolution and in most cases petitioners would be kept waiting for years for any news of how their complaint was being processed. But Feng, with his VIP suite and his mobile phone, was clearly a different sort of activist.

He was the representative of 10,000 or so private investors in about 6,000 small oil wells that had been confiscated without compensation by the authorities in fifteen counties in Shaanxi. The investors were a varied bunch. Some were wealthy entrepreneurs but the majority were peasant farmers who coaxed a living out of the inhospitable Yellow Earth Plateau, an eroded buffer that protects the central plains from the advancing sands of the Gobi Desert. Many of the farmer-investors had sold their land and furniture to raise money for prospecting. After losing their wells, their income had dried up and some had turned to loan sharks to fund their children's schooling. The aim of their collective petition was to implore the central government to intervene on their behalf and see that their wells were returned.

Disputes between individuals and local mandarins are common throughout the country, but in some ways this one was different. It was almost certainly the biggest concerted challenge by private-sector interests against their local authorities since private enterprise was first permitted in the early 1980s. To me, that made it an important story. It was a test of the tidy theory that sooner or later single-party politics would bump up against an increasingly free-market economy and when that happened, the Party would have to yield. Thus the Shaanxi oil well dispute seemed a manifestation of a crucial stage in the country's political evolution.

Feng was blunt about where I fitted in to his plans. He had considered appealing to the law courts in Shaanxi but dropped the idea because, as everyone knew, the judges were appointed and paid by the very officials whom the oil well investors wanted to sue. He had tried the State Petitions Office, but not yet to any avail. The local media had found his story too risky to run. So, he said with a worn smile, that left us, the foreign press. There was a chance that our articles, translated, would make it into the 'Big Reference', a confidential digest of foreign reports that is circulated only to top cadres. If they saw it, they might be sympathetic, he said.

I said that to write the story I needed to quote him by name and to get the Shaanxi government's version of events. After some persuasion, he agreed to let me use his name. A few days after my article was printed, he received an unexpected, late-evening knock at his hotel room door. Three men, all in black, told him that they were there to take him to a senior official who was interested to hear his case. The elevator that he took to the lobby was made of glass and ran down one side of the hotel's cavernous atrium. One of the men stood by the door, the other two close to Feng, who could see the lobby-level coffee lounge coming to meet him. Waitresses were wiping down the tables and, along the far wall, a fountain made of alabaster animal statues had fallen silent, turned off for the night.

But the elevator did not stop at the lobby. It went on to the basement car park, where Feng was bundled into the back of an official car and driven for more than twenty hours to Yulin City, northern Shaanxi. Without being charged, he was put in jail. At first his interrogators quizzed him about his contacts with a *Financial Times* journalist and then switched to investigating the tax returns from his oil well business. Shortly after his detention, his son called me and, scrupulously polite, asked if there was anything I could do to help. Sheepishly, I said there was not.

Almost a year later we met again in Beijing and, far from blaming me for the consequences of our first encounter, Feng punctuated his account of the abduction, detention and interrogation with bursts of laughter. He had been released after a month or so in jail on the condition that he would cease his activism. Since then he had lived an itinerant life, sleeping in the apartments of friends or on the office sofas of colleagues, fearful that the police would find him. But there was no question of him giving up. 'This used to be about oil wells. Now it is about our rights. This used to be a problem. Now it is a cause,' he told me.

Feng's new strategy was to lobby. He and a growing group of associates had decided to try to win the support of the central government in Beijing by moral suasion and behind-the-scenes activism. Achieving their aim would require turning Beijing against the local authorities in northern Shaanxi, an ambitious scheme that, in essence, amounted to asking the Communist Party to endorse the interests of private entrepreneurs over the actions of the state or, at least, one branch of it. But some of the activists felt they at least had a chance. One activist, Li Zhiying, put it this way: 'They say that the arm is unable to twist the leg. That is true. But I ask you, who is the arm and who is the leg?'

Indeed, not all the odds were stacked against the investors. The facts of the case seemed to favour them: in 1994 the oil ministry and the China National Petroleum Corporation (CNPC), the state-owned oil giant, agreed to turn over the prospecting and development rights for 1,080 square kilometres of territory in northern Shaanxi to the local authorities. This was an unusual step because oil was an asset over which the state had monopoly ownership. Nevertheless, the agreement was official and public and, in any case, CNPC had searched for oilfields in northern Shaanxi but found nothing tempting there.

With little delay, local authorities put the prospecting rights up for sale at around $10,000 for each square kilometre block. Initially investors were hesitant but after the first gushers spouted, the trickle of farmers trailing across the Loess plateau to buy drilling licences became a flow. 'Nodding donkey' derricks appeared on barren hillsides, their rhythmic pumping exerting a hypnotic pull on would-be wildcatters. Some lost everything. But around 10,000 struck lucky and more than 1,000 small oil companies were founded to operate about 6,000 wells. Soon, one of the poorest places in all China began to get rich. Some investors built new houses. Others sent their children off to the best local boarding schools. A few bought cars and Feng, who until then had done a series of dead-end jobs in state companies, developed the habit of staying in hotel suites.

But by 1999, their luck was turning. An order from the State Economic and Trade Commission, a ministry-level body in Beijing, instructed local authorities to renationalise the private wells, placing them under the control of the Shaanxi Yanchang Oil Industry Group, a new company to be run and owned by Shaanxi provincial authorities. The key provision of this order, however, was that the transference from private to state ownership should take place by 'acquisition, merger or share purchases', according to the document. It was here that the local authorities of Yulin and Yan'an in northern Shaanxi departed from their instructions. In the first place, they did not act on the order for four years, for reasons that remain unclear. Then, when they did act in early 2003, they simply seized the wells by force.

A few years earlier, they might have got away with it. But China in 2003 looked like it might have been changing. In March, the national legislature passed a landmark amendment to the Constitution that for the first time gave private property a legal status equal to that which had long been accorded to state property. In other words, private entrepreneurs for the first time enjoyed rights of ownership and legal action that were, on paper at least, not inferior to their cosseted cousins in state-owned enterprises.

Also around this time, Hu Jintao, newly installed as the General Secretary of the Communist Party, had upgraded the long-neglected Constitution by ordering that the politburo – the pinnacle of Chinese power – should study it and govern according to its principles. The *People's Daily* reflected the emerging zeitgeist by running front-page editorials lionising the inviolability of the country's basic law.

This provided Feng and his associates with an opportunity.

They formulated a plan to turn the Shaanxi oil issue into a case study, a litmus test of the Party's fealty to its own principles. To do this he tapped into what is perhaps the most economically liberal official body in China, the All-China Federation of Industry and Commerce, a Party organisation with considerable clout. At the federation, Feng found Bao Yujun, a former deputy editor of the *People's Daily* who had also founded the All-China Society of Private Economy Research in 1993. Bao, one of the first officials to call for constitutional protection for private property, saw the Shaanxi case as a natural extension of his work. 'This is a classic case of illegal administration and the misuse of administrative power,' Bao said.

He first aired the issue for public debate at a conference he was chairing a short time later in Taizhou, an eastern seaboard city famous as a crucible of private enterprise back in the 1980s. The issue attracted so much interest that Bao agreed to chair another meeting entirely devoted to the Shaanxi case in the Great Hall of the People in Beijing, the seat of China's legislature.

The academics who attended that meeting in the summer of 2004 were a virtual Who's Who of the country's top legal and economic thinkers. On a screen by the podium where Bao sat, they were shown video footage from the Shaanxi county of Ansai revealing evicted oil well investors being brutally treated at an open-air 'public arrest meeting'. Their transgression, according to the local officials who appear on the smuggled video, was to resist the seizure of their wells. The video over, the floor was opened to debate. One academic after another castigated the Shaanxi local authorities. 'You are the people's government. Your power is given to you by the people,' said Li Chengxun, a researcher at the Chinese Academy of Social Sciences, a top state think-tank. 'The local governments of northern Shaanxi have trampled on the law. The [oil production] contracts they themselves granted to the peasants, they themselves have torn up.' Li Yiping, a professor at the People's University in Beijing, saw a broader significance. 'China's democracy, future civilisation and future rule of law relies completely on us to rise up and struggle with law-breaking governments, including at this meeting today,' he said. 'Democracy and the rule of law is a process. It is not something that the government bestows.'

For Feng, the Great Hall of the People meeting was a watershed. It had imparted moral legitimacy to his cause and cast the problem of the confiscated wells in the wider context of constitutional loyalty. Securing the backing of prominent academics was a considerable achievement – many of them were from state-run think-tanks and some were even policy advisers to the central government.

But there was another windfall, a video compact disc. The meeting's proceedings were filmed and edited into a documentary narrated by a professional who had worked for China Central Television. This was then sent to government officials in Beijing and to all levels of the Shaanxi provincial administration. 'When they got the VCD, the pressure on the Shaanxi officials was mounting,' said Li, the activist.

My attempts to get the Shaanxi government's side of the story had been almost fruitless. Telephone calls to various offices in Xian, the provincial capital, had been met with blanket denials that any dispute existed. Eventually, a director of the Shaanxi provincial news office, Zhang Lin, agreed to answer my questions. He said the wells had been recovered after state television broadcast negative news about the private oil investors. What kind of negative news? 'Various. I have forgotten,' he said. Asked if it was true that local officials were running the newly established oil companies in northern Shaanxi and benefiting materially from them, Zhang made a clear denial. 'It is impossible that officials are directly involved in business. There is a government policy to separate politics from business,' he said.

I decided to travel to the area in October to check his assertions, as well as those of Feng and his associates. The route to northern Shaanxi from Beijing goes via Yan'an, the revolutionary base of Mao and his comrades during the most gruelling years of the Communists' guerrilla war against Chiang Kai-shek's Nationalists and the invading Japanese. That era is now bathed in nostalgia for many Chinese and the hillside caves that Mao and his generals once used have become tourist attractions.

Shops near the caves sold packets of coarse grain and other manifestations of the 'Yan'an Spirit' that in Mao's time had elevated 'eating bitterness and enduring labour' into a lofty ideal.

The few customers in the shops that Saturday in October were people from Beijing and Shanghai, and deprivation for them was a distant memory. One middle-aged man swayed gently to *Nanniwan*, a famous Yan'an song that played on the shop's stereo. '. . . there are crops everywhere, everywhere cattle and sheep. The Nanniwan of the past was all barren hills, with no wisp of humanity. But today's Nanniwan is just not the same as the past.'

Six hours north of Yan'an by car is Jingbian, the county that Feng's disputed oil wells are in. As my taxi climbed through the hills, passing 'nodding donkey' derricks to the left and right, I sought insights into local concerns by reading the slogans on walls and signposts by the side of the road. 'Having One Child Is Good,' said one. 'Everybody Takes Care of Underground Cables,' read another. My driver said that, to be understood, their meaning had to be inverted. People here wanted several children because that meant more labour, he said. Telecoms cables were often dug up and sold. In Ansai county, the scene of violent confrontations between the local government and oil well investors, there was a large sign reading 'Put People First', the Hu Jintao formulation for a kinder, gentler government.

In Jingbian I went to the office of Gao Zhongcheng, concurrently the deputy mayor and general manager of the Jingbian Oil Drilling Company. Metal plaques on the gate identified the company as both a government and Communist Party concern. When I entered his office, Gao was not pleased to see me. 'What the hell are you up to?' he shouted, breaking up a meeting. I identified myself as a journalist and he said he was calling the police. I told him that I had come to get the Jingbian government's side of the story, but his irritation seemed to deepen. 'These are illegal reporting activities. The police will settle this,' he said. I was escorted down the corridor to wait in a separate room, and left alone. Open on a desk in front of me were stacks of accounting documents detailing production from the confiscated wells. The revenue of Gao's company, according to my hurried calculations, ran to millions of renminbi a day.

I was not sure what the police, when they turned up, would do with me and I tried to listen through the door to a conversation in the corridor for clues. After a while, one of Gao's assistants appeared with a cup of hot water. When the police arrived after another half-hour, the water was replaced by tea. 'Jasmine,' said the assistant as he put the cup down next to me. An hour of questions later, I was ordered to return to Yan'an by car.

At the time of writing, some three years after Feng and his fellow petitioners had started their campaign, the case had still not been resolved. There had been no court hearing and no ruling by Beijing on whether the constitutional protection extended to private property applied in this instance or not. Instead, the battle of attrition between the activists and the Shaanxi authorities dragged on and on. But fortune appeared to be on the side of the authorities. For even as they arrested Feng, Zhu the lawyer and others, only to re-release them without charges and then re-arrest them again, they were earning millions of US dollars every month from the output of the wells that they had seized. Meanwhile, the savings that Feng and the others had put aside from their now-distant days as local oil barons were dwindling fast. When they ran out of money, their quest to hold the government accountable for its crimes would become a freedom they could not afford.

NINE

A beaten-up red taxi took me home one afternoon as spring was turning to summer. The driver's accent, which tagged a lazy 'er' sound onto the end of most words, identified him as 'lao Beijing', or 'old Beijing' – a singular description. In English we differentiate between London and Londoners, and between New York and New Yorkers. But the Chinese language makes no distinction between the alleyways and courtyard houses that make up the old quarters of the national capital and the people whose families have lived in them for generations. Both are called 'old Beijing', as if long association has somehow fused one with the other. The alleys in which 'old Beijing' have traditionally lived are called 'hutong' and their layout has helped to mould the city's soul. They are long, narrow and lined sometimes with ginkgo or other broadleaf trees. In the summer, when the heat of the day is subsiding, the inhabitants of the courtyard houses carry low stools out of their front doors, place them in the shade of the trees and sit down to chat. Their conversations can be long and rambling, a Beijing speciality called 'kan da shan', or 'chatting a big mountain', in which robust views, cursing-for-the-fun-of-it and cutting-through-the-bullshit are intermingled with local gossip, old stories and political satire. Humour is never far from the surface.

Most of the alleyways in Beijing's old quarters have been bulldozed over the last decade, sweeping away hundreds of years of history. The graceful eaves of the old houses, the pomegranate trees in their carefully tended beds and the carved stones from which inhabitants in other times mounted their horses have all fallen to a modernising zeal. A city with an antique charm that rivalled Venice is preserved only in photographs. With the disappearance of its physical contours, the old town's soul resides now mainly in its human manifestation. The people of 'old Beijing' can still be seen walking to the imperial parks dedicated to the sun, earth, moon and sky to fly their kites on the light breezes that arrive in the spring and autumn. They also wander with songbirds in rattan cages or Pekinese dogs tucked under their arms to their other old haunts – places that once had some local significance but are now road intersections or the forecourts of soaring new office towers. Once in these modern surroundings they appear a little bereft, as though they have been drawn by the topography of their memories; the knowledge that the stretch of anonymous concrete beneath their feet used to be 'dragon's whisker ditch' or 'tributary rice store hutong' or the old mosque on Bull Street.

In the years that I have lived in Beijing, one of the things I have enjoyed most has been the company of such people. Thus whenever I get into a taxi and hear that the driver is 'lao Beijing', I feel a small swell of pleasure. More often than not it means I am in for a fun and interesting conversation. And so it was on this day in the late spring. My ride started with the usual mixture of cursing at other motorists, swearing at the Beijing government for letting the traffic get out of control and some general expressions of dismay at the general state of the world. But in among this banter were the things that made some 'old Beijing' taxi drivers special: snatches of poetry, four-character-phrases, fragments of ancient lore and wise old saws. Listening to the driver talk, it occurred to me that I was being treated to the linguistic equivalent of an archaeological dig. Layer after layer, the inherited wisdom of an unbroken culture was being peeled back to reveal its artefacts. In one sentence there lay buried a saying from Confucius, followed a few minutes (and 2,500 years) later by a nugget from Chairman Mao and then, a bit later than that, there were a couple of things that I could not place or date. It was not that the driver was being pretentious, only that the Chinese language is a heavy loam.

When I happened upon a particularly shiny linguistic relic, I would take out my notebook and store it away for posterity. On this day, I wrote down 'throwing a meat dumpling to hit a dog', which is how the driver spoke of the futility of protesting against the government. Then there was 'Ou duan si lian' or 'lotus broken skeins join', which described the way small viscous strands, almost invisible to the eye, join two halves of a lotus root after it has been broken in two. It describes the emotional tug that exists between estranged lovers. That one took a while for the driver to explain, and I had not yet finished writing it down when, all of a sudden, I heard the radio being turned up. It was a 'xiangsheng', a rapid-fire comic dialogue that is also part of the 'lao Beijing' lore. The driver fell silent and I craned over from the back seat so as to hear more clearly.

Although I missed some of it, I could comprehend that one comedian was asking the other to name his favourite animal. After some banter back and forth, the other comic answered that his favourites were monkeys, or 'hou' in Chinese. He then explained that he liked them because they were hairy and loud and boister-ous. In fact he liked them so much that one day, unaccountably, he found that he was missing them. So he went to the zoo to see if he could find any. But when he got there, there was not a monkey in sight. So he called out: 'hou!', 'hou!', 'hou'. But still nothing came, so he amplified the volume. 'Hou!', 'hou er!', 'hou er o!', 'houero!', 'horro!', 'hello!'. The laughter from the audience started as murmur. But when he said 'hello' again the volume of laughter grew as everybody evidently understood the implied comparison between Westerners and monkeys.

The end of my taxi ride coincided almost exactly with the punchline. The taxi driver smiled a little bashfully as he took my money and we said goodbye. I was not in the least offended; in fact I too had laughed. I had long since left behind the hurt I used to feel when my foreignness was mocked. There had been times in my student days, and occasionally later, when I had felt humiliated. Once in 1982, a few weeks after I arrived at Shandong University, campus administrators had taken my intake of foreign students to the theatre. I did not understand much of the play, but I do recall that the stock joke of the evening was that foreigners had big noses. I also remember the university running coach, a kind and dedicated man, taking me aside one day after training to explain that negroes and Caucasians tended to be better sprinters than Chinese because, it had been scientifically proven, we shared more chromosomes with apes. As the years passed, however, I accepted that some Chinese felt different from the rest of us, and that was just the way things were.

However, the monkey 'xiangsheng' put me into a pensive mood, perhaps because at the time of my taxi ride anti-Japanese demonstrations had been raging day after day in Beijing and other mainland cities. Marches against the Japanese, which were among the few public protests that the authorities sanctioned, had been a periodic feature of the political scene for decades. But these were uglier than others I had witnessed. The vitriol of the taunts, the fact that many of the protestors were still in their twenties and the twisted expressions of hatred and fury on their faces had unsettled me in a way that took me by surprise. No matter how much I tried to rationalise things, I was beset for weeks by questions that were as insistent as they were banal: 'Do they like us?', 'Are we friends?', 'Are we going to be friends?'.

Friendship. It means different things to different people. One variant describes the diplomatic relations between states. Another deals with the feelings between individuals. The first is hard work; structured and scripted down to the smallest detail. The second is spontaneous, haphazard and voluntary. But in China the boundaries between the two have been blurred by dint of a strenuous, state-sponsored drive to nurture 'friendship' between Chinese and foreign individuals as an important instrument of foreign policy. Such efforts are called 'waishi', or 'foreign affairs', the remit of which is to try to manage the way that China is seen by the outside world, not only by foreign governments but also by the public. The head of the 'waishi' system in government is China's top leader and virtually every government organisation, urban authority and state enterprise has an office designated to deal with foreign affairs. Friendship was not something that the Communist Party was willing to leave to chance.

In some ways this is not so unusual. The Soviet Union had a similar system for dealing with foreign guests. But what is, perhaps, revealing about the Chinese effort is the way that foreigners are described in the training manuals distributed to 'waishi' operatives. These books are designated as 'internal', or secret from the foreigners they are intended to help influence. However, several of them have been obtained by Anne-Marie Brady, author of *Making the Foreign Serve China*, an impressively researched recent book.[1] The rules of engagement contained in the training manuals are intricate and all-pervasive. They stress that intimacy is forbidden and that making friends with foreigners is 'work'. One phrase that keeps cropping up is 'nei wai you bie' (foreigners and Chinese are different). There are also quoted injunctions from Zhou Enlai, Mao's urbane Premier, to the effect that making 'friends' with foreign journalists required thorough research and investigation because 'waishi' workers needed to 'know your enemy and know yourself'. Adding to the sense that 'waishi' workers were somehow crossing an elemental divide, was the cover of one handbook from the mid 1990s. It showed two hands shaking. One was smooth and the other covered in thick black hair.

In the same book, a 'waishi' aficionado, Zhao Pitao, summed up the mission of foreign affairs workers: 'To make friends with foreigners is the effective way to strive for international sympathy and support. It is an important task of foreign affairs work.'[2]

One way to cultivate 'friendship', the handbooks say, is to create feelings. This can be done in a number of ways, one of which is to find things in common, or 'qiu tong'. This does not have to involve politics. It can be related to children, gardening, sports and other things. But whatever form it takes, eliciting some sense of commonality is essential in the creation of favourable feelings. 'Feelings are the response of people to objective events. They are an important motivation for human activity. In order to work on people, we first of all need to establish feelings,' says one passage in a 'waishi' book called *Zhou Enlai's Diplomatic Art*. Other ways to nurture feelings included convincing foreigners that they are special. At times, this resulted in a form of theatre. In the late 1970s and early 1980s, a favoured device was a kind of charade that involved some small item – a discarded sock, a spent razor or a pack of postcards – that had been left by a foreigner in a hotel room. Shortly after the foreigner had checked out, someone (usually a local 'waishi' official) would jump into a car and rush after the foreigner's taxi or bus, slow it down and then hand over the item to the embarrassed but thankful visitor.

Later in the 1980s, foreigners who exhibited 'friendship' would be given privileges. Mostly this involved the deployment of China's most powerful chimera: its population. The foreigner would be either charmed by the adulation of crowds or seduced by the exclusivity of a one-in-a-billion reception. Examples of the former variant in this genre included the 'spontaneous' crowd of tens of thousands that hailed Craig Barrett, the then CEO of Intel, in the southwestern city of Chengdu. They surrounded him in the streets chanting 'in-te-er, in-te-er' (Intel, Intel) until Barrett, by his own admission, began to feel like Elvis Presley.[3] Later, Intel approved the chip-packaging plant investment that Chengdu had been angling for. Edgar Bronfman, the then sixty-eight-year-old chairman of Seagram Co., had a similar experience in a remote village by the Yangtze River in 1998. His drinks company had promised to invest in a $55 million orange orchard that would help transform the local economy. When he arrived off a five-storey cruise ship that took him downriver, he saw thousands of peasant farmers thronging the hillsides, in the streets and waving from the rooftops as his car passed. The feelings engendered in Bronfman were so strong that when Seagram was later bought by Vivendi, a media company, he insisted that the orange orchard be kept as a special unit, even though it was about as far from the core business as can be imagined.

Sometimes it is exclusivity rather than popular adulation that is employed. The foreigner can see the multitudes thronging about him as he is ferried around town in a limo with a police escort, but is kept discrete from the hoi-polloi in the manner of a mandarin in a sedan chair. More rarefied gradations of exclusivity are reserved for people like Rupert Murdoch, the magnate who controls News Corporation, the media group. During the years he has been trying to crack the China market, he has gained access to most of the inner sanctums of Communist power. He has had dinner with the most powerful men in the country inside Zhongnanhai, which is guarded just as fiercely as the old, imperial Forbidden City ever was. He has also enjoyed the virtually unique privilege of addressing a lecture hall full of future leaders in the Central Party School. The theme of his speech – the efficacy of an open media – contrasted neatly with the fact that the school is strictly off-limits for both Chinese and foreigners unless they have secured prior approval.

Yet the privileges granted, the warmth, the closeness and respect that are simulated are all calculated to achieve utilitarian aims. That these 'friendships' are nothing more than temporary arrangements for mutual benefit is evident in example after example. Yet no case is clearer than that of Edgar Snow, an American journalist and author who became acquainted with Mao when the future Chairman was the leader of a guerrilla force based in Shaanxi. The following passage, recorded in Snow's unpublished diaries, shows just how powerful the 'waishi' principle of 'creating feelings' by making foreigners feel special can be. It describes the arrival after an arduous journey of Snow and George Hatem, a Lebanese doctor who was also to become a firm 'friend of China', at the Communist's revolutionary base.

The bands and troops fell behind us and marched up the main street to the accompaniment of slogans shouting, 'Welcome American comrades! Hurrah for the Chinese comrades! Hurrah for the world revolution!' etc and posters and banners of welcome decorated the walls of the town, some written in English, some in Latin-hua and many in Chinese. It was the first time I had been greeted by the entire cabinet of a government, the first time a whole city had been turned out to welcome me. The effect pronounced on me was highly emotional. Had I been called up to make any kind of speech I would have been unable to do so.[5]

Snow was to become China's most famous post-revolutionary friend. His book *Red Star over China* was to become a best-seller and Mao, who called him 'friend Snow', had him stand beside him on top of Tiananmen Gate on national day. But it was always inevitable that the time for a payback would come. When it did, Beijing took its payment in the most valuable currency that a journalist has to offer: his credibility. Unlike many other 'friends of China', Snow lived in the US. But he was given a special invitation to come back in 1960, when China was in the midst of the famine caused by Mao's industrialisation policies. Beijing hoped that the man who had done more to further the image of the Communists in the eyes of foreigners than anyone else would return to write another book supporting the regime. They wanted him to reinforce their claims that there was no trace of famine in China and that rumours of mass starvation in the media were rubbish. He was escorted around the country by George Hatem who had stayed on in Beijing after the revolution as part of a coterie of professional 'friends of China'. When Snow's book, *The Other Side of the River, Red China Today*, came out, it contained the whitewash the Chinese were looking for. Snow declared that he saw no starving people in China though 'isolated instances' of starvation may exist and considerable malnutrition was undoubted. 'Mass starvation? No,' he said. In fact, an estimated 30 million were dying of hunger.

The phenomenon of 'waishi' friendships is interesting on different levels. It can be looked upon as an aspect of public diplomacy, or as an exercise in social psychology. But I have found it absorbing for what it suggests about the Chinese government's attitude towards the outside world. Why was it that the state felt the need to steer personal friendships, and why did Beijing wish to discourage real friendships based on genuine feelings? Perhaps it had something to do with the 'patriotic education' that Chinese schoolchildren are taught and the anti-foreign propaganda that sometimes surfaces in state newspapers. In both cases, the foreigners portrayed were not people who were friendly to China. Rather, it was as Chairman Mao said on top of Tiananmen Gate as he declared the founding of the People's Republic on 1 October 1949: 'The Chinese have always been a great, courageous and industrious nation; it is only in modern times that they have fallen behind. And that was due entirely to oppression and exploitation by foreign imperialism and domestic reactionary governments . . . Ours will no longer be a nation subject to insult and humiliation. We have stood up.'

Over the last decade or more, Beijing has allowed the Chinese much greater freedom to make real friendships with foreigners and, of course, the personal bonds formed are as intimate, trusting and loyal as anywhere else on earth. Yet the state continues to try to use its people to contrive an image of China in foreign minds. The most recent example of this is a new set of handbooks published by the state to teach people how to make a good impression on foreigners when the Olympic Games are hosted in Beijing in 2008. The books urge scrupulous politeness, high standards of personal hygiene and the creation of 'warmth' towards visitors. To some extent, however, this is all an artifice. The state's real view of foreigners has not changed. Schoolchildren are still taught that the 109 years prior to the 1949 revolution were characterised by the treachery of a cabal of Western and Western-orientated countries – Russia, Great Britain, France, Germany, Japan and the United States – which attacked the old Chinese empire and seized hundreds of square miles of territory.[6] They forced the government to sign unequal treaties, resorted to gunboat diplomacy, fought two Opium Wars with the aim of peddling drugs, burned imperial palaces, looted priceless treasures and humiliated Chinese people. All of this, in fact, is true. But what is lacking in the textbooks, or in the stream of newspaper articles and television programmes on the same issue, is any sustained attempt to distinguish between historical crimes and current realities. Every schoolchild has to memorise passages of history in which Japanese are described as 'devils' and portrayed as evil. Elementary school students learn that the first among ten 'must-know' historical facts is that Communist China was founded on 'one hundred years of Chinese people opposing foreign aggression'.[7]

There is little official attempt to breed a spirit of reconciliation or forgiveness. As demonstrators outside the Japanese embassy in the late spring screamed 'devils', 'Japanese dwarfs', 'dogs' and other epithets, there was no move by the authorities to calm them down, or to educate them about all the aid and investment with which the Japanese government and companies have provided China over the last two and a half decades. There was no suggestion from Beijing that the Japanese people of today may be different in their attitudes to the soldiers of the Imperial Army that swept through China before and during World War Two. In fact, at times it appears that the government has nurtured nationalism into so potent a force that it is in danger of losing control of it. A senior official once told me that Beijing had no option but to allow days of violence by rock-throwing mobs outside the US and British embassies in 1999 after the Chinese embassy in Belgrade was bombed by NATO forces. When I asked him why, he said: 'Because we did not want to be called Li Hongzhang,' naming the arch-traitor of the Qing dynasty who is universally reviled for signing so-called 'unequal treaties' with foreign powers.

Issues of friendship and nationalism are difficult to pin down and describe. You may even feel foolish for posing unanswerable questions such as 'do they like us?'. Yet, in some way, such enquiries are the most important of all. History shows that the rise of great powers creates tensions, dislocations and antagonism among the pre-existing hierarchy of nations. The causes of the Great War had a lot to do with the rise of an assertive Germany, and the nationalism of a resurgent Japan did much to precipitate the Far Eastern theatre of World War Two. It is true that fostering warmth between peoples may not, ultimately, be sufficient to prevent outbreaks of violence between states, but it can inhibit the escalation of peacetime competition into outright hostility. And that could be crucial for China and the West, because the competition that is already roiling commercial and diplomatic relations is of a powerful nature and is set to intensify.

But before getting into that, some balance is required. It must be said that from a global perspective, China's emergence is of enormous economic benefit. The value created by the release of 400 million people from poverty, the migration of over 120 million from farms where they perhaps raised chickens to factories where they churn out electronics, the quantum leap in educational standards for tens of millions of children, the construction of a first world infrastructure, the growth of over forty cities with populations of over one million, the commercialisation of housing and the vaulting progress up the technology ladder have helped unleash one of the greatest ever surges in general prosperity. The prime beneficiary of this has been China itself, but the mobilisation of wealth on such a scale is necessarily, in aggregate terms, lifting the fortunes of the planet. Some specific advantages are already evident. Beijing's towering pile of foreign currency reserves, which in late 2005 stood at over $710 billion, has been used to a large extent to buy US Treasury bonds. Not only has that helped the American government to finance public spending and pay for the war in Iraq, but it has also assisted in keeping interest rates low. The depressed level of US interest rates has, in its turn, set a standard for the world and led to a property boom in most developed countries. At the same time, the manufacture of ever cheaper products such as those on sale in Yiwu has meant that people's purchasing power has strengthened.

Regionally, however, the benefits are unevenly spread. Generally, the countries that have gained most are those that are rich in energy and other resources but do little in the way of manufacturing. Africa has seen particular advantages. Trade between China and the countries on the African continent has tripled in the last three years and helped power a boom that was expected to carry African growth in 2005 to its highest level in thirty years.[8] In Asia, too, the picture is generally positive. Trade with the ten member nations of the Association of Southeast Asian Nations was expected to exceed $130 billion in 2005,[9] up by about a third over one year earlier. In northern Asia, things have been equally vibrant, with South Korea and Japan now both counting China as their largest trade partner. Australia has been a clear winner, exporting iron ore, alumina, natural gas and a host of other resources and commodities. In Latin America, the picture is more mixed, with a surge in commodity and resources trade offset somewhat by the impact of bruising competition with the manufacturing industries of Mexico and Brazil.

But Europe and America, as this book has discussed, have had a much more turbulent time. And, because of the way that global power is distributed, it is here that a key challenge to China's future may reside. With trade amounting to more than two-thirds of the size of China's economy (compared to around a quarter for other large economies), Beijing is clearly vulnerable to the protectionism that might follow a removal of the West's goodwill. Many of the achievements of the last twenty-seven years might not have been possible without the infusions of overseas capital, expertise, technology and the access to foreign markets. But America and Europe, in large part due to homegrown deficiencies, are finding it increasingly tough to identify a net advantage from their engagement with China. A key question for the future, therefore, is not so much how China's rise will affect the world but to what extent the world will *allow* China to continue its ascent. While a general shutdown in trade would have a catastrophic impact on the global economy and is therefore unlikely, even a partial pruning of commercial links or a gradual upsurge in Western protectionism towards China would have profound effects on the world's well-being and create tensions that could spill over into other areas. From an economic perspective, such an outcome would be irrational because a curtailment of trade hurts the protected as much as those they are seeking protection against. But such decisions rarely come down to dispassionate economic analysis; they turn instead on the perceptions of electorates – people such as those in Rockford, Illinois or Prato in Tuscany or a thousand other places reeling from China's manufacturing might. And therein lies the rub.

My (admittedly unscientific) impression is that Americans, and to a lesser extent Europeans, do not generally credit the Chinese for the improvements that they have brought to their lives. As a small indicator of this theory, I stood outside Wal-Mart in Rockford asking shoppers if they felt like saying 'thank you' to Chinese workers for reducing the price of their shopping. I got plenty of double takes, a few strange looks and one man turned on his heel and walked in the opposite direction. But only one or two people had a couple of words of gratitude. I suspect that if I had gone to a mortgage lender and asked home-buyers if they felt good about China buying US Treasuries, thereby helping to keep interest rates low, the reaction might have been even more muted. The point, without being flippant, is that a lot of the 'good' that China does to the economies of the US and the EU is less visible than the blame it attracts for its deleterious impact on jobs. Thus, if a politician runs for office promising to prevent the outsourcing of jobs under 'unfair' trade conditions to a Communist behemoth that fails to uphold intellectual property rights, fixes its currency's exchange rate and exploits its own workers, he can be virtually assured of tapping into a ready-made, populist agenda. By contrast, a case built on the accurate but more nebulous argument that free trade benefits those who engage in it may not achieve the same pulling power.

China is peculiarly vulnerable here. The shortcomings in its systems of governance mean that it finds it tough to respond to such criticisms. It cannot stamp out piracy, for example, because many of the abuses take place with the connivance of disobedient local governments. It cannot allow independent trade unions to be formed because they might pose an intolerable challenge to the Party's authority. Neither does it have much leeway to allow free fluctuation of the currency, because even a modest appreciation could wipe out the profit margins of manufacturers who have yet to build up their brands. And as for being a Communist behemoth, well, that is difficult for Beijing to address because although it is no longer Communist, it is still ruled by the Communist Party. All of this points to an uncomfortable paradox: that China owes its emergence in large part to the free-trade system created by America since the war, but in many ways it is still not a creature of that system. In several aspects, its economy, political system, culture, military posture and values are different from most of the other nations that have reached maturity under the Pax Americana.

In the past, this may not have mattered much. China's differences with the West have not caused the West to turn away from China during the last two and a half decades (with the exception of a brief period after the Tiananmen massacre in 1989), so why should they start to make a difference now. The answer to that question is linked to early 2004 when the manhole covers were disappearing from drains all over the world to feed the churning hunger of Asia's rising giant for scrap steel. At that time, a Rubicon was crossed. China's future was destined to be different from its past. Even though the central government did not control the nation's appetite, it had no option but to do everything in its power to satisfy it. Failing to do so could have precipitated panic or a sudden economic collapse of the sort that could shake the timbers of Party authority. Whatever else happened, China had to be fed.

A new era in international relations dawned, one defined by the geopolitics of scarcity.[10] Greater and greater competition, both commercial and political, began to set one country against another in pursuit of finite resources and energy. As recently as five years ago, Beijing's leaders hardly had to worry about where and how their companies would secure supplies of oil, gas and a host of traded commodities and resources. In those days, the country's demand, though significant, was relatively easily accommodated on world markets. But now it is the second-largest importer of oil in the world after the US. Its imports of aluminium, nickel, copper and iron ore have risen from an average 7 per cent of world demand in 1990 to a predicted 40 per cent by the end of this decade.[11] Beijing has therefore become anxious in case supplies of crucial inputs run out or are diverted to other countries, thus threatening the growth that produces the 24 million new jobs it must create every year. Thus scarcity, or finding ways to alleviate it, has in a few short years leapt up Beijing's agenda to become the key motivator of foreign and domestic policies.

The imperative to tend to its cravings has brought China more and more into strategic and diplomatic conflict with the US. Because it has no slack in the decisions of where to sate itself, Beijing has had to strike deals for access to resources as they have become available, wherever they have been.[12] Many have been with countries that are rivals of the US or designated as pariahs by Washington. Thus America is watching with rising angst to see if Beijing enters agreements that impinge upon vital interests or threaten its own established energy supply lines. So far, the situation has not revived the dynamics of the Cold War, when great powers jockeyed for influence in third-world countries around the world, but the conditions are there for it to become so. Take, for example, the Latin American nation of Venezuela, the world's fifth-largest oil producer. It is run by Hugo Chavez, a socialist ally of Cuba's Fidel Castro who accuses Washington of plotting a coup to kill him and seize his country's oil resources. He has used the forum of the United Nations to brand America a 'terrorist state' and has pledged at home to reorientate his economy away from its dependence on the US. But in spite of this, Venezuela is an important source of oil for the US, supplying some three million barrels a day to the world's superpower.

But recently Chavez started trying to find alternative clients for the oil exports and China is top of his list. He was invited to Beijing in 2004 for a warm welcome and, while there, signed agreements that could bring Chinese investments in Venezuela's oil sector to $3 billion, double the existing amount. In 2005, the new affinity continued, with Zeng Qinghong, the Vice-President, receiving a friendly welcome from Chavez in Caracas. The Venezuelan President told Zeng his country had an 'extreme interest in becoming a safe supplier of oil and oil derivatives to the People's Republic of

China'. The not-so-safe subtext, though, was that if long-term supply contracts with China are eventually signed, they may be honoured at the expense of the US supplies and Washington is already on tenterhooks. As Condoleezza Rice, the US Secretary of State, has said, the US 'welcomes the rise of confident, peaceful and prosperous China' but hopes it will be 'able and willing to match its growing capabilities to its international responsibilities'.[13] In other words, it does not want to see Beijing befriending Washington's rivals in order to divert away the oil supplies that sustain American growth.

Elsewhere, the issue is not that China may impinge on US supply lines, but that in its alacrity to shore up supplies, it is forging ties with countries that Washington has made a policy of isolating. Sudan is a case in point. In 1997, when the predominantly Muslim government in Khartoum was engaged in a gruesome war against Christian rebels in the south, Washington imposed a ban on US companies from doing business in the East African country. This gave the Chinese a clear run at tapping into its oil reserves. In the years since, Sudan has become China's largest overseas oil project and China has turned into Sudan's biggest supplier of arms. Chinese-made tanks, fighter planes, bombers, helicopters, machine guns and rocket-propelled grenades have added new impetus to the civil war between the north and south of the country which has already lasted for two decades.[14] The money to buy those weapons, meanwhile, has come from oil revenues generated largely by the activities of the state-run China National Petroleum Corporation.

China National Petroleum owns 40 per cent, the largest stake, of the Greater Nile Petroleum Operating Co., a consortium that dominates Sudan's oilfields. Another Chinese firm, Sinopec, is erecting a pipeline over hundreds of miles to Port Sudan on the Red Sea, where China's Petroleum Engineering Construction Group is building a tanker terminal. The total investment runs into billions of US dollars and as production increases, Sudan has come to furnish China with 10 per cent of its total oil imports. But the benefit derived from this has to be weighed against the cost to Beijing's reputation. Not only has China become the chief supporter of a government that has perpetrated repeated instances of genocide but, according to human rights groups and locals quoted by Peter Goodman, a reporter for the *Washington Post*, the construction of Chinese oil rigs has also led directly to the slaughter of Sudanese people.[15]

The US-funded Civilian Protection Monitoring Team, a non-governmental organisation, has asserted that government troops have sought to clear a cordon sanitaire around oil installations by moving out the mostly ethnic Nuer and Dinka tribes who lived there. On 26 February 2002, the Nuer town of Nhialdiu was wiped out during one such operation to make way for a Chinese well that now functions in the nearby town of Leal. Mortar shells landed at dawn, followed by helicopter gunships directing fire at the huts where people lived. Antonov aeroplanes dropped bombs and roughly 7,000 government troops with pro-government militias then swept through the area with rifles and more than twenty tanks, according to Goodman's report, which was based on numerous local sources. 'The Chinese want to drill for oil, that is why we were pushed out,' Goodman quoted a local, Rusthal Yackok, as saying. Yackok added that his wife and six children were killed in the operation. The chief of Leal, Tanguar Kuiyguong, who lost three of his ten children on that day, told Goodman that around 3,000 of the town's 10,000 inhabitants died and every house was burned to the ground.[16]

There is no evidence, however, that the Chinese government or its largest oil company had any advance notice of the Sudanese government's scorched-earth strategy at Leal. Beijing also brushes off any suggestion that it is complicit in Sudan's genocide. As Zhou Wenzhong, a Deputy Foreign Minister, said in 2004: 'Business is business. We try to separate politics from business. I think the internal situation in Sudan is an internal affair, and we are not in a position to impose upon them.' A few months later, though, Chinese diplomats successfully diluted the impact of a United Nations resolution condemning Khartoum, thereby undermining Washington's efforts to threaten sanctions against Sudan's oil industry in protest at other waves of genocide in the Darfur region of the country. Having watered the resolution down, however, Wang Guangya, the ambassador to the United Nations, denied that his actions had anything to do with a desire to protect Chinese state oil interests in the country.[17]

Sudan is by no means the only country in which Beijing has pursued energy and resources at the expense of its international reputation. When the President of Uzbekistan, Islam Karimov, visited Beijing in 2005, the government rolled out the red carpet for him in spite of the fact that just twelve days earlier the Uzbek army had killed hundreds of civilian protesters in a town square in the east of that Central Asian nation. The fêting that Karimov enjoyed in the Chinese capital contrasted with an outcry elsewhere in the world, and with the calls for an international inquiry from the US and its North Atlantic Treaty Organisation allies, which at that time maintained military bases on Uzbek soil. In Beijing, however, Karimov got a twenty-one-gun salute in Tiananmen Square and there was never a public mention of the events that had unfolded in Andijan, the city in the Fergana Valley where the atrocity had taken place. It was not long, however, before clues emerged as to the real motivations behind China's courting of a 'reliable friend', as the state media referred to Karimov. The Uzbek President had brought with him a $600 million deal that allowed China National Petroleum access to twenty-three Uzbek oilfields.[18]

A couple of months after Karimov, it was the turn of Zimbabwean dictator Robert Mugabe to accept a twenty-one-gun salute, a small loan and some encouraging words from Hu Jintao. Much more substantive than these ties with either Uzbekistan or Zimbabwe, however, has been China's warming relationship with Iran, another country high on Washington's list of pariah states. Iran supplies 11 per cent of China's oil imports, so it is already a crucial resource partner. But the level of reciprocal interest is set to surge as Sinopec, the second largest state oil firm, implements an oil and natural gas agreement with Tehran that is said to be worth as much as $70 billion – the biggest energy deal yet by any member of OPEC, the cartel of oil-producing companies.[19] Under this agreement, Beijing is committed to develop the giant Yadavaran oilfield and buy 250 million tonnes of liquefied natural gas over the next thirty years. Tehran has also agreed to export to China some 150,000 barrels of oil per day at market prices for twenty-five years.

The ballast that this deal has given to bilateral ties has made Beijing a loyal friend of Tehran in the UN Security Council, where China is one of only five countries with the power to veto any resolution that is proposed. It has put that power, or the aura of it, to work over the last couple of years in deflecting successive attempts by the US to impose sanctions through the UN on Iran's energy sector. Washington suspects that Iran may be developing nuclear weapons technology and had hoped to use the threat of sanctions to force Tehran to demonstrate to the UN's nuclear watchdog that it has not broken the Nuclear Non-Proliferation Treaty, an international agreement that seeks to stem the spread of nuclear weapons and weapons technology. But this avenue now appears effectively blocked by China's manoeuvring in the Security Council. The anxiety this causes in the White House is hard to overestimate: preventing Iran from developing the bomb has long been a cornerstone objective in the State Department's global view.

Tensions are rising palpably. China's willingness to elevate the agendas of resource-rich pariah states to the United Nations Security Council is a major departure in the way that it conducts itself. But so far, Washington's warnings have gone unheeded. In June 2005, Chris Hill, the Assistant Secretary of State for East Asian and Pacific Affairs, told a subcommittee of the US House of Representatives that an important task for the United States and its Asian allies was 'to ensure that in its search for resources and commodities to gird its economic machinery, China does not underwrite the continuation of regimes that pursue policies seeking to undermine rather than sustain the security and stability of the international community'.[20] A few months later, with no observable change in China's behaviour, Robert Zoellick, the US Deputy Secretary of State, was more blunt. 'China's involvement with troublesome states indicates at best a blindness to consequences and at worst something more ominous,' he said. He added that if Beijing tried to use its influence to 'push the US out, they would get a counter-reaction'.[21]

The first ripples of that 'counter-reaction' may already be evident. The failure of the bid by CNOOC, the oil firm, for its US counterpart, Unocal, in the summer of 2005 was an indication of how sensitive American public opinion has become towards a rising and potentially threatening China. That is because by objective reckoning, the approach of China's third-largest oil company to the mid-tier American producer did not represent a threat to US national security in any way at all. The total output from Unocal's American oil wells, after all, satisfied just one per cent of US consumption. But in a democracy, it is emotion rather than objectivity that counts. With China courting US rivals in several parts of the world, issuing statements calling upon the US to get out of its military bases in central Asia and absorbing outsourced American jobs, Congressmen, understandably, did not find themselves in a mood to assist its oil companies. Neither was CNOOC's cause enhanced by the comments of a Chinese general just days before Congress was due to vote for or against CNOOC's bid proceeding. In prepared remarks to international journalists, the general, Zhu Chenghu, warned that if 'the Americans draw their missiles and position-guided ammunition onto the target zone on China's territory, I think we will have to respond with nuclear weapons. We Chinese will prepare ourselves for the destruction of all the cities east of Xian [in central China]. Of course, the Americans will have to be prepared that hundreds of cities will be destroyed by the Chinese.' It was no surprise after that, that the House of Representatives voted 398 to 15 to refer CNOOC's bid for review by the President on national security grounds.

Statements such as General Zhu's make a strong impression, no real matter how representative or otherwise they may be of Beijing's real intentions. The CNOOC failure, though important, was just one deal. But it illuminates the much larger and very real danger that, one day, the US Congress and the American electorate will come to see China unequivocally as an enemy in prospect. If that perception begins to gel, then it may start to condition Washington's thinking on a panoply of strategic and commercial issues and lead to the step-by-step reversal of the policy of engagement that has underpinned China's rise over the past twenty-seven years. If the sense of China as an adversary permeates deeply enough into the US political psyche, then a whole range of familiar anti-Beijing arguments – that it is an unfair trader, a manipulator of its currency's value, a pirate of intellectual property, an exploiter of its own workers, a beneficiary of subsidised financing from its state banks and others – may grow in potency. But Beijing, goaded on by its insatiable appetite, may have no room to concede ground to American public opinion, creating an impasse that could trigger progressively stronger counter-reactions from the White House.

To some, this scenario will seem far-fetched. But there is in fact ample justification for the view that strategic and military competition between China and the United States is intensifying. There are two interrelated issues that underlie this competition. The first is an established but incendiary rivalry over Taiwan and the second is a much newer expression of Beijing's growing assertiveness: the desire to guarantee the safe passage back home of the oil and resources it acquires in foreign climes.

On Taiwan, things are regressing appreciably. The background to the problem is ostensibly straightforward: China claims that Taiwan is part of its territory and threatens to invade if the island's leaders ever declare formal independence. The US accepts that Taiwan geographically belongs to China but wants reunification to happen peacefully and is obliged under an American law, the Taiwan Relations Act, to come to Taipei's assistance if the mainland ever decides to attack. Beyond these outline dimensions, however, things get more nuanced and emotional. Taiwan's position bestride the sea lanes that skirt through the South China Sea and then head towards Japan make it of crucial strategic importance for trade and the projection of military power in the region. Its attraction to Washington is further enhanced by its democratic government and the assiduous courting of US Congressmen by its senior officials. For China, the issue is also highly emotional and nationalistic. Beijing sees the island as a lingering slight on its prestige, a reminder that the humiliations it suffered at the hands of foreign powers in the 109 years before 1949 have yet to be reversed. The cause of reclaiming Taiwan, which it lost in 1895 after a war with Japan, has become a shibboleth of Communist rule.

With the two powers so implacably opposed, any shift in the military balance across the Taiwan Straits is a cause for concern throughout the Asia-Pacific region. That shift has now unambiguously taken place. David Shambaugh,[22] a US expert on the Chinese military, says that following the aggressive upgrading of the People's Liberation Army's capabilities, the balance of military power across the strait has tilted decidedly in China's favour. According to estimates by the US Pentagon, China now has more than 700 missiles near its southeast coast facing Taiwan and is accelerating the build-up by adding seventy to seventy-five missiles a year, up from its previous annual increase of around fifty.[23] Such a deployment, some US and Taiwanese analysts say, could be consistent with intentions to launch a lightning 'decapitation' strike against Taiwan, using accurate, guided weapons to disable the government, disrupt communications and force Taiwan to the negotiating table within hours – before the US Navy has had time to sail to Taipei's rescue.

In spite of the stand-off over Taiwan, though, the US and China have managed since they established diplomatic ties in 1979 to avoid painting each other as future enemies. But this too may be subtly changing. On a visit to Singapore in 2005, Donald Rumsfeld, the US Defense Secretary, asked an open forum why it was that China was expanding its missile forces so that it could reach targets in many parts of the world, not just the Pacific region: 'Since no nation threatens China, one must wonder: Why this growing investment?' A senior Foreign Ministry official in the audience countered him, also with a question: 'Do you truly believe that China is under no threat whatsoever from any part of the world?' Later in the year, on a visit to Beijing, Rumsfeld returned once more to the theme, asking his senior army inter-locutors why China was spending, by the Pentagon's estimate, as much as $90 billion a year on strengthening its military. His host told him that the Pentagon had got its figures wrong, and that the Chinese military budget for 2005 was actually only $29 billion, a mere fraction of what the US spends every year.[24] Nevertheless, these exchanges serve to underline America's growing anxiety.

Anxiety levels are set to rise further as Beijing seeks to deepen its military footprint in the Asia-Pacific, a region in which the US has been the undisputed arbiter of security since the war. China is not trying to incite Washington, but it has no option but to seek to shore up its oil supply lines from the Middle East through the Strait of Malacca, the sea channel between Indonesia and Malaysia through which almost all of Asia's imported oil passes. The potential for a conflict with the US over Taiwan means that Beijing cannot rely on American ships to police the Strait of Malacca for it. It needs to set down its own naval support network in the region, and it has gone about this task with speed and determination.

China has started to implement a strategy to strengthen diplomatic and military ties with countries dotted like a 'string of pearls' along the route that its oil tankers take on their journey from the Middle East, according to a report prepared for the Pentagon by Booz Allen Hamilton, the defence contractor.[25] Each pearl denotes a military facility or a listening-post that the Chinese may use or are in the process of building. One pearl is Gwadar, a Pakistani naval base that Beijing is helping to construct. When it is finished, diplomats assume, the Chinese Navy will enjoy regular access to dock its vessels. In nearby Bangladesh, a container port is under construction with Chinese help in Chittagong, another strategic port along the vital sea artery from the Middle East. In Myanmar (Burma), where the government receives generous military assistance from Beijing every year, electronic listening posts have been installed on islands in the Bay of Bengal so that the Chinese can monitor the activities of the Indian and US Navies in the areas around the Strait of Malacca.

Of course, none of this means that a conflict between China and the US is imminent or even likely. But it does represent a significant heightening of tensions and mutual suspicions. If these spill over into the realm of commerce, as they did quite clearly during the CNOOC bid for Unocal, then slowly but surely, the free-market assumptions of the West that have facilitated China's remarkable ascent since 1978 could start to be undermined. If this happens, the biggest economic event of the second half of the twemtieth century could be thrown off-course in the first half of the twenty-first, causing dislocations that would convulse not only China but also much of the rest of the world. That prospect, so damaging for so many hundreds of millions of people, is made possible by globalisation's most fundamental limitations – which is that, although trade increases the mutual economic dependence of the countries that engage it in, it does not make the peoples of those nations any fonder of each other. Thus, when relations deteriorate because of issues that have nothing to do with commerce, each side starts to resent its dependence on the other, and goodwill can rapidly unravel.

The most worrying contemporary example of this is the relationship between Japan and China. The two countries are engaged in an economic convergence unprecedented in its rapidity and depth. Some 16,000 Japanese firms do business in the Chinese mainland and sharply increased trade with China has lifted Japan's economy out of a decade of feeble growth and recurring recessions, while imports from China have lowered costs for Japanese consumers. More than 150,000 Chinese students attend Japanese universities and a million Chinese work in Japanese companies. In Shanghai, where their business presence is growing sharply, there may be as many as 100,000 Japanese residents. But in spite of all this, the two Asian giants are no better reconciled diplomatically or emotionally than they were in 1978, when Japanese business involvement in China was virtually zero.

In fact, politically, the neighbours are diverging as fast as they are coalescing commercially. Popular nationalism in both countries is driving politicians to pander to their constituencies, exacerbating the existing ill will. In Japan, Junichiro Koizumi, the Prime Minister, makes regular visits to the Yasukuni Shrine, thus insulting Chinese who know all too well that several of the war criminals who committed atrocities during the Sino-Japanese war are commemorated there. In China, senior officials who normally prevent street demonstrations from taking place, grant regular permission for screaming crowds of anti-Japanese protesters to gather outside Tokyo's embassy. It stands to reason that at some stage deteriorating political and diplomatic ties will spill over into commerce, and the Chinese people may launch sporadic boycotts of Japanese goods just as they did in the 1930s and 1940s when the war was being fought. One day, it is possible that one of these boycotts could flare into something bigger, more long-term and more damaging.

Maybe, however, the scenario I have painted is too pessimistic, too black. Indeed, when I think of all the issues described above, of how the acrimony, ill will and strategic competition could one day rupture China's trading relationship with the West, a particular memory recurs to me suggesting that these concerns may be overblown.

The memory in question is set in the embassy quarter of Beijing in the aftermath of NATO's bombing of the Chinese embassy in Belgrade. With smoke still rising from the rubble of the Chinese embassy complex, Washington issued a statement saying that the bombing had been a tragic mistake, a case of a pilot under pressure using an outdated map. But Beijing scorned this notion; a politburo meeting was held during which it was decided that the Pentagon had deliberately targeted their embassy, killing some of the staff inside. When this was announced to the people, genuine fury engulfed not only Beijing but most of the country. Indignant crowds of students and ordinary citizens gathered outside the US and UK embassies within hours of the news being released, and as the first day of protests wore on, the frenzy mounted. The Chinese military and police guards who are stationed all year round to protect foreign embassies just stood by as the demonstrators started to hurl rocks, paint and bottles over the walls. When a good thrower managed to hurl a projectile across the width of the embassy forecourts and smash a window, triumphant cries welled up from the rest of the crowd and at times, even the guards would join the jubilation.

Meanwhile, foreign residents of Beijing found themselves sub-ject to closer than normal questioning from Chinese as to which country they came from. If the answer was the UK, the US or other NATO countries, the reaction was never favourable. Suddenly, the number of self-professed British and Americans in Beijing started to drop precipitously, while those calling them-selves Australians, South Africans and Canadians surged. One senior British diplomat I knew, when accosted by an angry mob not far from the embassy's front gates, said that he was Albanian. Others in their desire for bland anonymity adopted an Icelandic identity. But as dusk was falling on the evening of the first day of protests, I had not known how identities were migrating all over town. I felt no animosity to the Chinese and, naively, could not really see why they would feel it towards me – after all, whether the bombing in Belgrade was a mistake or not was an issue for my government. I had nothing to do with it. So when I was standing making notes in the middle of a crowd of several hundred rock-throwing people outside the British embassy and somebody asked me where I was from I answered 'Britain'. There was a sudden silence from those around me, and they began to back away. Then someone said 'English pig'. Somebody else added 'English dog'. A third said 'English running dog'. The chant began to ripple through the crowd: 'English pig, English dog, English running dog'. With each refrain, it built in intensity and menace. I could see that something was going to happen, so I pushed my way outwards, and the crowd let me pass with only a few kicks, shoves and punches. When I broke free I ran as fast as a running dog could go. Rocks brushed my legs and hit my left shoulder as I went, and the crowd roared triumphantly at my departure.

The next morning I had become South African. I was outside the American embassy watching the rocks sail through the windows of the ambassador's study. I knew he was in the building because the British military attaché, using skills he had picked up in Northern Ireland, had managed to evade the crowds, slip down a side alley and over a high-security fence with sleeping bags for the besieged ambassador and his staff. Then, just as I was interviewing the protesters, I bumped into someone I knew. She was an influential official in the Chinese Ministry of Foreign Trade and Economic Co-operation, and a leading light in the ongoing negotiations to win China access to the World Trade Organisation. I counted her as a friend and was happy to see her there. We normally met over coffee in Häagen-Dazs and, in between mulling trade issues, we would chuckle over whether we felt brave enough to eat one of the fattening ice creams on the menu. But as I walked towards her, I could see that she did not share my feelings. When we got to within two feet of each other, she started to rant. I do not have the exact words in my notebook because I just stood there gaping. But I do remember that the Opium Wars came up several times, the century and a half of shame and humiliation, how we should realise that the Chinese would one day have their revenge and then we would know what it was to suffer. I asked her, when she had finished, whether the negotiations to enter the WTO would be derailed because of this. 'Of course, how can you talk about trade when the other side is bombing your embassy,' she shouted.

But the episode does not end like that. A month or so later we were back in Häagen-Dazs and she informed me that the deliberations on joining the WTO were proceeding. When I asked her when and how they had resumed, she replied that they had never stopped. 'We are prepared to make concessions to benefit ourselves in the long run,' she said.

It is this flexibility and pragmatism, visible in China's transformation over and over again, that supplies the counter-argument to future scenarios full of doom and gloom. China is perhaps too much wedded to the world, too deeply insinuated into its organisations and treaties, and too dependent on others to bite the hands that feed it.

BIBLIOGRAPHY

Banister, Judith, *China's Changing Population*, Stanford University Press, Berkeley, 1987

Becker, Jasper, *The Chinese*, John Murray, 2000

Bonavia, David, *The Chinese*, Allen Lane, 1981

Brady, Anne-Marie, *Making the Foreign Serve China*, Rowman & Littlefield, 2003

Brown, Lester R., *Who Will Feed China? Wake up Call for a Small Planet* (*Worldwatch Environmental Alert* series), W.W. Norton, New York, 1995

Burstein, Daniel and de Keijzer, Arne, *Big Dragon*, Simon & Schuster, 1998

Buzan, Barry and Foot, Rosemary (eds), *Does China Matter? A Reassessment*, Routledge, 2004

Cabestan, Jean-Pierre, *L'Administration Chinoise après Mao: Les Réformes de Deng Xiaoping et leurs limites*, Editions du Centre National de la Recherche Scientifique, Paris, 1992

Chang, Gordon G., *The Coming Collapse of China*, Arrow Books, 2002

Chase, Michael S., Pollpeter, Kevin L., Mulvenon, James C., *Shanghaied: The Economic and Political Implications of the Flow of Information and Investment Across the Taiwan Straits*, Rand, 2004

Chetham, Deirdre, *Before the Deluge, The Vanishing World of the Yangtze's Three Gorges*, Palgrave Macmillan, 2002

China, Air, Land and Water, World Bank, 2001

China's Economic Future, ed. The Joint Economic Committee of Congress of the United States, M.E. Sharpe, 1997

Clissold, Tim, *Mr China*, Constable & Robinson, 2004

Commission Hearings before the US-China Review Commission, 2001–2002, Compilation of Hearings

Cronin, William, *Nature's Metropolis*, W.W. Norton, 1991

Economy, Elizabeth C., *The River Runs Black*, Cornell University Press, 2004

Faber, Marc, *Tomorrow's Gold*, CLSA Books, 2002

Farrell, Chris, *Deflation*, Harper Business, 2004

Gerth, Karl, *China Made*, Harvard University Asia Centre, 2004

Giley, Bruce, *Tiger on the Brink, Jiang Zemin and China's New Elite*, University of California, Berkeley, 1998

Gittings, John, *Real China*, Pocket Books, 1997

Hersey, John, *A Single Pebble*, Bantam, 1956

Hu Angang, *Great Transformations in China*, Centre for China Studies, 2004

Huang, Yasheng, *Selling China*, Cambridge University Press, 2003

Hutchings, Graham, *Modern China*, Penguin Books, 2000

Jenner, W.J.F., *The Tyranny of History. The Roots of China's Crisis*, Allen Lane, London, 1992

Landes, David S., *The Unbound Prometheus*, Cambridge University Press, 2003

Lardy, Nicholas R., *Integrating China into the Global Economy*, Brookings Institution Press, 2002

Li Zhisui, *The Private Life of Chairman Mao: The Inside Story of the Man Who Made Modern China*, Chatto & Windus, 1994

Lieberthal, Kenneth, *Governing China*, W.W. Norton, 2004

Link, Perry, *Evening Chats in Beijing: Probing China's Predicament*, W.W. Norton, 1992

McGregor, James, *One Billion Customers*, Wall Street Journal Books/ Free Press, 2005

Miles, James A.R., *The Legacy of Tiananmen. China in Disarray*, University of Michigan Press, 1996

Miller, Donald L., *City of the Century*, Simon & Schuster, 2003

Moore, Oliver, *Reading the Past. Chinese*, British Museum Press 2000

Mosher, Steven W., *Hegemon*, Encounter Books, 2002

Nathan, Andrew J. and Ross, Robert S., *The Great Wall and the Empty Fortress*, W.W. Norton, 1997

Ngai Pun, *Made in China*, Duke University Press, 2005

Nolan, Peter, *China and the Global Economy*, Palgrave Macmillan, 2001

Nolan, Peter, *China at the Crossroads*, Polity Press, 2003

Overholt, William H., *China. The Next Economic Superpower*, Weidenfeld & Nicolson, London, 1993

Pomeranz, Kenneth, *The Great Divergence*, Princeton University Press, 2000

Pomeranz, Kenneth and Topik, Steven, *The World that Trade Created*, M.E. Sharpe, 1999

Richardson, Philip, *Economic Change in China 1800–1950*, Cambridge University Press, 1999

Sachs, Jeffrey, *The End of Poverty*, Penguin Books, 2005

Saich, Tony, *Governance and Politics of China*, Palgrave Macmillan, 2004

Short, Philip, *Mao. A Life*, John Murray, 1999

Spence, Jonathan, *The Search for Modern China*, W.W. Norton, 1990

Spence, Jonathan, *The Chan's Great Continent*, Penguin, 1998

Studwell, Joe, *The China Dream*, Profile Books, 2002

Sull, Donald N., *Made in China*, Harvard Business School Press, 2005

US-China Trade and Investment: Impact on Key Manufacturing and Industrial Sectors: Field Hearing in Akron, Ohio. US-China Economic and Security Review Commission, September 2004

Waley, Arthur, *Three Ways of Thought in Ancient China*, Routledge, 1939

Walter, Carl E. And Howie, Fraser J.T., *Privatising China*, John Wiley, 2003

White, Theodore H. And Jacoby, Annalee, *Thunder Out of China*, Victor Gollancz, 1947

Wilson, Dick, *China. The Big Tiger*, Abacus, 1997

Wolf, Martin, *Why Globalisation Works*, Yale University Press, 2004

Woetzel, Jonathan R., *Capitalist China*, John Wiley, 2003

Wood, Frances, *No Dogs and Not Many Chinese*, John Murray, 2000

Zhongguo Ke Chizu Fazhan Zhanlue Baogao, Kexue Chuban She, 2004

Zweig, David, *Freeing China's Farmers*, M.E. Sharpe, 1997

SOURCE NOTES

CHAPTER ONE

1 'Shagang Group purchases German plant from ThyssenKrupp Stahl', China Business Information Network, 31 December 2002.
2 Shown on the photographic website '26 things in one abandoned steel mill' at http://www.hebig.org/photos/26things/index.php.
3 These figures come from a meeting with Shen and other announcements by Shagang. Other details of the Shen Wenrong and Shagang story come from Yang Shilin, Chen Liming, Yang Zhiqiang in *Kua shiji de chaoyue, shen wenrong yu shagang de qiji* (Metallurgical Industry Press, 2000).
4 Joe Studwell, *The China Dream* (Profile Books, 2002), pp. 31, 32, 33.
5 Matthew Forney, 'It Takes a Village. A band of hungry farmers in Anhui launched China's economic revolution', *Time International*, 15 August 2005 and Jim Mann, 'China denies return to collectives', *Los Angeles Times*, 9 May 1986.
6 Matthew Forney, op. cit.
7 This phenomenon has been noticed by several researchers, including Professor Yang Dali, Political Science department, University of Chicago, and David Zweig, director of the Centre on China's Transnational Relations at Hong Kong University of Science and Technology.
8 James Kynge, 'Chinese eye SE Asia buys', *Financial Times*, 25 February 1998 and interview with the author. Also, Benjamin Kang Lim, 'China tycoon hails legal changes', Reuters, 3 February 1999.
9 John Pomfret, '"Reform hero" gets life term for fraud', *Washington Post*, 31 May 2000 and Andrew Higgins, 'Enemies close in on China's whiz-kid', *Guardian*, 17 September 1996.
10 Ling Zhijun, *Lian Ziang Feng Yun*, 2005.
11 James Kynge, 'Hope holds out for triumph over adversary', *Financial Times*, 29 April 1998 and 'China's public show of capitalism', *Financial Times*, 18 December 2000. See also Russell Flannery, 'Not just chicken feed', *Forbes*, 14 November 2005.
12 Peter Wonacott, 'Shopping for China: A Scourge of the Rust Belt Offers Some Hope There, Too – Auto-Parts Maker Wanxiang Invests in US Partners as Its Ambitions Expand', *Wall Street Journal*, 26 November 2004.
13 Elaine Kurtenbach, 'China's tiny automakers set their sights on the whole world', Associated Press, 24 July 1005.
14 'Chinese Business: Li makes some costly calls', *The Edge Singapore*, 20 September 2004.
15 'China at 50. Nation builders. Zong Qinghou. A toast to daring ventures', *Asiaweek*, 24 September 1999.
16 Interview with a former classmate of Shen Wenrong in Jinfeng. He declined to be identified by name.
17 Yang Shilin, Chen Liming, Yang Zhiqiang, op. cit.

CHAPTER TWO

1 Theodore H. White and Annalee Jacoby, *Thunder Out of China* (William Sloane Associates, 1946), p. 13.
2 Quoted in Donald L. Miller, *City of the Century* (Simon & Schuster, 2003), p. 188.
3 Ibid.
4 Niu Wenyuan and others, *Zhongguo ke chixu fazhan zhanlue baogao* (Science Press, 2004), pp. 227 and 228.
5 Ibid., p. 236.

6 Doug Peacock, *Cotton Times* (http://www.cottontimes.co.uk/workers1.htm).

7 William Cronin, *Nature's Metropolis* (W.W. Norton, 1991), p. 164.

8 Speech in 1924 by Sun Yat-sen, as quoted by Deirdre Chetham, *Before the Deluge* (Palgrave Macmillan, 2002).

9 Marc Faber, *Tomorrow's Gold* (CLSA Books, 2002), p. 52.

10 The story of porcelain told here is discussed at length in Christopher Cullen, *The Dragon's Ascent* (Pacific Century Publishers, 2001), p. 127.

11 Joe Studwell, *The China Dream* (Profile Books, 2002), p. 4.

12 Angus Maddison, *Dynamic Forces in Capitalist Development. A long-run comparative view* (Oxford, Oxford University Press, 1991), p. 10.

13 Adam Smith, *The Wealth of Nations*, Book 1, Chapter 9, in paragraph 1.9.15.

14 Jeffrey Sachs, *The End of Poverty* (Penguin, 2005), p. 150.

15 I am indebted to research conducted by Zhang Lijia in White Horse village in 2004 for several of the details in this account.

16 Elizabeth Rosenthal, 'Study links rural suicides in China to stress and ready poisons', *New York Times*, 29 November 2002.

CHAPTER THREE

1 Joe Studwell, *The China Dream*, p. 19.

2 Ibid.

3 Graham Hutchings, *Modern China* (Penguin, 2000), p. 340.

4 Author interview and taped transcript, 1999.

5 This figure of $60 billion is taken from remarks made by William Lash, Assistant Secretary of Commerce from the US, at a news conference in Beijing on 12 April 2005, the transcript of which was published by the US embassy in Beijing. As an estimate of the damage caused by piracy, it is at the conservative end of the spectrum. Necessarily, such estimates are extremely rough and the true losses due to piracy of various sorts may indeed by much higher.

6 Anne Stevenson-Yang and Ken DeWoskin, 'China Destroys the IP Paradigm', *Far Eastern Economic Review*, March 2005.

7 Author interview, 1999.

8 A good account of the deflationary conditions in the latter part of the nineteenth century can be had in Chris Farrell, *Deflation* (HarperCollins, 2004).

9 Quoted in *Hearing on China's impact on the US manufacturing base*, p. 17, 30 January 2004 at the US-China Economic and Security Review Commission. Testimony of Ernest F. Hollings, a US senator from the State of South Carolina.

CHAPTER FOUR

1 There are various estimates of the size of the Chinese immigrant population in Prato and all are complicated by the fact that many illegal immigrants do not register with the local authorities. The estimate of 20,000 is based on official publications and may well be on the conservative side. Prato has the second-largest Chinese population of any city in Italy, after Milan.

2 Bruce Stokes, 'Italian textile town braces for the worst', *National Journal*, 2 October 2004.

3 I am indebted here to Antonella Ceccagno of the Università di Bologna, author of 'The Economic Crisis and the Ban on Imports. The Chinese in Italy at a Crossroads', a paper providing an in-depth account of Chinese immigrants working in Italy.

4 Local details such as these come from interviews with Francesco Delfino, general manager of the province of Prato, and his staff as well as from local government literature.

5 For a further account of these and other dynamics see Suzy Menkes, 'China: Catastrophe for creativity or luxury opportunity?', *International Herald Tribune*, 27 September 2005.

6 This passage describing and quoting Moritz Mantero and aspects of the Como silk industry comes extensively from Peter S. Goodman, 'China's Silk Noose Tightens', *Washington Post*, 18 December 2003.

7 Wei Jingsheng, 'Chirac is making a fool of himself', *Agence France-Presse*, 24 October 1999.

8 'Chirac calls for closer ties', *Shanghai Daily*, 12 October 2004.

9 James Kynge and Martin Arnold, 'Chirac hails Beijing as trade deals are set up', *Financial Times*, 11 October 2004 and 'French firms sign big deals with China', *Business Daily*, 11 October 2004.

10 'Chinese president's visit throws Chirac into hot water', *Agence France-Presse*, 22 October 1999.

11 Wei Jingsheng, op. cit.

12 'Chirac says EU measures on Chinese textiles not enough', AFX Asia, 19 May 2005.

13 'Europe's new protectionism – Charlemagne', *The Economist*, 2 July 2005 and, among many others that reported this speech, Nicholas Watt, 'Wake up and change, Blair tells EU', *Guardian Weekly*, 1 July 2005.

14 'March Champion. French Socialist Works to Keep Voters in "No" on EU Constitution – Legislator Taps European Frustration with Leaders, Bloc's Recent Growth – Chirac Makes a Televised Appeal', *Wall Street Journal Europe*, 27 May 2005.

15 Jack Ewing and Dexter Roberts, 'The Chinese Are Coming . . . to Germany; Mainland companies are opening up shop – and setting their sights on the manufacturing sector', *Business Week*, 21 February 2005.

16 Interview with the author, Beijing, November 2004.

17 James Kynge, 'Zhu warns rural poverty poses threat to future', *Financial Times*, 5 March 2003.

18 Total government expenditure has been around 21 per cent of China's gross domestic product in recent years. See 'China risk: Macroeconomic risk', Economist Intelligence Unit, 15 November 2005.

19 Stefan Theil, 'Capitalism? Nein! Schröder and his Social Democrats rediscover Karl Marx. Alas, it's more than election opportunism', *Newsweek International*, 9 May 2005.

CHAPTER FIVE

1 Testimony of Bruce A. Cain, President Xcel Mold and Machine, Canton, Ohio. Hearing before the US-China Economic and Security Review Commission, Akron, Ohio, 23 September 2004.

2 'Magnum Integrated Technologies becomes lead bidder for Ingersoll Metalworking Insiders', report, 17 July 2003.

3 Al Frink said in this speech and in remarks to the media before the dinner that laws and regulations plus red tape added 22 per cent to the cost of doing business in the US. This and other remarks made to the author before, during and after the Rockford dinner are on tape.

4 Peter Cowhey, Dean of Graduate School of International Relations and Pacific Studies at University of California. Testimony to US-China Economic and Security Review Commission, 12–13 February 1004.

5 'China industry. Chery's big expansion plans', Economist Intelligence Unit, 7 February 2005 and Mark O'Neill, 'Chery gears up for US roll-out', *South China Morning Post*, 26 April 2005.

6 Brian Bremner and Kathleen Kerwin, 'Here Come Chinese Cars; China aims to be a big auto exporter, with help from big names manufacturing in the country', *BusinessWeek Online*, 26 March 2005. See also Alysha Webb, 'Chery: Big ambition or a pipedream? Tiny provincial automaker wants to win in Europe, US', *Automotive News Europe*, 18 April 2005.

7 Michael S. Chase, Kevin L. Pollpeter, James C. Mulvenon, *Shanghaied?*, Rand, July 2004.

8 Author interview.

9 Kathryn Kranhold, 'China Sets a High Price to Gain Market Entry', *Wall Street Journal*, 27 February 2004.

10 I am indebted to Rupert Wingfield-Hayes, the BBC bureau chief in China, for letting me listen to the tape of his interview with Bo Xilai in May 2005.

11 Diana Farrell, 'Trends', *The Milken Institute Review*, Second Quarter 2005.

12 McKinsey Global Institute surveys and reports can be found through http://www.mckinsey.com/mgi/.

CHAPTER SIX

1 James Kynge, 'China is the workshop of the world. But it is becoming the rubbish tip too', *Financial Times*, 27 July 2004. This article quotes a research paper from the Chinese Academy of Environmental planning that says costs to human health from air pollution in the early twenty-first century accounted for 2 to 3 per cent of annual gross domestic product and will reach 13 per cent of GDP by 2020 if China fails to curb a worsening trend. In the country's eleven largest cities some 50,000 people die prematurely and 400,000 people are infected by chronic bronchitis each year because of soot and other tiny airborne particles. If things do

not change, some 380,000 people will be dying prematurely each year by 2010 and that figure will rise to 550,000 people annually by 2020, the research paper suggests.

2 'From T-shirts to T-bonds – China and the world economy', *The Economist*, 30 July 2005 and also David Zweig and Bi Jianhai, 'China's global hunt for energy', *Foreign Affairs*, September/October 2005, p. 25.

3 Elizabeth Economy, *The River Runs Black* (Cornell University Press, 2004, p. 48).

4 Most of the details of Wang Jinxi's life contained here are gleaned from photographs, pamphlets, booklets, recordings and photocopies on display at the Iron Man Wang Museum in Daqing.

5 Kenneth Pomeranz, *The Great Divergence. China, Europe and the Making of the Modern World Economy* (Princeton University Press, 2000), p. 226.

6 'Kashagan Sale Completed', *International Petroleum Finance*, 11 April 2005. This article describes how the Western oil companies that owned stakes in the Kashagan oilfield used their pre-emption rights to prevent China National Offshore Oil Corp (CNOOC) and Sinopec from buying into the field.

7 Gavin Menzies, *1421. The Year China Discovered America* (Harper Perennial, 1 January 2004).

8 Francesco Guerrera, Joe Leahy, Richard McGregor and Enid Tsui, 'The maverick oil mandarin', *Financial Times*, 25 June 2005.

9 Francesco Guerrera, Stephanie Kirchgaessner, Joe Leahy, Sheila McNulty and James Politi, 'Twists and turns in log of Treasure Ship's transglobal journey', *Financial Times*, 14 July 2005.

10 Ibid.

11 'Chevron confident about bid for Unocal', AFX Asia, 24 June 2005.

12 Enid Tsui, 'CNOOC executive speaks out about failed bid', *Financial Times*, 16 September 2005.

13 Andrew Gowers, Editor of the *Financial Times*, and Mure Dickie, Beijing Correspondent, had this experience in October 2003. I experienced a similar explanation in June 1999.

14 Richard McGregor, 'Hope for parched cities springs from canal project', *Financial Times*, 9 June 2005.

15 This comment was made 'off the record' and I am therefore not at liberty to disclose which official said this to me.

16 Matthew Pottinger, Steve Stecklow, John F. Fialka, 'Invisible Export: A Hidden Cost of China's Growth: Mercury Migration', *Wall Street Journal*, 17 December 2004.

17 Ibid.

18 Tim Radford, 'Huge rise in Siberian forest fires puts planet at risk, scientists warn', *Guardian*, 31 May 2005.

19 Venessa Leevenessa, 'Giant strides and a colossal fallout; China's miracle economy may be planet's greatest threat', *Newstoday.com.sg*, 22 October 2005. See also Michael Richardson, 'Illegal logging: calls to give it the chop', *Straits Times*, 14 May 2005 and 'China's Need for Wood Imperils Other Nations' Forests', *Dow Jones International News*, 8 March 2005.

20 Michael McCarthy, 'Your planet: The state we're in', *Independent*, 25 September 2005.

21 'Renewable Energy. China pledges $180B for initiatives', *Greenwire*, 7 November 2005.

22 Richard Lloyd Parry, 'Himalayas' melting glaciers will open floodgates to catastrophe', *The Times*, 12 July 2005. See also Janet Larsen, 'Ice Melt Alert', *USA Today*, 1 May 2005.

CHAPTER SEVEN

1 Arthur Waley, *Three Ways of Thought in Ancient China* (Routledge, 1939, p. 115).

2 Ibid., p. 116.

3 James Kynge, 'Phoney police add to China's fakes list', *Financial Times*, 21 June 2002.

4 This assertion is based on personal experience and on testimony from people within public relations companies in Beijing.

5 Author interview.

6 'Local officials given imprisonment for fake milk powder cases', Xinhua News Agency, 12 August 2004.

7 Pierre Haski, *Le Sang de la Chine* (Grasset, 2005). See also Philip P. Pan, 'China's AIDS Orphans Feel Brunt of Power – Communist Party Thwarts Activist's Unofficial School, Efforts to Draw Attention to Disease', *Washington Post*, 14 September 2004.

8 James Kynge, 'The Pearl River Delta attracting $1bn of investment a month', *Financial Times*, 4 February 2003.
9 Author interview, October 2004.
10 Mure Dickie, 'China's high-tech hero', *Financial Times*, 11 December 2004.
11 Fareed Zakaria, Melinda Liu, Christian Caryl, Karen Lowry Miller, Rukhmini Punoose, John Barry, 'Does the Future Belong to China? A new power is emerging in the East. How America should handle unprecedented new challenges, threats – and opportunities', *Newsweek*, 9 May 2005.

CHAPTER EIGHT

1 Nicholas D. Kristof, 'China update: How the hardliners won', *New York Times*, 12 November 1989.
2 A transcript of this speech was given to the author by Cao.
3 Yasheng Huang, *Selling China* (Cambridge University Press, 2003), pp. 343–50. This book deals extensively with the ideological, structural and political impediments hampering the development of the private sector.
4 'Dialectical materialism', *The Economist*, 3 July 1999.
5 A full account of the Zhengzhou Baiwen scandal is contained in Carl E. Walter and Fraser T.J. Howie, *Privatising China* (John Wiley and Sons, 2003), p. 190.
6 Hu Shuli, 'Enrons of China; Scoops: They reveal a business culture that is now teetering on the brink between cronyism and capitalism', *Newsweek International*, 1 December 2004. See also 'China's bourses are looking up', *Business Times Singapore*, 3 February 2004.
7 David Barboza, 'Wave of Corruption Tarnishes China's Extraordinary Growth', *New York Times*, 22 March 2005.
8 Ibid.
9 China kicks off trial over $3.1 bln finance fraud', Reuters, 10 June 2004.
10 'China's bourses are looking up', op. cit.
11 Andrew Yeh, 'Bank refinance may cost Beijing Dollars 190bn', *Financial Times*, 29 April 2005.
12 James Kynge, 'Officials in China face "mafia" probe', *Financial Times*, 22 June 2001. See also Larry Teo, 'Triads could overwhelm China's local govts', *Straits Times*, 20 November 2004.
13 Liu Li, 'Audit reveals breadth of fund abuse', *China Daily*, 29 June 2005.
14 Pei Minxin, 'China is paying the price of rising social unrest', *Financial Times*, 7 November 2005.

CHAPTER NINE

1 Anne-Marie Brady, *Making the Foreign Serve China* (Rowman & Littlefield, 2003). I am indebted to Brady's research for much of the material on 'waishi', or foreign affairs, mentioned in this chapter.
2 Ibid., p. 18.
3 Author interview.
4 Kathy Chen, 'Seagram Wants Orange Juice to be Chinese Staple', *Dow Jones*, 2 January 1998.
5 Quoted from the unpublished diaries of Edgar Snow in Anne-Marie Brady, op. cit., pp. 44–5.
6 Leslie Chang, 'China Battles the Present with the Past – "Us Against the World" Mentality Dominates the Nation's History Lesson', *Asian Wall Street Journal*, 24 June 1999.
7 Ibid.
8 Ernest J. Wilson III, Senior Research Fellow, Center For International Development and Conflict Management, University of Maryland. Influence of China in Africa. Congressional Testimony. Committee on House International Relations Subcommittee on Africa, Human Rights and International Operations, 28 July 2005.
9 'Asian-China ties in 2020: stronger and deeper?' *The Nation* (Thailand), 29 November 2005.
10 I first heard this phrase spoken by Lester Brown, President of the Earth Policy Institute, a non-governmental environmental organisation based in Washington. Brown, who was speaking at a meeting in Beijing in early 2005, noted that China consumes more grain, meat, coal, steel, copper, cement, fertiliser, cell phones and refrigerators than the United States.
11 David Zweig and Bi Jianhai, 'China's global hunt for energy', *Foreign Affairs*, September/October 2005, p. 25. I am indebted to this fine, comprehensive article for many of the points quoted in the next several paragraphs.

12 Ibid.
13 Glen Kessler, 'Rice Puts Japan at Center of New US Vision of Asia; China Challenged in Major Speech', *Washington Post*, 19 March 2005.
14 Peter S. Goodman, 'Blood and oil: China's involvement in the Sudan oil industry contributes directly to a regime that is widely accused of systematically massacring civilians, critics charge', *Washington Post*, 24 April 2005.
15 Ibid.
16 Ibid.
17 'UN Security Council Deadlocked over New Sudan Resolution', *Dow Jones International*, 18 March 2005. See also Evelyn Leopold, 'UN Council votes for sanctions on Darfur offenders', Reuters, 29 March 2005.
18 'China Strengthens Alliance with Embattled Uzbekistan Leadership', *Voice of America*, 26 March 2005. See also 'Guest of dishonour', *Globe and Mail*, 28 May 2005 and Mark Magnier, 'Slaking the dragon's thirst. China's energy quest', *Los Angeles Times*, 7 August 2005.
19 'Iran Leaves Europeans Out in the Cold', *Petroleum Intelligence Weekly*, 7 March 2005.
20 'US seeks China as global partner, assistant secretary of state for East Asian and Pacific Affairs says', *US Fed News*, 7 June 2005.
21 Daily Press Briefing for 8 March – Transcript, State Department Press Releases and Documents, 8 March 2005.
22 David Shambaugh, 'Lifting the China arms ban is only symbolic', *Financial Times*, 5 March 2004. The point about the shift in the military balance was made in conversations with the author in late 2005.
23 Robert S. Ross, 'Assessing the China Threat', *The National Interest*, 1 October 2005.
24 James Boxell, Demetri Sevastopulo, Daniel Dombey, 'China's defence spending more than double disclosed', *Financial Times*, 26 October 2005. The London-based International Institute of Strategic Studies estimated that China spent $62.5 billion on defence last year, compared with the Beijing government's official figure of $25 billion. Indeed, most independent estimates are considerably higher than the official figures released by Beijing.
25 Jonathan Broder, 'Balancing Fuel and Freedom', *CQ Weekly*, 13 September 2005.

INDEX

mercury, 144
Mexico, 212
Microsoft Corp., 114
Middle East, 125, 145, 222–3
Midea company, 60–1
migrant workers, 40–4, 160, 176
Milan, 77
military, 154
milk powder scandal, 57, 158
Ming dynasty, 36, 40, 81, 131
Mingshan, Yin, 52–5, 58–9, 61–3
Ministry of Foreign Trade and Economic
    Co-operation, 226
Ministry of Public Security, 193
Mitsubishi, 55, 113, 162
Modena, 80
Mongolia, 6, 80, 125
monkeys, 41, 204
Montebelluna, 82
Montreal, 6
Moscow, 76
motorbikes, 54–5, 57–9, 61
Motorola, 114
Mugabe, Robert, 218
multinational companies, 107, 119
Müntefering, Franz, 96
Murdoch, Rupert, 63, 207
Myanmar, 145, 223

Nanking, 24–5, 33
Nantong, 80
Napoleon Bonaparte, 7
National Bureau of Statistics, 47
National People's Congress (NPC), 180, 182,
    192
nationalism, 211, 221, 224
NATO, 218, 225
Natural Science Research Society, 127
Navy, Chinese, 223
Netherlands, 92
New Hope group, 19
New York, 24, 33, 98–100, 182, 202; Stock
    Exchange, 9; Rockefeller Center, 162
News Corporation, 207
newspapers, see media
Newton, Sir Isaac, 62
Nhialdiu, 217
Nigeria, 62
Nile, River, 139
Nissan, 110, 162
non-governmental organisations, 142, 144,
    186
Northern Ireland, 226
nuclear power, 115
nuclear weapons, 219–20

oil, 14, 121, 125–36, 184, 214–18; wells,
    193–201
Olson, Dean, 103

opium, 37, 116
Opium Wars, 116, 210, 226
Organisation for Economic Co-operation and
    Development, 109, 192
Other Side of the River, The (Edgar Snow), 209
outsourcing, 106–8, 119–20, 213, 220
outward investment, 162–3
oversupply, 52, 59–61, 163, 168
Oxford University, 169, 170–1

Pacific Ocean, 125
Pacyna, Josef, 144
pandas, 159
Pao Chen company, 160
Papua New Guinea, 125
Pasteur, Louis, 98
Pax Americana, 214
Pearl Harbor, 55
Pearl River, 15, 22, 42, 44, 60, 63, 94, 137,
    160
Pekin, Illinois, 97
Peng, Li, 141, 180
pensions, 55, 95
People's Bank of China, 156, 189
People's Daily, 187, 197–8
People's Liberation Army, 22, 179–80, 222
people-smuggling, 74–8
Persian Gulf, 172–3
PetroChina, 130, 163, 185
Petroleum Engineering Construction Group,
    216
Philippines, 109
philosophy, Chinese, 148–9
Phoenix steel plant, see ThyssenKrupp
    (Phoenix) steel mill
Phuket, 173
Pingxiang, 123, 125
Pinochet, Augusto, 91
piracy, 56–8, 64–5, 107, 110; and crisis of trust,
    154, 159, 175–6, 213, 220; see also DVDs;
    intellectual property
Pitao, Zhou, 206
Plato, 148
Pliny the Elder, 84
Poland, 94
police, 154, 191, 200
pollution, see environmental degradation
population, 37–9, 45–6, 49–52, 127, 132, 206
porcelain, 35–7
Port Sudan, 216
Prato, 71–2, 74–5, 77–83, 85, 87, 92, 213
printing, 35
privatisation, 182–4
propaganda, 129, 141, 154, 209
protectionism, 212
publishing, 56–7, 184

Qianlong, emperor, 115–18, 121
Qiling, Wang, 40–2

241